Creative Beading

Compiled by Julia Gerlach

Acknowledgements: Tea Benduhn, Mindy Brooks, Terri Field, Lora Groszkiewicz, Kellie Jaeger, Carrie Jebe, Diane Jolie, Patti Keipe, Alice Korach, Patricia Lantier, Tonya Limberg, Debbie Nishihara, Cheryl Phelan, Carole Ross, Salena Safranski, Candice St. Jacques, Maureen Schimmel, Kristin Schneidler, Lisa Schroeder, Terri Torbeck, Elizabeth Weber

Printed in Singapore

06 07 08 09 10 11 12 13 14 15
10 9 8 7 6 5 4 3 2 1

Publisher's Cataloging-In-Publication Data
(Prepared by The Donohue Group, Inc.)

Creative beading / compiled by Julia Gerlach.

   p., : col. ill. ; cm.
   Includes index.
   Summary: Projects from last year's Bead&Button magazine.
   ISBN: 0-87116-228-8

1. Beadwork--Handbooks, manuals, etc. 2. Beads--Handbooks, manuals, etc. 3. Jewelry making--Handbooks, manuals, etc. I. Gerlach, Julia. II. Title: Bead&Button magazine.

TT860 .C74 2006
745.594/2

Senior art director: Lisa Bergman
Book layout: Sabine Beaupré
Editors: Julia Gerlach, Pam O'Connor, Lesley Weiss
Photography: Jim Forbes and Bill Zuback

Cont

ents

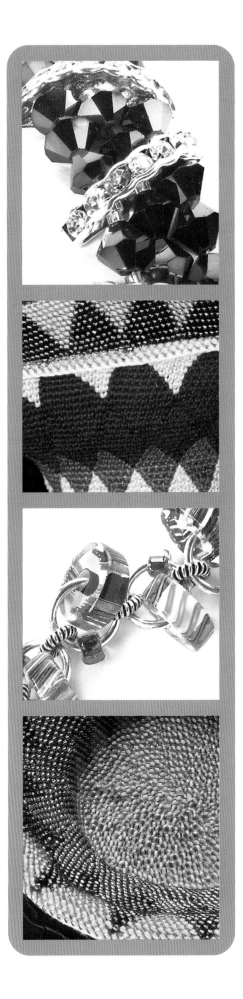

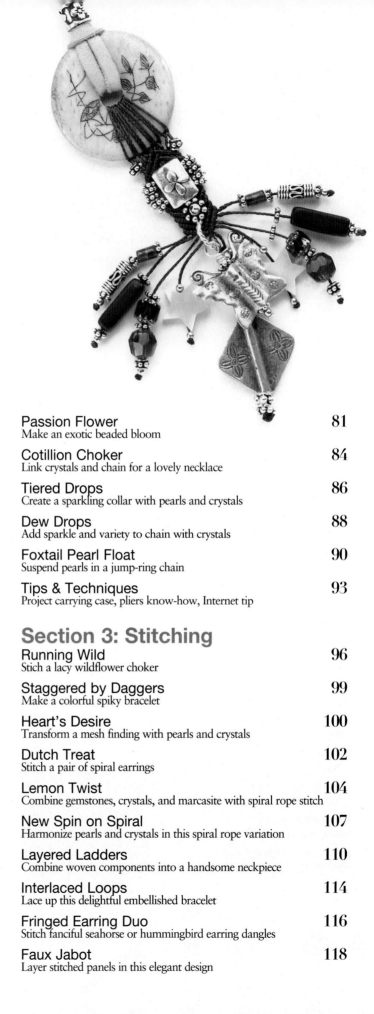

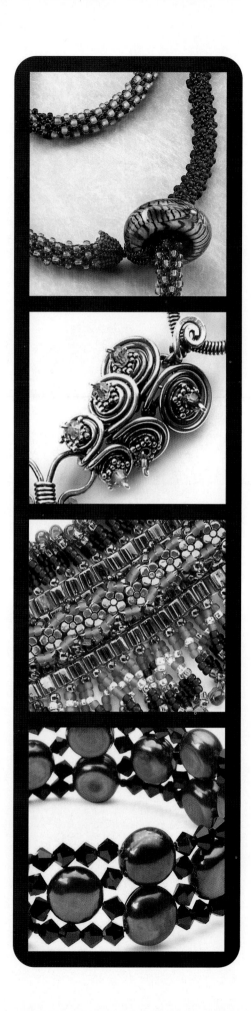

Section 4: Bead Crochet, Embroidery, and Macramé

Introduction

For more than a decade, *Bead&Button* magazine has been a relentless advocate for the art/craft/hobby of beading. We've published hundreds of articles for beading enthusiasts, delivering the best that beading has to offer to readers around the world. From the start, our emphasis has been on presenting beading projects with meticulous accuracy, and over the years we have covered every popular beading technique.

With great joy we have watched beading grow from a fledgling interest area to its current worldwide popularity. More classes, shops, websites, books, and certainly more beads are available than ever before. The beading community is now larger than at any time in the past, and our numbers are still growing. We're delighted to be a part of it.

Creative Beading is a compilation of more than 90 projects from the past year. The articles range from simple, introductory-level projects to challenging pieces for experienced beaders. The techniques in this book include stringing, loomwork, bead embroidery, bead crochet, and the most popular off-loom stitches — peyote, brick stitch, Ndebele herringbone, right-angle weave, and square stitch — with scores of variations, combinations, and embellishments. Most of the book is dedicated to jewelry making, although the techniques shown here can easily be adapted to other types of accessories.

The majority of *Bead&Button*'s articles come from outside submissions, a fact that surprises many of our readers. Staff editors design only a few of the magazine's projects. As a result, we're always on the lookout for interesting and creative beading ideas, and they come from a wide spectrum of sources. Some of our authors are professional beaders with a long list of teaching credentials, awards, and commercial success, but by no means do we limit our articles to the pros. We frequently publish articles from casual beaders who send us a terrific piece of original beadwork.

No matter what the source, before we publish any project in *Bead&Button*, our editors test the directions by making the featured piece. We simplify techniques as needed and supplement written directions with precise how-to photos and illustrations. Our readers know they can count on us for accuracy. We've built our reputation on getting the instructions right.

Throughout these pages, you'll find many wonderful projects and ideas. We hope you enjoy every one of them.

Mindy Brooks

Mindy Brooks
Editor
Bead&Button magazine

Tools

Tools

Excellent tools for making jewelry are available in bead shops, catalogs, and on the Internet. Hardware stores and craft stores also yield great finds.

A. **Roundnose pliers** have smooth, tapered, conical jaws and are used to form loops in wire. Choose a pair with narrow jaws so you can turn small loops when needed.

B. **Chainnose pliers** have smooth, flat inner jaws, and the tips taper to a point so you can get into small spaces. Use them for gripping wire, closing bead tips, and for opening and closing loops and rings. (Hardware-store pliers often have ridges on their jaws. Chainnose pliers for jewelry and wirework must have flat inner surfaces.)

C. On **diagonal wire cutters**, the backs of the blades meet squarely, yielding a flat-cut surface. The fronts make a pointed cut. Always cut with the back against the section you want to finish so that the wire end will be flat. Never use jewelry wire cutters on memory wire, which is extremely hard; use heavy-duty cutters or bend the memory wire until it breaks.

D. **Crimping pliers** have two grooves in their jaws — one presses an indentation into the crimp bead, and the other folds the crimp into a compact, cylindrical shape.

E. Use **thread snips** or small scissors for cutting bead-stringing cord.

F. An **awl** has a handle and a sharp, pointed metal tip. It is the easiest tool to use when knotting between beads.

G. A **twisted wire needle** is simply a length of fine wire folded in half and twisted tightly together. It has a large, open eye at the fold, which is easy to thread, and it accommodates thicker cords than conventional beading needles.

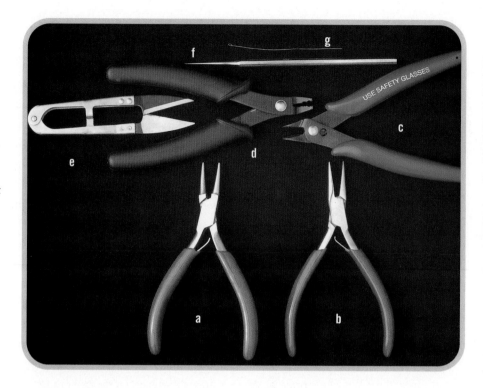

Findings

Findings are the components that link beads into a piece of jewelry. Always buy the best you can afford. Inexpensive metal clay findings may soon discolor. Sterling silver and gold-filled findings are slightly more expensive, but they look good for many years.

A. A **head pin** looks like a thick, blunt sewing pin with a flat or decorative head on one end to keep the beads from falling off. Head pins come in different gauges and in lengths ranging from 1-3 in. (2.5-7.6cm).

B. **Eye pins** are like head pins with a round loop on one end instead of a head. Once you are comfortable making wire loops, you can easily make your own eye pins.

C. A **jump ring** is a small wire circle or oval with a split that you can twist open and closed. It connects loops with loops or loops with other findings. A **soldered jump ring** has had its opening soldered shut and is often used as part of a clasp.

D. **Split rings** look like tiny key rings. They are more secure than jump rings and a good substitute for them.

E. **Crimp beads** are round or tube-shaped beads designed for use with flexible beading wire. They can be flattened with chainnose pliers or folded into a roll with crimping pliers.

F. **Bead tips** or calottes are small metal beads primarily used to link a strand of beads on cord to a clasp. Bead tips come in a clamshell shape or as a basket. Clamshell bead tips close over the knot and hide it. The knot rests against the basket in basket-shaped bead tips.

G. **Clasps** come in an extensive range of shapes, sizes, materials, and prices. Some of the most common are toggles, consisting of a ring and a bar; lobster claws and spring rings, which open when you push on a tiny lever; S-hooks; and hook-and-eye clasps.

H. **Earrings** also come in many shapes, sizes, and styles, including posts, French hooks, kidney wires, and hoops. Post earrings require a loop if you plan to attach any kind of dangle.

I. **Cones** have openings at both ends. They are ideal for concealing the knotted ends of a tassel or a multistrand necklace.

Stringing and Stitching Materials

A steady supply of new stringing materials is available to beaders, so experiment to find the cords you prefer. Look for products that are durable, come in several weights or sizes, and offer a good selection of colors.

Flexible beading wire consists of very fine wires twisted or braided together and covered with a smooth plastic coating. The wires come in several diameters, depending on the brand, but range from .010 in. (the thinnest) to .036 in. (the thickest). Most come in 7-wire, 19- or 21-wire, and 49-wire grades. The 49-wire beading wire is the highest grade and the most expensive. Finish beading wire projects with crimp beads.

Beading cords and threads come in many materials, but nylon is the most common since it is both strong and supple. Cord size is indicated either by a number or letter — the lower the number or letter, the thinner the cord. (The exception is O, which is very thin.) Use these doubled for extra security.

High-tech fishing lines, particularly Fireline, are a popular choice for stringing and stitching. They're strong, fray-resistant, and won't stretch. Never string beads on monofilament because it becomes brittle over time.

Pearls are traditionally strung on **silk**, but many of the new nylons are almost as supple and much less fragile.

Wire is used to make clasps, dangles, and many decorative elements. It is sold by gauge, with thinner-gauge wires having higher numbers. For making jewelry, common sizes are 16- to 28-gauge. Sterling silver and gold-filled wire are designated dead soft or half hard. The two are often interchangeable, but half-hard wire holds its shape better in the thinner gauges.

Memory wire is steel spring wire. It comes in several sizes and can be used without clasps to make coiled bracelets, necklaces, and rings.

Beading threads, used mainly for off-loom beadweaving, often are made with nylon. Nymo is the most common brand. Nymo comes in sizes O, B, and D, listed from thinnest to thickest size. These threads must be conditioned before use to prevent fraying, separating, and tangling.

Beading needles look like thin sewing needles. The sizes most often used are # 10 to 13.

What does it take to make beautiful jewelry? The secret is knowing which tools and materials will give you the best results.

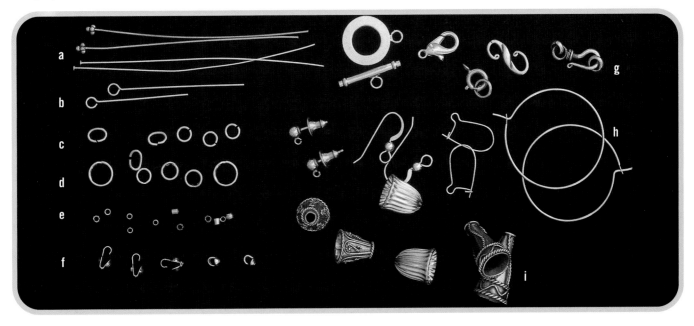

Basics

KNOTS

Half-hitch knot

Figure 1: Come out a bead and form a loop perpendicular to the thread between beads. Bring the needle under the thread away from the loop. Then go back over the thread and through the loop. Pull gently so the knot doesn't tighten prematurely.

FIGURE 1

Lark's head knot

A lark's head knot is commonly used to start macramé projects.

Figure 2: Fold a cord in half and lay it behind a ring, loop, bar, etc., with the fold pointing down. Bring the ends through the ring from back to front, then through the fold and tighten.

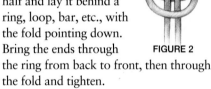

FIGURE 2

Square knot

Figure 3: Bring the left-hand cord over the right-hand cord and around.

FIGURE 3

Figure 4: Cross right over left and go through the loop.

FIGURE 4

Surgeon's knot

Figure 5: Cross the right end over the left and go through the loop. Go through again. Pull the ends to tighten. Cross the left end over the right and go through once. Tighten.

FIGURE 5

Overhand knot

Figure 6: Make a loop in the cord and bring the end that crosses on top behind the loop. Then pull the end through to the front.

FIGURE 6

STITCHES AND THREAD

Conditioning thread

Use either beeswax (not candle wax or paraffin) or Thread Heaven to condition thread. Beeswax adds tackiness that is useful if you want your beadwork to fit tightly and stiffly. Thread Heaven adds a static charge that causes the thread to repel itself, so it can't be used with doubled thread. Stretch the nylon thread, then pull it through beeswax or Thread Heaven, starting with the end that comes off the spool first.

Ladder

Figure 7: A ladder of seed or bugle beads is often used to begin brick stitch and Ndebele herringbone. Pick up two beads, leaving a 4-in. (10cm) tail. Go through both beads again in the same direction. Pull the top bead down so the beads are side by side. The thread exits the bottom of the second bead **(a–b)**. Pick up a third bead and go back through the second bead from top to bottom. Come back up the third bead **(b–c)**.

Figure 8: String a fourth bead. Go through the third bead frombottom to top and fourth bead from top bottom **(c-d)**. Continue adding beads until you reach the desired length.

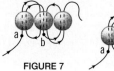

FIGURE 7

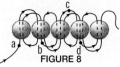

FIGURE 8

Figure 9: To stabilize the ladder, zigzag back through all the beads.

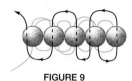

FIGURE 9

Brick stitch

Work off a stitched ladder (see **Figures 7-9**).

Figure 10: Begin each brick-stitch row so no thread shows on the edge: String two beads. Go under the thread between the second and third beads on the ladder from back to front. Pull tight. Go up the second bead added, then down the first. Come back up the second bead.

Figure 11: For the row's remaining stitches, pick up one bead. Pass the needle under the next loop on the row below from back to front. Go back up through the new bead.

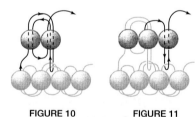

FIGURE 10   FIGURE 11

Ndebele herringbone, flat

Figure 12: Start with an even number of beads stitched into a ladder. Turn the ladder, if necessary, so your thread exits the end bead pointing up.

Pick up two beads and go down through the next bead on the ladder **(a–b)**. Come up through the third bead on the ladder, pick up two beads, and go down through the fourth bead **(b-c)**. Repeat across the ladder.

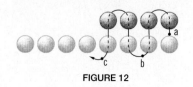

FIGURE 12

Figure 13: To turn, come back up through the second-to-last bead and continue through the last bead added in the previous row (**a–b**). Pick up two beads, go down through the next bead in that row, and come up through the next bead (**b–c**). Repeat across the row.

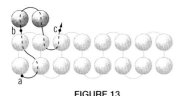

FIGURE 13

Ndebele, tubular

Figure 14: To work tubular Ndebele, make a ladder of the desired number of beads (an even number, in this case four) and join it into a ring. String two beads and go down the next bead on the row below (the ladder). Come up the next bead and repeat. There will be two stitches when you've gone down the fourth bead (**a-b**).

You need to work a "step up" to be in position to start the next row. To do this, come up the bead next to the one your needle is exiting and the first bead of the first stitch (**c-d**).

Continue adding two beads per stitch and stepping up at the end of each round.

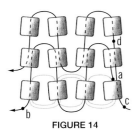

FIGURE 14

Ndebele herringbone, adding and ending thread

Figure 15: Thread the needle on the tail end (where you cut it from the spool). Insert the needle in the bead where the old thread exits and go down four beads (**a–b**). Go up three beads in the adjacent stack (**b–c**). Go down two beads in the first stack (**c–d**). Go up

three beads in the second (**d–e**). Go down four to six beads in the third (**e–f**). Then trim the short tail off and thread the needle on the long end. Follow a similar path to end the old thread, working in the opposite direction.

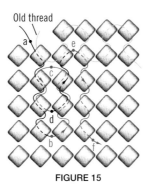

FIGURE 15

Peyote: flat even-count

Figure 16: String one bead and loop through it again in the same direction. String beads to total an even number. These beads comprise the first two rows. (Remove the extra loop and weave the tail into the work after a few rows.)

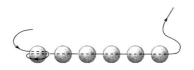

FIGURE 16

Figure 17: Every other bead from **figure 16** drops down half a space to form row 1. To begin row 3 (count rows diagonally), pick up a bead and stitch through the second bead from the end. Pick up a bead and go through the fourth bead from the end. Continue in this manner. End by going through the first bead strung.

FIGURE 17

Figure 18: To start row 4 and all other rows, pick up a bead and sew through the last bead added on the previous row.

Weave through the work in a zigzag path to end thread. Begin a thread the same way, exiting the last bead added in the same direction to resume.

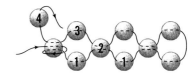

FIGURE 18

Peyote: flat odd-count

Begin as for flat peyote (even count), but string an odd number of beads. Work row 3 as shown in **figure 17**. Since the first two rows total an odd number of beads, you won't have a place to attach the last bead on odd-numbered rows.

Figure 19: Work a figure-8 turn at the end of row 3, which will position you to start row 4: String the next-to-the-last bead (#7) and go through #2 then #1. String the last bead (#8) and go through #2, #3, #7, #2, #1, and #8. You can continue to work this turn at the end of each odd-numbered row, but this edge will be stiffer than the other.

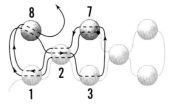

FIGURE 19

Basics

Figure 20: For a modified turn, string the last bead of the row then loop through the edge thread immediately below. Go through the last bead to begin the new row. Then turn at the end of even-numbered rows as shown.

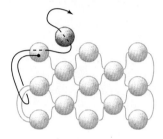

FIGURE 20

Peyote: circular (tubular) even-count

Figure 21: String an even number of beads to equal the desired circumference. Tie in a circle, leaving some ease.

FIGURE 21

Figure 22: Even-numbered beads form row 1 and odd-numbered beads, row 2. (Numbers indicate rows.) Put the ring over a form if desired. Go through the first bead to the left of the knot. Pick up a bead (#1 of row 3), skip a bead, and go through the next bead. Repeat around until you're back to the start.

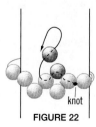

knot

FIGURE 22

Figure 23: Since you started with an even number of beads, you need to work a step up to be in position for the next round. Go through the first beads on rounds 2 and 3. Pick up a bead and go through the second bead of round 3; continue. (If you begin with an odd number of beads, there won't be a step up; you'll keep spiraling.)

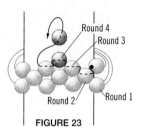

Round 4
Round 3
Round 2
Round 1

FIGURE 23

Peyote: rapid increase

Figure 24: At the point of the increase, pick up two beads instead of one. Pass the needle through the next bead.

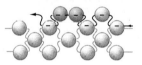

FIGURE 24

Figure 25: When you reach the double bead space on the next row, go through the first bead, add a bead, and go through the second bead.

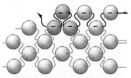

FIGURE 25

Peyote: gradual increase

Figure 26: The gradual increase takes four rows. At the point of the increase, pick up two thin beads. Go through the next high bead.

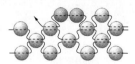

FIGURE 26

Figure 27: When you get to the two thin beads on row 2, go through them as if they were one bead.

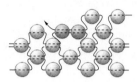

FIGURE 27

Figure 28: On row 3, place two regular-size beads in the two-thin-bead space.

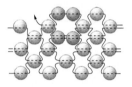

FIGURE 28

Figure 29: When you get to the two beads on the next row, go through the first, pick up a bead, and go through the second.

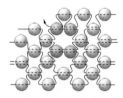

FIGURE 29

Peyote: rapid decrease

Figure 30: At the point of the decrease, don't pick up a bead. Instead, go through two beads on the previous row.

FIGURE 30

Figure 31: When you reach the point where you went through two beads, pick up one bead; continue peyote stitch.

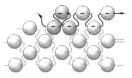

FIGURE 31

Peyote, two-drop

Work two-drop peyote stitch just like peyote stitch, but treat every pair of beads as if it were a single bead.

Figure 32: Start with an even number of beads divisible by four. Go through the first 2 beads. Pick up two beads (stitch 1 of row 3), skip two beads, and go through the next two beads. For odd-count turns, see **Figures 19 and 20**.

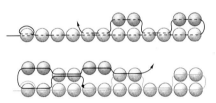

FIGURE 32

Peyote: zipping up or joining

Figure 33: To join two sections of peyote stitch invisibly, begin with a high bead on one side and a low bead on the other. Go through each high bead, alternating sides.

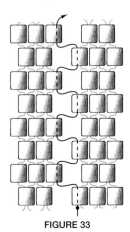

FIGURE 33

Right-angle weave

Figure 34: To start the first row, string four beads and tie into a snug circle. Pass the needle through the first three beads again.

FIGURE 34

Figure 35: Pick up three beads (#5, 6, and 7) and sew back through the last bead of the previous circle and #5 and 6.

FIGURE 35

Figure 36: Pick up three beads and sew back through #6 and the first two new beads. Continue adding three beads for each stitch until the first row is the desired length. You are sewing circles in a figure-8 pattern and alternating direction with each stitch.

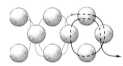

FIGURE 36

Figure 37: To begin row 2, sew through the last three beads of the last stitch on row 1, exiting the bead at the edge of one long side.

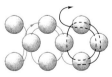

FIGURE 37

Figure 38: Pick up three beads and sew back through the bead you exited in **figure 37** (the first "top" bead of row 1) and the first new bead, sewing in a clockwise direction.

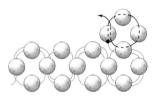

FIGURE 38

Figure 39: Pick up two beads and sew through the next top bead of the row below and the last bead of the previous stitch. Continue through the two new beads and the next top bead of the row below, sewing counter-clockwise.

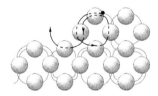

FIGURE 39

Figure 40: Sewing clockwise, pick up two beads and go through the side bead of the previous stitch, the top bead on the row below that you exited in **figure 39**, and the first new bead. Keep the thread moving in a figure-8. Pick up two beads for the rest of the row. Don't sew straight lines between stitches.

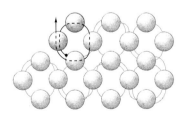

FIGURE 40

Basics

Beaded backstitch embroidery

Figure 41: To stitch a line of beads, come up through the fabric from the wrong side. String three beads. Stretch the bead thread along the line where the beads will go, and go through the fabric right after the third bead. Come up through the fabric between the second and third beads and go through the third bead again. String three more beads and repeat. For a tighter stitch, string only two beads at a time.

FIGURE 41

Whipstitch

Figure 42: Whipstitch is a method of hand-sewing seams. Bring the needle through the material on the bottom side of the opening, and push it through the material on the upper side of the opening at an angle as shown. Repeat until the opening has been closed.

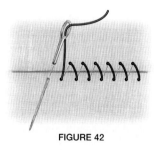

FIGURE 42

WIRE & METAL TECHNIQUES

Crimping

To crimp with chainnose pliers, simply mash the crimp as flat as possible, making sure the wires aren't crossed inside the crimp. Crimping with crimping pliers has two steps. It's also a good idea to place a bead between the crimp and the clasp to ease strain on the wire.

Figure 43: String a crimp bead and a large-hole bead on one end of a length of flexible beading wire. Go through one end of the clasp. Bring the wire back through both beads. Slide the bead and crimp close to the clasp, leaving a small space. Mash the crimp firmly in the hole closest to the handle, which looks like a half moon.

FIGURE 43

FIGURE 44

Figure 44: Hold the wires apart so one piece is on each side of the deep dent.

Figure 45: Put the dented crimp bead in the front hole of the pliers on end and press as hard as you can. This rolls the crimp into a cylinder.

FIGURE 45

Loops: plain

Figure 46: Cut a head or eye pin, leaving a ⅜-in. (1cm) tail above the bead. Bend it against the bead at a right angle.

FIGURE 46   **FIGURE 47**

Figure 47: Grip the tip of the wire in roundnose pliers. If you can feel the wire when you brush your finger along the back of the pliers, the loop will be teardrop-shaped. Press the pliers downward slightly to avoid pulling and rotate the wire into a loop.

Figure 48: Let go, regrasp the loop at the same place on the pliers, and keep turning to close the loop.

FIGURE 48   **FIGURE 49**

Figure 49: The closer to the pliers' tip that you work, the smaller the loop.

Loops: wrapped

Figure 50: Make sure you have no less than 1¼ in. (3.2cm) of wire above your bead. With the tip of your chainnose pliers, grasp the wire directly above the bead. Bend the wire (above the pliers) into a right angle.

FIGURE 50   FIGURE 51

Figure 51: Using roundnose pliers, position the jaws in the bend.

Figure 52: Bring the wire over the top jaw of the roundnose pliers.

FIGURE 52   FIGURE 53

Figure 53: Reposition the pliers so the lower jaw fits snugly in the loop. Curve the wire downward around the bottom of the roundnose pliers. This is the first half of a wrapped loop.

Figure 54: Position the jaws of your chainnose pliers across the loop.

FIGURE 54   FIGURE 55

Figure 55: Wrap the wire around the wire stem, covering the stem between the loop and the bead. Trim the excess wire and gently press the cut end close to the wraps with chainnose pliers.

Rings: opening and closing

Figure 56: Hold the jump ring with two pairs of chainnose pliers or chainnose and roundnose pliers, as shown.

FIGURE 56   FIGURE 57

Figure 57: To open the jump ring, bring one pair of pliers toward you and push the other away.

Figure 58: Reverse the steps to close the jump ring. ❂

FIGURE 58

S

tringing

Play on Color

Mix a lively palette of seed beads to complement candy-colored lampwork beads

by **Carol Pulk**

MATERIALS

both projects

- crimping pliers
- diagonal wire cutters
- **2** pair chainnose pliers or
  1 pair chainnose and
  1 pair bent chainnose (optional)

necklace 21½ in. (55cm)

- **11** 8–15mm lampwork beads
- 2g seed beads, size 11º, **12–24** colors to complement the lampwork beads
- **2** size 6º triangle beads or 5mm square beads
- **22** bead caps
- **4** spacer beads
- flexible beading wire, .010–.012
- toggle clasp (Bead Paradise, 440-775-2233, beadparadise.com)
- charm (optional)
- 6mm jump ring (optional)
- **2** crimp beads

bracelet 8 in. (20cm)

- **7** 8–15mm lampwork beads
- 2g seed beads, size 11º, **6–12** colors to complement the lampwork beads
- **2** size 6º seed beads
- **10** bead caps
- **4** spacer beads
- flexible beading wire, .010–.012
- self-closing clasp
- 6mm soldered jump ring
- **2** crimp beads

step*by*step

Necklace

You can substitute up to three small lampwork beads for one large bead. Or use other types of colorful beads instead of lampwork beads.

[1] Cut three 26-in. (66cm) lengths of flexible beading wire. Lay the wires together.

[2] String a bead cap, a lampwork bead, and a bead cap on the three wires.

[3] Center the beads and tape one end **(photo a)**.

[4] String 20 seed beads on each wire, alternating the colors **(photo b)**.

[5] Repeat steps 2 and 4 five times.

[6] String a spacer, a triangle or square bead, a spacer, a crimp, and a clasp loop over all three wires. Go back through the crimp and the next few beads, tightening the wire to form a small loop (photo c).

[7] Crimp the crimp bead (Basics, p. 10), then trim the excess wire close to the beads (photo d).

[8] Attach an optional charm to the clasp loop (photo e). My charm has a spring ring (photo above), which can be opened by hand. If yours does not have a spring ring, open a jump ring (Basics) to connect the clasp and the charm. Close the jump ring (Basics).

[9] Repeat these steps to make the second half of the necklace. Omit the charm.

Bracelet

[1] Cut three 12-in. (30cm) lengths of flexible beading wire. Lay the wires together.

[2] Repeat steps 2–3 of the necklace instructions.

[3] String eight seed beads on each wire, alternating the colors (photo f), then a bead cap, a lampwork bead, and a bead cap (photo g).

[4] Repeat step 3 three times, but use two spacers instead of bead caps with the final lampwork bead.

[5] String a size 6º seed bead, a crimp, and the clasp. Go back through the crimp and next few beads. Tighten the wire and beads, then crimp the crimp bead (photo h).

Trim the excess wire.

[6] Repeat steps 4–5 on the other end of the bracelet, but string a jump ring instead of the clasp. ●

To contact Carol, email chloeandcarol@netscape.com or call (330) 650-0122.

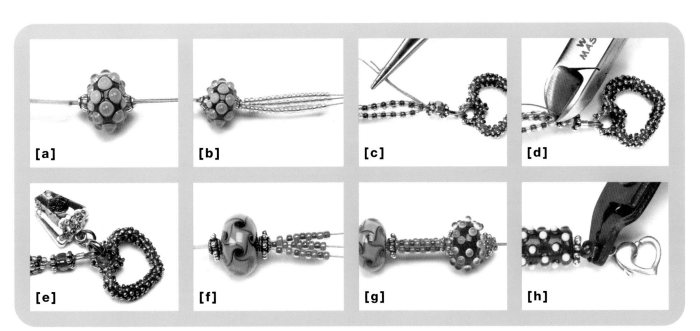

[a]

[b]

[c]

[d]

[e]

[f]

[g]

[h]

Charmed, I'm Sure

Make these fun and easy beaded charms with crystals, lampwork beads, and silver bead caps

by **Bindy Lambell**

step*by*step

Make the charms

[1] String an accent color (AC) crystal and a five-point bead cap (points up) on a 2-in. (5cm) head pin.

[2] String a main color (MC) crystal on a 1-in. (2.5cm) head pin. Make a small plain loop (Basics, p. 10) above the crystal. Slide the dangle onto the head pin prepared in step 1 and make sure the crystal sits in the bead cap as shown in **photo a**. Adjust the loop size

if necessary. Make four more dangles.

[3] Stack the four crystal dangles on the head pin as in step 1 **(photo b)**. String a five-point bead cap (points down), arranging the dangles so they nestle between the points on the two bead caps **(photo c)**. String an AC.

[4] Start a wrapped loop (Basics) about ⅛ in. (3mm) above the AC, slide a soldered jump ring into the loop, and finish with three to four wraps at the base of the loop **(photo d)**.

[5] Make three more crystal charms as

in steps 1–4, but substitute a jump ring or a split ring for the soldered ring on the last charm.

[6] String an AC, a spacer, a 10mm lampwork bead, a spacer, and an AC on a head pin. Start a wrapped loop, slide a soldered ring onto the loop, and finish with three to four wraps at the base of the loop **(photo e)**.

[7] Make three additional lampwork charms.

Assemble the bracelet

[**1**] String a crimp bead and half the clasp to about 1½ in. (3.8cm) from the end of the flexible beading wire. Go back through the crimp bead and crimp it (Basics). Trim the short tail.

[**2**] String an MC, an AC, an MC, a 4mm bead cap, an 8mm lampwork bead, and a 4mm bead cap.

[**3**] String an AC, a lampwork dangle, an MC, a 4mm bead cap, an 8mm lampwork bead, and a 4mm bead cap.

[**4**] Repeat step 3, alternating between crystal charms and lampwork charms **(photo f)** until you have four lampwork and three crystal charms strung.

[**5**] String an AC, an MC, and an AC. Then string a crimp bead and the other half of the clasp. Go back through the crimp bead and crimp it. Trim the tail.

[**6**] Open the jump ring on the remaining crystal charm and attach it to the loop end of the toggle **(photo g)**. ●

Bindy created the lampwork beads on p. 20. See more of her work at www.bindy.com or contact her at bindy@bindy.com.

EDITOR'S NOTE:
To make a pair of matching earrings, follow the directions for the desired charm, but slide an earring finding into the wrapped loop instead of a soldered jump ring.

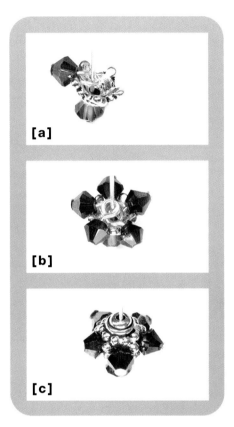

[a]

[b]

[c]

MATERIALS
bracelet 7½ in. (19cm)
- 4mm bicone crystals
  30 main color
  26 accent color
- **12** 8mm lampwork beads (or any 8mm beads or crystals)
- **8** five-point bead caps
- **16** 4mm bead caps
- **8** 4mm spacers
- **8** 2-in. (5cm) head pins, 22-gauge
- **20** 1-in. (2.5cm) head pins, 22-gauge
- **2** crimp beads
- **7** 3mm soldered jump rings
- 3mm jump ring or split ring
- 12 in. (30cm) flexible beading wire, .019
- toggle clasp
- crimping pliers
- wire cutters
- roundnose pliers
- chainnose pliers

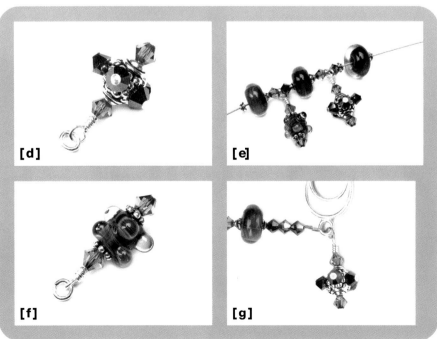

[d]

[e]

[f]

[g]

Color in Context

by **Cheryl Phelan**

Patti Cahill's fantastic bead creations are the culmination of years of studying color and color combinations, both on paper and at the torch. She takes her cue from the world around her, observing everything from people's clothing to their dinnerware, and then expands on those ideas in the many notebooks that line her shelves. While some beadmakers are archaeologists, Patti's more of a mad scientist when she works her glass; distilling what she sees today into a diary she'll take out of the kiln tomorrow. A Mexican kitchen, a flower, a swimsuit, a spaceship. You can always tell where Patti's been by looking at her beads. Although she gladly makes matched pairs, her beads come in such a variety of interesting shapes, it's more fun to mix and match them.

step*by*step

Amber necklace

[1] Cut three 24-in. (61cm) lengths of .010 flexible beading wire. Fold the wires in half and pass all six ends through a crimp bead. Slide the crimp bead to ⅛ in. (3mm) from the fold to form a loop **(photo a)**. Crimp the crimp bead (Basics, p. 10).

[2] String 8½ in. (22cm) of 2mm amber beads and 3mm and 4mm crystals in a random pattern on each strand as shown in **photo b**. Tape the end of each strand before stringing the next.

[3] Remove the tape and pass the wire ends through a crimp bead. Bring the wires back through the crimp bead to make a loop. Tighten the wires so the beads are snug. Crimp the crimp bead and trim the wires close to the crimp bead.

[4] Repeat steps 1-3 using two or three strands per crimp until you have a total of 12-16 strands.

[5] Cut a 24-in. length of .014 flexible beading wire. Pass the wire through a loop on each of the beaded strands. Center the strands on the wire and pass both ends through a cone-shaped lampwork bead. String a rondelle, a 4mm bicone, a rondelle, and a 5mm amber bead over both wires **(photo c)**. Continue stringing the pattern for approximately 5 in. (13cm), then tape the ends of the wire.

[6] Cut a 20-in. (51cm) length of .014 flexible beading wire, so the necklace is asymmetrical. Pass the wire through the remaining loops on the beaded strands and center them on the wire. String an 8-12mm lampwork bead over both wire ends **(photo d)**, then string the following pattern for approximately 7 in. (18cm): a 5mm crystal, a rondelle, a 5mm amber bead, a rondelle, a 5mm crystal, a flower, a 3mm crystal, an 8-10mm lampwork bead, a 3mm crystal, and a flower.

[7] String a 4mm crystal, a crimp bead, and a 4mm crystal. Pass the wires through the loop on one of the toggle components and back through the crystals and crimp bead. Crimp the crimp bead and trim the excess wires.

[8] Repeat step 7 with the remaining toggle component at the other end of the necklace.

Black necklace

[1] Cut a 22-in. (56cm) length of .014 beading wire.

String a pattern of Czech glass and seed beads for 16½ in. (42cm).

[2] String a crimp bead and pass the wire through a loop on the clasp and back through the crimp. Crimp the crimp bead and trim the wire.

[3] Repeat step 2 with the other end of the necklace and the remaining clasp half.

[4] Repeat steps 1–3, stringing a different pattern so the beads are staggered **(photo e)**.

[5] Cut a piece of chain

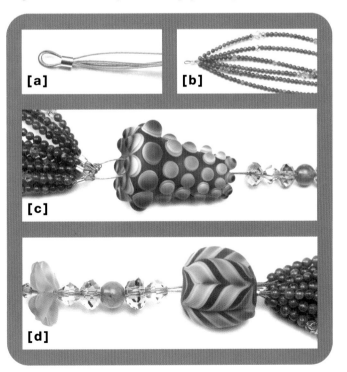

[a]

[b]

[c]

[d]

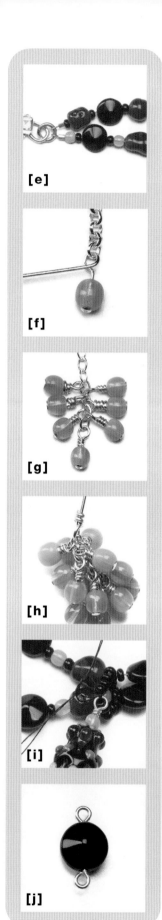

[e]

[f]

[g]

[h]

[i]

[j]

seven links long.

[6] String a 4mm bead on a head pin and make the first half of a wrapped loop (Basics).

[7] Slide the end link of chain on the loop (photo f) and finish the wraps.

[8] Connect two dangles to each of the remaining chain links (photo g) for a cluster of 13 dangles.

[9] Cut a 3-in. (7.6cm) piece of 22-gauge wire. Make the first half of a small wrapped loop about an inch (2.5cm) from the end of the wire. Connect the loop to the end link of chain between the two dangles and make two or three wraps (photo h).

[10] String a cone-shaped lampwork bead and a 4mm bead on the wire and against the loop. Make a wrapped loop above the 4mm bead.

[11] Cut a 12-in. (30cm) length of thread and, working with it doubled, string enough 8° seed beads to make a ring around both strands at the center of the necklace.

[12] Pass the needle through the wrapped loop of the cluster unit and tie the beads into a ring with a square knot (photo i and Basics). Sew through the ring of beads again, tie a few half-hitch knots (Basics) between beads, and trim the threads.

Cluster earrings

[1] Follow steps 5-8 for the black necklace.

[2] Cut a 1-in. piece of 22-gauge wire and make a plain loop (Basics) at one end.

[3] String an 8-12mm bead and make a plain loop on the same plane as the first (photo j).

[4] Open one of the loops and connect it to the end link of chain between the dangles, as you did for the necklace.

[5] Connect the remaining loop to the ear wire.

[6] Make a second earring to match the first. ●

Cheryl is an associate editor at Bead&Button magazine. Contact her at editor@beadandbutton.com.

MATERIALS

amber necklace 24 in. (61cm)
- cone-shaped lampwork bead (Patti Cahill beads, Dyed in the Fire Designs, 828-689-8934)
- 12-15mm lampwork bead
- 4-10mm lampwork beads
- Swarovski crystals
  80-100 3mm bicones
  15-25 4mm bicones
  20 5mm bicones
  20 6mm rondelles
- **8** 16-in. (41cm) strands of 2mm round amber beads
- **10** 5mm round amber beads
- **8** 12mm pressed glass flowers
- flexible beading wire 16 ft. (4.9m) .010

44 in. (1.1m) .012-.014
- **8** crimp beads
- toggle clasp
- crimping pliers

black necklace 18 in. (46cm)
- cone-shaped lampwork bead
- **100-125** assorted Czech glass beads, size 4-10mm
- **16** 4mm beads
- 2g seed beads, size 8°
- **4** crimp beads
- clasp
- 1 in. (2.5cm) small-link chain
- 44 in. (1.1m) flexible beading wire, size .012-.014
- 3 in. (7.6cm) 22-gauge wire, sterling silver, half hard

- Nymo B or Fireline, 6 lb. test
- beading needles, #12

cluster earrings
- **2** 8-12mm Czech glass beads
- **30** 4mm beads
- **30** head pins
- pair of ear wires
- 2 in. (5cm) 22-gauge wire, sterling silver, half hard

black necklace and earrings
- crimping pliers
- chainnose pliers
- roundnose pliers
- wire cutters

Better in Blue

When working with a large blue focal piece, such as this dramatic dichroic pendant, it can be hard to match the color with one strand of complementary beads. By using five strands of seed beads dressed up with a few crystals, simulated opals, and silver, you can pick up several of the shades in the pendant with a necklace that won't overpower it.

by **Debbie Nishihara**

step*by*step

Setting it up

[1] Cut two 3-in. (7.6cm) lengths of 22-gauge sterling silver wire. (Your wires should be 2 in./5cm longer than your cones to leave sufficient room for wrapped loops.)

[2] Make a wrapped loop at one end of each wire (Basics, p. 10).

[3] This necklace is 19 in. (48cm) long without the clasp. Cut five 22-in. (56cm) lengths of flexible beading wire. If you find it's easier to pull the wires through the crimps when you've got lots left over, allow for those extra inches now.

EDITOR'S NOTE:
Finished jewelry should end with a bang. The person who wears your work will appreciate your going that extra step to finish your pieces with beautiful findings.

Stringing patterns

[1] Gather the strands and slide the following to the center: 5mm crystal, 4mm spacer, an opal, a saucer bead, an opal, the pendant, an opal, a saucer bead, an opal, 4mm spacer, and 5mm crystal (photo a). Starting from either 5mm crystal, string one side of the necklace at a time.

[2] On strand 1, string ten blue 11ºs then the following pattern: 3mm spacer, 8º, 3mm spacer, ten blue 11ºs, 4mm spacer, cat's eye, silver saucer, cat's eye, 4mm spacer, and ten blue 11ºs (photo b). Repeat three times then string a 3mm spacer, 8º, 3mm spacer, and fifteen blue 11ºs.

[3] On strand 2 string the following pattern: 15 blue 11ºs, cat's eye, 4mm spacer, an opal, 4mm spacer, cat's eye, 15 blue 11ºs, 3mm spacer, 8º, 3mm spacer (photo c). Repeat three times, then string five blue 11ºs.

[4] Strand 3 is identical to strand 2.

[5] On strand 4 string three 3-cut seeds, a 3mm spacer, 4mm crystal, 3mm spacer, and 15 3-cut seeds. Then string the following pattern: 3mm spacer, 8º, 3mm spacer, 15 3-cut seeds, 3mm spacer, 4mm crystal, 3mm spacer, 15 3-cut seeds (photo d). Repeat twice, then string a 3mm spacer, 8º, 3mm spacer, and 25 3-cut seeds.

[6] Strand 5 is identical to strand 4.

Add or remove seed beads to make the strands even.

[7] String the other side of the necklace to mirror the first.

Finishing

[1] Hold the necklace up and adjust as necessary so both sides are even. By playing with the bead counts at the ends, you can stagger the opals and other elements exiting the cone (photo e).

[2] Gather the ends from one side of the necklace. String at least two strands through a crimp bead, the wrapped loop, and back through the crimp bead. I string all five strands through one (photo f), but multiple crimp beads may be preferable and won't be visible inside the cones. Because the strands tend to slip here, I like to hold the necklace up and pull each wire through with a pair of pliers before I crimp. Pull the strands tight, crimp the crimp bead(s), and trim the tails.

[3] Slide a cone over each silver wire and pull the strands all the way in (photo g).

[4] Start a wrapped loop and attach one end of a toggle clasp (photo h). Finish the loop and trim the end of the wire.

[5] Repeat step 4 with the other end of the toggle clasp. ●

Debbie is an associate editor at Bead&Button. Contact her at editor@beadandbutton.com.

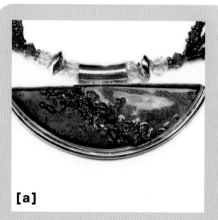

[a]

[b]

[c]

[d]

[e]

[f]

[g]

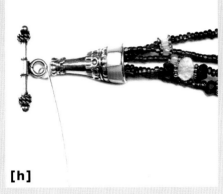

[h]

EDITOR'S NOTE:
When stringing into cones, adjust your bead counts so you don't waste spacers or expensive beads by hiding them.

MATERIALS

- dichroic pendant (Eclectica, 262-641-0910, eclecticabeads.com)
- 16-in. (41cm) strand 6mm simulated opals
- 16-in. strand 5mm royal blue faceted fiber optic (cat's eye) beads
- Swarovski crystals, sapphire
  16 4mm bicone
  2 5mm bicone
- seed beads
  hank size 11º, royal blue
  hank 12º 3-cut, purple/blue
  50 size 8º silver-lined white

- **10** 10mm sterling silver saucer beads (Rio Grande, 800-545-6566, riogrande.com)
- **115** 3mm daisy-shaped silver spacers
- **50** 4mm daisy-shaped silver spacers
- flexible beading wire, size .014
- pair of inlaid silver cones (Scottsdale Bead Supply, 480-945-5988, scottsdalebead.com)
- silver toggle clasp
- 6 in. (15cm) 22-gauge sterling silver wire
- **4–6** silver crimp beads
- chainnose pliers
- roundnose pliers
- wire cutters

Style

String art glass, crystals, and silver for a pair of elegant necklaces

by Susan Tobias

step*by*step

Blue necklace

[1] To prepare the pendant, start a wrapped loop (Basics, p. 10) on one end of the 20-gauge wire, string a small finding or accent bead, then finish the wraps. String a focal bead on the wire **(photo a)**.
[2] String a silver bead cap on the wire, then make a wrapped loop.
[3] Center a liquid silver bead or bugle on 20 in. (51cm) of flexible beading wire, then string the pendant over it **(photo b)**.
[4] String the following sequence of beads: a 4mm crystal, a bead cap, a 12mm crystal, a bead cap, a 4mm crystal, five 3mm crystals, a 4mm crystal, a bead cap, a 12mm crystal, a bead cap, a tube bead, a bead cap, a 12mm crystal, a bead cap, a 4mm crystal, ten 3mm

crystals, and a 4mm crystal **(photo c)**.
[5] String a crimp bead and a jump ring, then go back through the crimp and the next few crystals. Crimp the crimp bead (Basics) and trim the excess wire **(photo d)**.
[6] Repeat steps 4-5 on the other end, tightening all the beads before crimping.
[7] Attach the S-hook clasp to either jump ring **(photo e)**.

Red necklace

[1] Cut an 8-in. (20cm) piece of 20-gauge wire and make a wrapped loop on one end.
[2] Cut a 5-in. (13cm) piece of flexible beading wire, then string a crimp bead. Go

through the loop then back through the crimp, leaving a 1-in. (2.5cm) tail. Crimp the crimp bead, then string 3 in. (7.6cm) of seed beads and a crimp. Crimp the crimp bead and cut the excess wire **(photo f)**.
[3] Repeat step 2 five times, varying the fringe length slightly (as on the red necklace above).
[4] To make the pendant, string a cone, a 5mm crystal, the focal bead, and a 5mm crystal on the wire. Make a second wrapped loop.
[5] Cut a 4-in. (10cm) piece of 20-gauge wire. Start a wrapped loop, string the

pendant's loop, then finish the wraps. String a 5mm crystal, a disc, and a 5mm crystal. Make another wrapped loop **(photo g)**.
[6] Cut an 8-in. piece of 20-gauge wire and make the first half of a wrapped loop

[a]

[b]

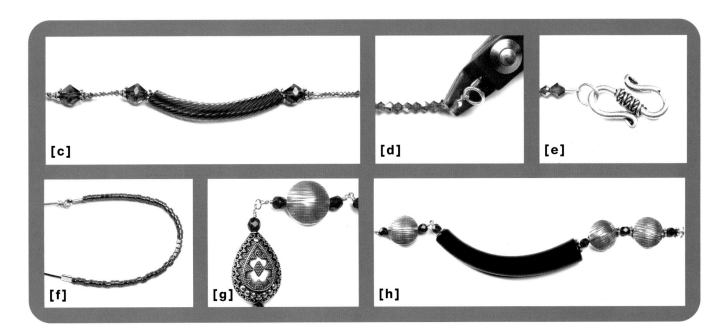

[c]   [d]   [e]

[f]   [g]   [h]

ubstance

on one end. Connect this loop to the second loop made in step 5. String a 5mm crystal, an 8mm spacer, a tube bead, an 8mm spacer, and a 5mm crystal. Make another wrapped loop.
[7] String a crimp bead on an 8-in. length of beading wire. Go through the wrapped loop then back through the crimp bead. Crimp the crimp bead and trim the excess wire.
[8] String a disc over the wrapped loop. String a 6mm spacer, a 5mm crystal, a 6mm spacer, a disc, a 6mm spacer, a 5mm crystal, a 6mm spacer, a crimp, and a jump ring. Go back through the crimp and the next few beads. Tighten the wire, crimp the crimp bead, then trim the excess wire (photo h).
[9] Repeat steps 5–8 on the other end of the necklace.
[10] Attach the S-hook clasp to either jump ring. ○

Contact Susan at dktobias@prodigy.net.

MATERIALS
both projects
- flexible beading wire, .014
- crimping pliers
- roundnose pliers
- chainnose pliers
- wire cutters

blue necklace 16 in. (41cm)
- **2** matched tube beads (Olive Glass, 360-468-2821)
- art glass focal bead (on necklace: Tom Boylan, tomboylan.com; in step-by-step shots: Kim Wertz, heartbead.com.)
- **6** 12mm vintage crystals
- **30** 3mm Swarovski crystal bicones

- **10** 4mm Swarovski crystal bicones
- **12** silver bead caps
- silver bead or bead cap (to fit top of focal bead)
- small finding or accent bead, sized to fit in the focal bead
- liquid silver bead or bugle
- **2** 4mm soldered jump rings
- **2** crimp beads
- S-hook clasp
- 6 in. (15cm) 20-gauge wire

red necklace 16 in. (41cm)
- **2** matched tube beads (Olive Glass, 360-468-2821)

- silver focal bead (Singaraja Imports, 800-865-8856)
- **14** 5mm vintage crystals
- **6** 19mm silver discs, flat (Singaraja Imports)
- 2g Czech 3-cut beads, size 12º
- silver cone
- **8** 6mm spacers
- **4** 8mm spacers
- **2** 4mm soldered jump rings
- **16** crimp beads
- S-hook clasp
- 46-in. (1.2m) 20-gauge wire

Watch

Don't be surprised if you keep getting asked for the time while wearing this sparkling watchband. The crystal sections string up so quickly, you'll be able to make one for every outfit and still have time on your hands.

by **Anna Nehs**

step*by*step

[1] Cut a 12-in. (30cm) length of flexible beading wire.

[2] Pass the wire through a loop on the watch face so it is centered on the wire. String a 5mm crystal, a seed bead, and a 5mm crystal on each end of the wire (photo a).

[3] String a seed bead over both wires and against the crystals (photo b).

[4] String a bead cap, a 10-12mm bead or crystal, a bead cap, and a seed bead over both wires (photo c).

[5] String a 5mm crystal, a seed bead, and a 5mm crystal on each wire (photo d).

[6] Repeat steps 3-5.

[7] String a seed bead over both wires and tape the end of the wires so the beads don't fall off.

[8] Repeat steps 1-7 with the other loop on the watch face.

[9] Check the length against your wrist and add or remove beads from each side until you reach the desired length minus the length of the clasp.

[10] Remove the tape from one side of

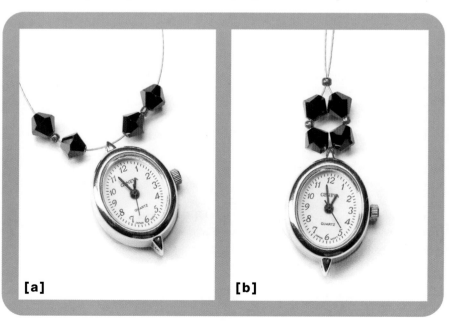

[a]   [b]

Out

the band. String a crimp bead and seven to nine seed beads. Pass the wire through the loop on one of the clasp components and back through the crimp bead **(photo e)**. If the loop on the clasp is small and doesn't slide over the seed beads, remove half of the seeds, string the clasp, and restring the second half of the seeds, so the clasp is centered.

[11] Adjust the tension of the wires so the crystals form a square and all the beads are snug.

[12] Crimp the crimp bead (Basics, p. 10) and trim the excess wires as close to the crimp as possible **(photo f)**.

[13] Repeat steps 10-12 to finish the other end. ●

Anna is an associate editor at Bead&Button magazine. Contact her at editor@beadandbutton.com.

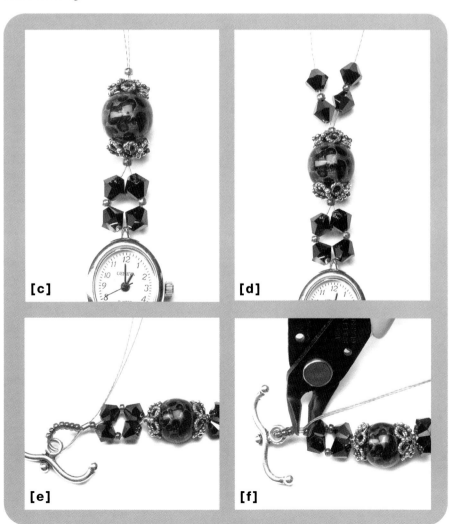

[c]

[d]

[e]

[f]

EDITOR'S NOTE:
A toggle clasp with three rings (at left) makes the length of the watchband adjustable, and the rings add weight to the clasp, keeping the watch face on top of your wrist.

MATERIALS
watchband 7½-8 in. (19-20cm)
- watch face
- **4** 10mm Swarovski bicone crystals or 10-12mm beads
- **24** 5mm bicone crystals
- **8** bead caps
- **1g** Japanese seed beads, size 11º
- toggle clasp
- **2** crimp beads
- **24** in. (61cm) flexible beading, size .012-.014
- crimping pliers
- wire cutters

A Fine

A fine-linked chain accents borosilicate beads from Eister Glass. Aquamarine gemstones pick up the lovely sea-green color that swirls throughout the beads.

by **Mindy Brooks**

step*by*step

[1] Determine the finished length of your necklace (mine is 16 in./41cm), add 5 in. (13cm), and cut a piece of beading wire to that length.
[2] String the end chain link, crystal, art bead, and crystal on the beading wire. Skip about an inch (2.5cm) of chain and go through another link **(photo a)**. Don't allow the chain to twist. Adjust the chain's length so it loops under your art bead without touching it.

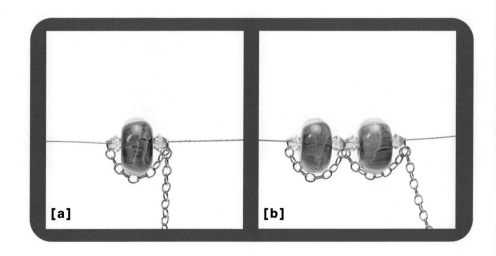

[a]

[b]

Line

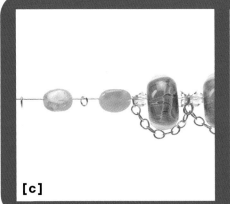

[c]

[d]

[e]

[3] String another crystal, art bead, and crystal and go through a chain link as before **(photo b)**. Repeat with the remaining crystals and art beads.

[4] Slide the beads and chain to the center of the beading wire. Cut off the excess chain.

[5] On each end of the beading wire, string an alternating pattern of gemstones and soldered jump rings. For the necklace shown here, I cut apart an 8-in. (20cm) chain and used the individual links in place of jump rings **(photo c)**.

[6] When the necklace is the desired length, string a crimp bead and lobster claw on one end. Go back through the crimp bead **(photo d)**. If possible, continue through one more bead past the crimp. (The holes in your gemstones may be too small for the wire to pass through twice.) Crimp the crimp bead (Basics, p. 10) and trim the excess wire.

[7] Repeat on the other end, using a soldered jump ring in place of the clasp **(photo e)**. Trim the excess wire. ◗

Mindy is the editor of Bead&Button *magazine. Contact her at* editor@beadandbutton.com.

EDITOR'S NOTE: You can easily substitute other styles of chain for the simple round cable chain shown here. Be sure to choose a chain that's in proportion to the size of your beads.

MATERIALS

necklace 16 in. (41cm)

- **6** 8 x 13mm (approx.) art glass beads (Eister Glass, 805-461-5445, artist1@fix.net)
- 16-in. (41cm) strand small oval gemstones to match art beads
- **12** 4mm bicone crystals
- 16 in. or more fine-linked cable chain or 8 in. (20cm) or more fine-linked cable chain
- **48** or more 3mm soldered jump rings
- lobster claw clasp with soldered jump ring
- flexible beading wire, .014–.015
- **2** crimp beads
- chainnose or crimping pliers
- diagonal wire cutters

Si

Multiple strands
drape gracefully in a
graduated necklace
of liquid silver

Simply strung, this
necklace can go from
casual to dramatic by
changing the length
and quantity of
strands. Make one
with strands of all
the same length to
support a pendant.
String short strands
for a coordinating
bracelet.

ver cascade

by **Glenda Payseno**

step*by*step

Necklace

Measure your neck to determine the length of the shortest strand. This one is 16 in. (41cm). To start with a different length, adjust the number of bugles until the strand fits comfortably around your neck. Make each subsequent strand five liquid-silver bugle beads longer than the one before.

[1] Start with a 1½-yd. (1.4m) length of thread. Tie the end of the thread to the first loop on the clasp with a surgeon's knot (Basics, p. 10 and **photo a**), leaving a 4-in. (10cm) tail.

[2] Pick up a 4mm bead, 70 liquid silver beads, and a 4mm bead. Sew through the corresponding loop on the other half of the clasp.

[3] Sew back through the 4mm bead **(photo b)**. Pull the beads snug against the clasp. Pick up 75 liquid silver beads and sew through the 4mm bead and the first loop on the first side of the necklace.

[4] Tie the working thread and the tail together with a surgeon's knot. To complete the first pair of strands, thread a needle on each end and pull the tails into the 4mm bead and the first few liquid silver beads. Dot the knot with glue if desired and pull so the knot slips into the 4mm bead **(photo c)**.

[5] Add strands to each clasp loop as in steps 1–4. Increase the length of thread by 5 in. (13cm) for each new pair of strands. Increase the liquid silver beads by five for every strand. Trim the tails.

Bracelet

Work the bracelet in the same manner as the necklace, but make all the strands the same length. You can also add more strands to each loop of the clasp to make a more substantial bracelet. ●

Contact Glenda via email at glendapayseno@comcast.net

MATERIALS

both projects
- Nymo D conditioned with beeswax, Power Pro 10 lb. test, or Fireline 6 lb. test
- beading needles, #12 sharps
- G-S Hypo Cement (optional)

necklace
- 4–8-strand silver clasp
- 1½ oz. 6mm liquid silver bugle beads (beadboppers.com)
- 8–16 4mm silver beads (firemountaingems.com)

bracelet 7 in. (18cm)
- 4-strand silver slide clasp
- ½ oz. 6mm liquid silver bugle beads
- 8 4mm silver beads

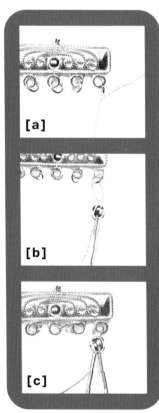

[a]

[b]

[c]

EDITOR'S NOTE: The liquid silver beads can slip into the hole of the 4mm beads, which makes the necklace more difficult to string. You can avoid this by using beads with smaller holes or by stringing a 2mm silver bead or 11º seed bead between the liquid silver beads and the 4mm beads.

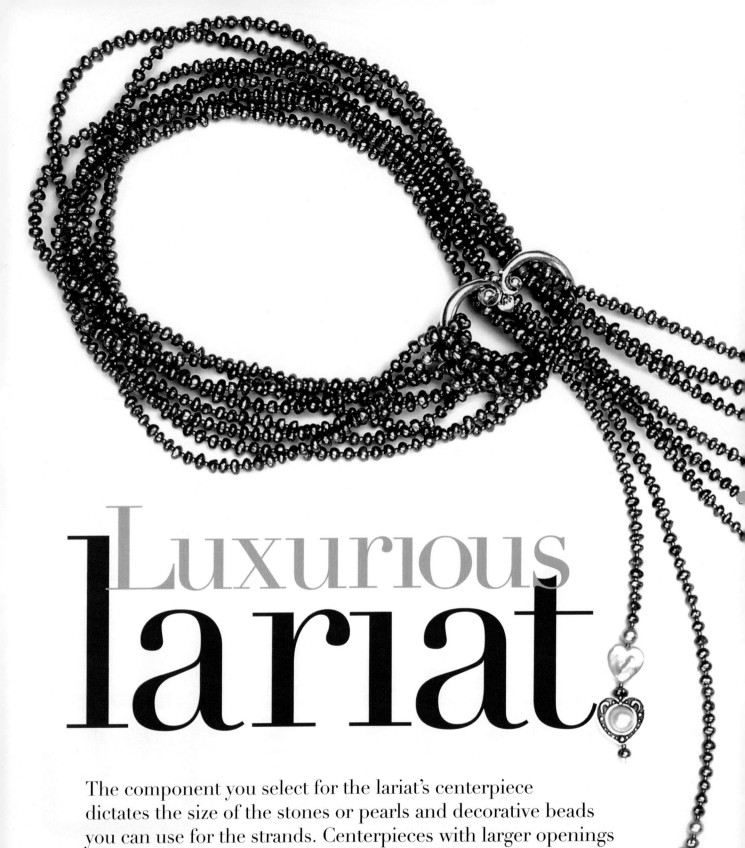

Luxurious lariat

The component you select for the lariat's centerpiece dictates the size of the stones or pearls and decorative beads you can use for the strands. Centerpieces with larger openings accommodate more strands and larger beads.

A pearl cascade falls through silver

by **Kelly Charveaux**

MATERIALS

lariat

- circular centerpiece
- 5-6 decorative beads
- 10 16-in. (41cm) strands of pearls or gemstone beads
- hank of seed beads, size 11º
- 5-6 beads to cover crimps
- flexible beading wire, .012-.014
- 10-12 crimp beads
- chainnose or crimping pliers
- wire cutters

step*by*step

[1] Cut a 34-in. (86cm) piece of flexible beading wire.

[2] String enough seed beads or pearls to go around the centerpiece. End with a crimp bead **(photo a)**. Slide the beads to about 2 in. (5cm) from the end of the wire, then pass the wire through the centerpiece.

[3] Slide the end of the wire through the crimp bead and pull tight **(photo b)**. Crimp the crimp bead (Basics, p. 10).

[4] String a bead to cover the crimp.

[5] String an alternating pattern of pearls or gemstones and seed beads **(photo c)** until the strand measures 26 in. (66cm).

[6] String a decorative bead, a pearl, a seed, a pearl, a seed, a pearl, and a crimp. (You can string any pattern of beads for the end of the strand; just make sure to end with a crimp bead.)

[7] Crimp the crimp bead and trim the excess wire **(photo d)**.

[8] Repeat steps 1-7 four or more times. Vary the lengths of the strands, but keep them in the 23-27 in. (58-69cm) range. ◓

Contact Kelly at 3625 N. Marshall Way, Scottsdale, Arizona 85251 or scottsdalebeadsupply @msn.com.

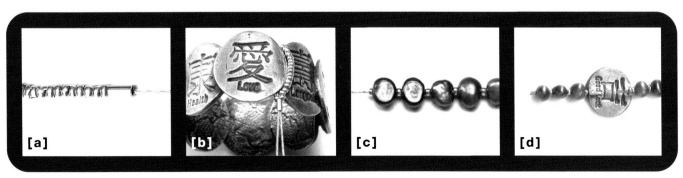

[a] **[b]** **[c]** **[d]**

Make a sophisticated bracelet in less than an afternoon with this quick technique. You can also lengthen the pattern to make a choker or condense it to create a pair of earrings to match.

by **Anna Nehs**

Easy Elegance

step*by*step

Bracelet

[1] Cut four strands of beading wire 12 in. (30cm) long. String a crimp bead on one strand and go through the first loop of the clasp and the crimp bead. Repeat for the other strands, sharing loops of the clasp if necessary **(photo a)**.

[2] String four crystals on the first and fourth strands **(photo b)**.

[3] String one crystal on the second and third strand, a double-drilled pearl over both strands, then one crystal on each strand **(photo c)**.

[4] String one double-drilled pearl over the first and second strands and one over the third and fourth strands **(photo d)**. If any beading wire shows on the first and fourth strands, fill in the gaps with 15° beads.

[5] Repeat steps 2–4 until you have six sets, then repeat steps 2–3.

[6] String a crimp bead on the first strand, go through the corresponding loop on the clasp, and back through the crimp bead. Crimp the crimp bead (Basics, p. 10) and trim the tail. Repeat for the other three strands.

Earrings

[1] Cut the wire into four 4-in. (10cm) pieces. Make a plain loop (Basics) at one end of each wire. Set two aside.

[2] String a 4mm crystal on each of two wires, a double-drilled pearl on both wires, and a 4mm crystal on each wire. Make a plain loop next to the end crystal on each wire.

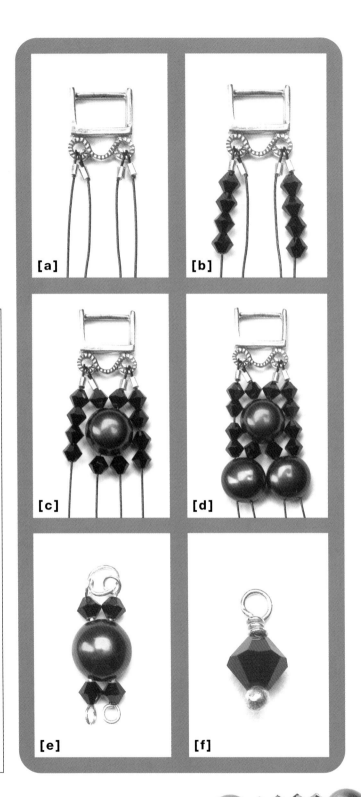

[a]

[b]

[c]

[d]

[e]

[f]

MATERIALS

bracelet 7 in. (18cm)
- **84** 4mm crystals, bicone
- **19** 6mm pearls, double-drilled
- 1g Japanese seed beads, size 15º (optional)
- multistrand clasp (2 or 4 strands)
- **8** crimp beads
- flexible beading wire, .012
- crimping pliers
- diagonal wire cutters

earrings one pair
- **2** 6mm pearls, double-drilled
- **22** 4mm crystals, bicone
- **14** head pins, 24-gauge
- 16 in. (41cm) 24-gauge wire
- **2** 4mm soldered jump rings
- **2** earring findings
- chainnose pliers
- roundnose pliers

[3] Open the loops (Basics) on one end, attach a soldered jump ring to both loops, and close the loops **(photo e)**.

[4] String a 4mm crystal on a head pin. Make a wrapped loop (Basics) above the crystal **(photo f)**. Make six more crystal dangles.

[5] Open the loops on the other end of the pearl component, slip three dangles onto each loop, and close the loops.

[6] Open the loop on the earring finding and attach the jump ring and a dangle. Close the loop.

[7] Make a second earring to match the first. ◗

Anna is an associate editor at Bead&Button *magazine. Contact her at editor@beadandbutton.com.*

Sparkling

step*by*step

Bracelet

[1] Cut three 12-in. (31cm) strands of flexible beading wire. String a crimp bead and one loop on one half of the clasp on each strand. Go back through the crimp beads, tighten the wire, and crimp the crimp beads (Basics, p. 10, and **photo a**).
[2] String two 3mm silver beads, a crystal, and two cylinders on the outer (first) strand. String a silver bead, two crystals, and a cylinder on the middle (second) strand. String three crystals on the last (third) strand. Thread each strand through the corresponding hole on the spacer bar **(photo b)**.
[3] String three crystals on the first strand. On the second, string a cylinder, two crystals, and a cylinder. On the third, string two cylinders, a crystal, and two cylinders. Thread each strand through the spacer

as before **(photo c)**.
[4] String two cylinders, a crystal, and two cylinders on the first strand. On the second, string a cylinder, two crystals, and a cylinder. On the third, string three crystals. Thread each strand through the spacer **(photo d)**.
[5] Repeat steps 3 and 4 until you've strung the last spacer bar. To finish, string

two cylinders, a crystal, and two silver beads on the first strand. On the second, string a cylinder, two crystals, and a silver bead. On the third, string three crystals **(photo e)**.
[6] String a crimp bead on each wire. Crimp each strand to the corresponding hole on the remaining clasp section.

MATERIALS

bracelet 7½ in. (19cm)
- **66** 6mm crystal bicones
- **10** 3-hole crystal spacers
- **6** 3mm silver beads
- **60** (approx.) Japanese cylinder beads, silver-lined
- 3-strand clasp
- flexible beading wire, .014
- **6** crimp beads
- crimping pliers

earrings
- **14** 6mm crystals bicones
- **4** 2-hole crystal spacers
- **4** 22-gauge head pins
- pair of ear wires
- **2** in. (5cm) fine chain
- roundnose pliers
- wire cutters

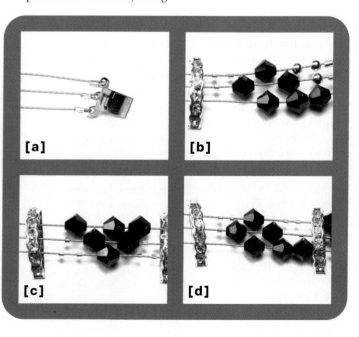

[a]   [b]

[c]   [d]

Spacers

Crystal spacers add light and definition to an easy bracelet and earring ensemble

by **Anna Nehs**

Earrings

[**1**] String a crystal onto a head pin. Repeat. Slide both head pins through a spacer.

[**2**] String a crystal on one of the head pins and two crystals on the other. Go through the second spacer.

[**3**] String a crystal on each head pin **(photo f)**.

[**4**] Trim each head pin, leaving ¼ in. (6mm) of wire above the end bead and turn a small loop (Basics).

[**5**] Cut the chain in half. Count the links and remove one, if necessary, so you are working with an odd number of links.

[**6**] Open one head pin loop (Basics) and attach the end chain link. Close the loop. Repeat with the other head pin **(photo g)**.

[**7**] Attach the ear wire to the middle chain link **(photo h)**. Check that the earring hangs straight. You may need to adjust the chain length on one side.

[**8**] Make the second earring the mirror image of the first. ●

Anna is an associate editor at Bead&Button *magazine. Contact her at editor@beadandbutton.com.*

EDITOR'S NOTE: Check the length before you finish. You may have to adjust the bead count or the design to suit your wrist size, but that's the only way to get the right fit.

[e]

[f]

[g]

[h]

Cool Dip

Dip into your bead stash for crystals and seed beads in cool, refreshing colors. String them quickly and spend the rest of the day relaxing in your hammock.

by **Carol Pulk**

step*by*step

Necklace

[1] Determine the desired finished length of your necklace (This one is 19 in./48cm) and add 6 in. (15cm). Cut three pieces of beading wire to that length.

[2] Center the following beads over all three wires: a 3mm crystal, an 11º seed bead, a 4mm crystal, an 11º, a 3mm crystal, an 11º, a 4mm crystal, an 11º, and a 3mm crystal (photo a).

[3] Work on one side of the necklace at a time. String ten 11ºs, a 3mm crystal, and ten 11ºs on each wire (photo b).

[4] Over all three wires, string a bead cap, a 6mm bead, a flat spacer, a 10–12mm bead, a flat spacer, a 6mm bead, and a bead cap (photo c).

[5] Separate the wires and string 11ºs between a repeating pattern of a 3mm crystal, an 11º, a 4mm crystal, an 11º, and a 3mm crystal. Adjust the placement of the crystals as you work so they are randomly spaced on the strands (photo d).

[6] Repeat steps 3–5 on the other end of the necklace.

[7] Check the length and adjust the number of beads on each strand as necessary. String a silver bead, a crimp bead, and one clasp half over all three wires on one end. Bring the wires back through the crimp and the silver bead (photo e).

[8] Adjust the tension of the strands so the beads are snug and crimp the crimp bead (Basics, p. 10). Trim the excess wires. Repeat on the other end of the necklace.

Centerpiece

[1] String an assortment of glass beads, crystals, and silver beads on a head pin. Make a wrapped loop (Basics) above the beads.

[2] Make a total of five dangles, varying the bead combinations and length of each one. Before finishing the loops on three of the dangles, slide the end link of a ½–¾-in. (1.3–2cm) piece of chain into the loop (photo f).

[3] Open the large jump ring (Basics). Slide the dangles and charms onto it. Attach the jump ring to the center of the necklace (photo g) and close the jump ring. ●

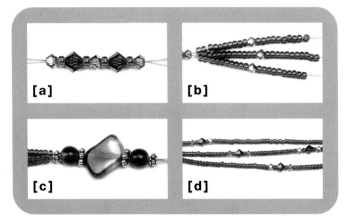

[a] [b] [c] [d]

[e] [f] [g]

Carol Pulk lives in Hudson, Ohio. Contact her at (330) 650-0122 or chloeandcarol@netscape.com.

MATERIALS

necklace 17 in. (43cm)

- 2 10–12mm glass beads
- 3–9 assorted glass beads and crystals for dangles
- 4 6mm glass beads
- 18–28 4mm bicone crystals
- 45–60 3mm bicone crystals

- 7–9 4–6mm silver beads
- 5g seed beads, size 11º
- 4 5mm flat spacers
- 4 bead caps or spacers
- 2 silver charms
- flexible beading wire, size .010
- 2 in. (5cm) chain

- 5 2-in. (5cm) head pins
- 6–8mm jump ring
- toggle clasp
- 2 crimp beads
- crimping pliers
- wire cutters
- roundnose pliers
- chainnose pliers

Make a luxurious scarf necklace with long, flowing strands of seed beads. String a second necklace in a coordinating color and enjoy the flexibility of interchangeable components.

by **Linda Arline Hartung**

Great Lengths

step*by***step**

[1] Cut 40 24-in. (61cm) pieces of nylon beading cord.

[2] Separate one strand of seed beads from its hank. Tape one end to secure the beads. Tie the other end to a piece of beading cord using the first half of a square knot (Basics, p. 10). Slide the beads off the original strand, over the knot, and onto the cord **(photo a)**.

[3] Slide the last bead about 1 in. (2.5cm) from the rest and make a square knot over it **(photo b)**.

[4] Place the tail against the exposed cord. Slide eight beads

MATERIALS

necklace 38½ in. (98cm)

- **2** hanks (24 strands each, 20 in./51cm long) seed beads, size 13º or smaller in coordinating colors
- Hastings bonded nylon cord, 1/0x (Shor International Corp., 914-667-1100, shorinternational.com)
- magnetic barrel clasp* with dimpled magnets (Alacarte Clasps, 707-887-2825, alacarteclasps.com)
- **2** 3 x 2mm crimps (2mm hole)
- Bond 527 Cement
- G-S Hypo Cement
- two-part epoxy
- rubbing (isopropyl) alcohol (optional)
- toothpick
- diagonal wire cutters
- bentnose pliers
- file or emery board
- bead reamer (optional)
- *** Note:** Pregnant women and people with pacemakers should consult their physicians before wearing magnetic jewelry.

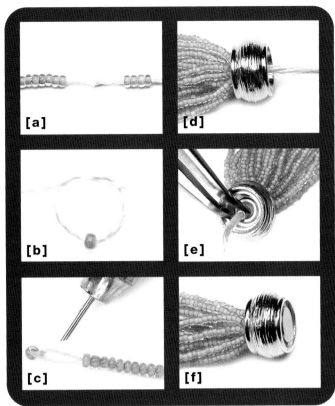

[a] [d]

[b] [e]

[c] [f]

over the tail and position them about ¼ in. (6mm) from the knotted bead. To secure the beads on the nylon, dab the exposed cords with G-S Hypo Cement **(photo c)**, then slide the beads against the knotted bead. Trim the tail. Push all the remaining beads flush against the others at the knot.

[5] Repeat steps 2–4, making a total of 20 beaded cords.

[6] Gather the 20 cords and glue the tips together using Bond 527 Cement. When the glue is dry, trim the tip of the glued section at an angle with diagonal wire cutters.

[7] String half the clasp on the glued cords **(photo d)**. If needed, use a bead reamer to enlarge the clasp's hole.

[8] String a crimp bead over the glued cords. Pull each cord so the beads are inside the clasp. Dab the cords at the bottom of the clasp with Bond 527 Cement, then push the crimp against the cords while still wet. Crimp the crimp bead (Basics) using bentnose pliers **(photo e)**. Allow the adhesive to dry, then cut the cords close to the crimp.

[9] Repeat steps 2–8 to make the second half of the necklace.

[10] Lightly file the dimpled sides of the magnets. Place them dimpled-side down into the clasps **(photo f)**. Test the fit by putting the two clasps together, making sure there are no gaps. If the clasp halves are not flush, trim the string closer to the crimp, then retest the fit.

[11] Remove the magnets. Mix a small batch of two-part epoxy according to the manufacturer's instructions. With a toothpick, place a liberal amount of glue in the clasp cavity. The glue should overflow slightly.

[12] Press a magnet into a clasp, dimpled-side down. Apply pressure. Wipe off the excess glue, then apply pressure until the glue sets. Remove any glue residue by wiping the clasp and magnet with a cloth slightly dampened with rubbing alcohol. Repeat with the second magnet and clasp. ●

For kits, contact Linda Arline Hartung at Alacarte Clasps, alacarteclasps.com, info@alacarteclasps.com, or (800) 977-2825.

EDITOR'S NOTE: The beads shown here are Italian seed beads, available through Alacarte Clasps. You can substitute Czech beads in size 13º or smaller for these diminutive beauties.

Garland
Necklace

String a strand of easy-to-make components to create the illusion of an intricate necklace.

by **Sharon Lester**

step*by*step

Large cluster

[1] Thread a needle with a 2-ft. (61cm) length of Nymo conditioned with beeswax (Basics, p. 10). Pick up a drop bead and slide it to 3 in. (7.6cm) from the end of the thread. Tie an overhand knot (Basics) above the drop.

[2] Pick up a 6mm round bead. Slide it next to the drop over both threads **(photo a)**. Trim the tail to just beyond the 6mm round.

[3] Pick up three size 11º seed beads, a bugle, an 11º, a flower, and a drop **(figure 1, a–b)**.

[4] Skip the drop and go back through all the beads, exiting the top of the 6mm bead **(b–c)**. Go through the first drop and back down the 6mm bead **(c–d)**.

[5] Repeat steps 3 and 4, but start with two 11ºs.

[6] Repeat steps 3 and 4, but start with one 11º.

[7] Pick up one 11º, a bugle, an 11º, four 15ºs, a leaf, and four 15ºs **(figure 2, a–b)**.

[8] Go back through to the first 11º, sew through the 6mm bead, and exit the drop **(b–c)**. Tie several half-hitch knots (Basics) around the main thread between the drop and the 6mm

bead. Dot the knots with glue and let them dry. Exit the 6mm bead and trim the tail. Make a total of 24 large clusters.

Small cluster

[1] Start the small cluster as in step 1 above. Pick up three 11ºs, a flower, and a drop **(figure 3, a–b)**. Skip the drop and go back up the flower, the three 11ºs, and the top drop **(b–c)**.

[2] Pick up two 11°s, four 15°s, a leaf, and four 15°s (c–d). Go back through the two 11°s and the drop (d–e). Tie several half-hitch knots and dot the knots with glue. Sew down through several beads and trim the tail. Make a total of 23 small clusters.

String the necklace

This necklace is 15 in. (38cm) long without the clasp. For a longer necklace, string more seed beads before adding the clusters or make additional clusters as desired.
[1] Cut a length of flexible beading wire 6 in. (15cm) longer than the desired finished length. String an 11°, a crimp bead, and an 11°. Go through the loop on one end of the toggle clasp. Go back through the 11° and crimp bead. Crimp the crimp bead (Basics and **photo b**) and trim the tail.
[2] String nine 11°s. String through the drop of a small cluster (**photo c**).
[3] String three 11°s and a large cluster (**photo d**). Continue stringing. Alternate between large and small clusters, with three 11°s between each, until all the clusters are strung. End with a small cluster.
[4] String ten 11°s, a crimp bead, and an 11°. Go through the loop on the other end of the toggle clasp and back through the 11° and the crimp bead.
[5] Tighten the wire and crimp the crimp bead. Hide the tail in several seed beads and trim the excess.

Earrings

[1] Tie the end of a 2-ft. length of conditioned Nymo to the loop on the earring finding with an overhand knot.
[2] Make a large cluster as before, but omit the drop

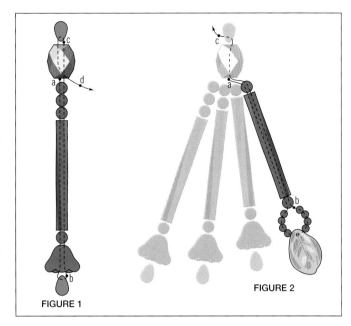

FIGURE 1

FIGURE 2

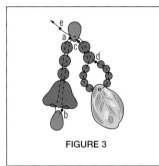

FIGURE 3

and start with the 6mm bead (**photo e**).
[3] Make a second earring to match the first. ●

Contact Sharon Lester at 706 S. Harrison Road, Houghton Lake, Michigan 48629 or via email at mamalester@yahoo.com.

MATERIALS

both projects
- Nymo B, color to match beads, conditioned with beeswax
- beading needles, #12
- G-S Hypo Cement

necklace 15 in. (38cm)
- **92** 10mm twisted bugle beads, purple
- **47** 10mm leaves, drilled front to back
- **93** 6mm flowers, purple
- **23** 6mm round glass beads, purple
- **140** drop beads, purple
- seed beads
  20g size 11°, purple
  10g size 15°, purple
- flexible beading wire, .014
- **2** crimp beads
- toggle clasp
- crimping pliers
- wire cutters

earrings
- **8** 10mm twisted bugle beads, purple
- **2** 10mm leaves, drilled front to back
- **2** 6mm round glass beads, purple
- **6** 6mm flowers
- **6** drop beads
- seed beads
  22 size 11°
  16 size 15°
- pair ball post earring findings with loop (Rio Grande, 800-545-6566, riogrande.com)

Note: Some suppliers sell the earring backs separately.

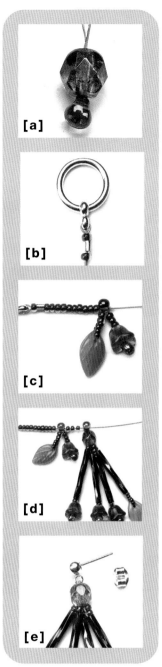

[a]

[b]

[c]

[d]

[e]

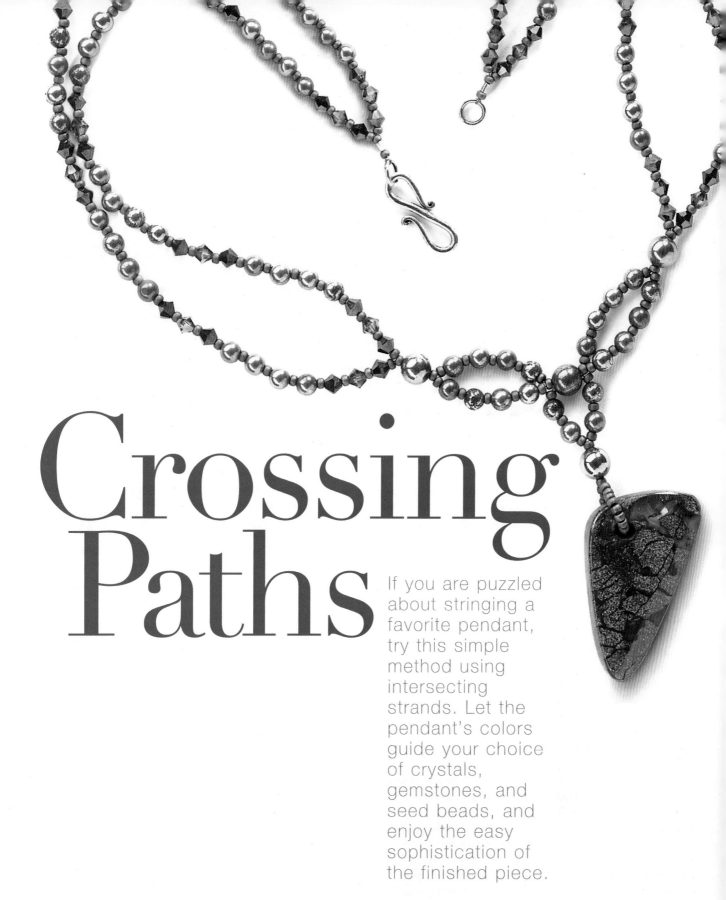

Crossing Paths

If you are puzzled about stringing a favorite pendant, try this simple method using intersecting strands. Let the pendant's colors guide your choice of crystals, gemstones, and seed beads, and enjoy the easy sophistication of the finished piece.

by **Anna Nehs**

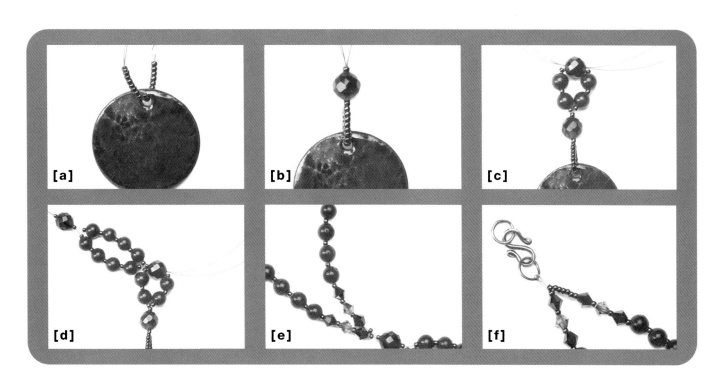

[a]

[b]

[c]

[d]

[e]

[f]

step*by*step

[1] Cut two 1½ yd. (1.4m) strands of beading wire. String enough seed beads to the center of the two strands to make a bail around the pendant. String the pendant over the seed beads **(photo a)**.

[2] String a seed bead, a 6mm stone, and a seed bead over all four strands. Split the four strands into two pairs **(photo b)**.

[3] On the first pair, string a seed bead, a 4mm stone, a seed bead, a 4mm stone, and a seed bead. Repeat on the second pair.

[4] Cross the pairs through a 6mm stone **(photo c)**.

[5] On the first pair, string one seed bead, then split the pair apart. On one strand, alternate a seed bead and a 4mm stone four times and end with a seed bead. Repeat on the second strand. Then string a seed bead, a 6mm stone, and a seed bead over both strands **(photo d)**.

[6] Split the first pair of strands apart again. On the first strand string a seed bead, a main color crystal, a seed bead, an accent color crystal, a seed bead, a main color crystal, and a seed bead. Then alternate a 4mm stone and a seed bead three times and end with a 4mm stone **(photo e)**. Repeat the sequence four times or to the desired length, ending with the seed bead and crystal section. Repeat for the second strand.

[7] String a seed bead, a crimp bead, and half the clasp over both strands. Check the fit and add seed beads to the strands, if necessary. Go back through the crimp with both strands, adjust the tension, and crimp the crimp bead (Basics, p. 10). Trim the tails **(photo f)**.

[8] Repeat steps 5–7 to finish the other side of the necklace. ◉

Anna is an associate editor at Bead&Button *magazine. Contact her at editor@beadandbutton.com.*

MATERIALS

necklace 17 in. (43cm)
- 2-in. (5cm) pendant with a top-drilled hole
- gemstone beads
  4 6mm round
  84 4mm round
- 4mm bicone crystals
  40 main color
  20 accent color
- Japanese seed beads, size 11º or 15º
- flexible beading wire, size .010
- **2** crimp beads
- clasp
- crimping pliers
- wire cutters

Pearl
Garden

Create a stunning pearl necklace from a collection of sparkling components

by **Christine Strube**

Like many who design jewelry, I rarely know what I'm going to do before I do it. I usually have an idea that starts with something I've seen, such as a kimono pattern, the stain of oxidized copper on a brick wall, or a collection of leaves floating in a puddle. This piece was inspired by the late afternoon sunlight on a vase of Lady Diana roses. Since pearls in every size, shape, and color fill my studio, it was only natural that these pale, rose-colored stick pearls helped determine my design.

step*by*step

Make the dangles
Save time when you make the dangles by completing all the tasks that require one set of tools before picking up the next. Or, make wrapped loops on each dangle as you work.
[1] Stack a spacer, a rondelle, a spacer, and a 4mm bicone on a head pin **(photo a)**. Make 15.
[2] Stack a 4mm pearl and a rondelle on a head pin **(photo b, page 52)**. Make 14.
[3] Stack a 2mm silver bead, a spacer, and a coin pearl on a head pin **(photo c, page 52)**. Make eight.
[4] String a coin pearl on a head pin **(photo d, page 52)**. Make seven.
[5] Stack a 4mm pearl and a cloisonné bead on a head pin

[a]

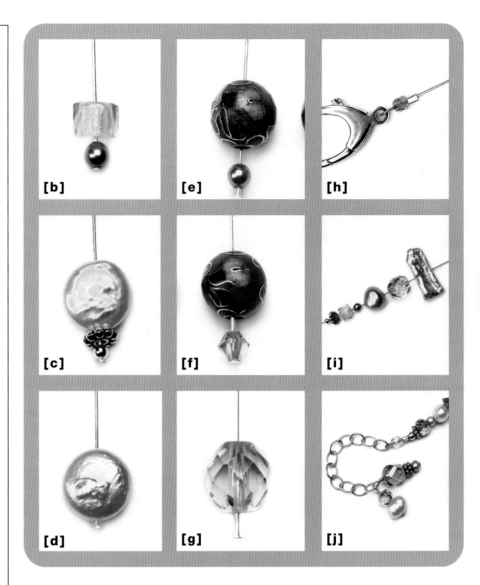

[b] [e] [h]

[c] [f] [i]

[d] [g] [j]

(photo e). Make seven.

[6] Stack a 4mm bicone and a cloisonné bead on a head pin (photo f). Make six.

[7] String an 8mm fire-polished bead on a head pin. Make six (photo g).

[8] Make wrapped loops (Basics, p. 10) above the beads on all the dangle components. Trim the excess wire and file any sharp edges as necessary.

EDITOR'S NOTE: Christine uses the large opening on her crimping pliers to compress the cut-wire ends on her wrapped loops to make filing the sharp edges unnecessary.

String the necklace

[1] String a crimp bead and a 4mm fire-polished bead on a 22-in. (56cm) length of flexible beading wire. Go through the loop on the lobster clasp and back through the 4mm bead and the crimp bead. Crimp the crimp bead (Basics and **photo h**).

[2] String a 2mm silver bead, a spacer, a rondelle, a 4mm pearl, an 8mm pearl, an 8mm fire-polished bead, and a stick pearl (**photo i**).

[3] String 17 in. (43cm) of pearls, crystals, beads, and dangles, alternating the components. This necklace does not have a set pattern, but the elements are spaced evenly, with the stick pearls strung about every inch (2.5cm).

[4] Mirror the start of the necklace by stringing a stick pearl, an 8mm fire-polished bead, an 8mm pearl, a 4mm pearl, a rondelle, a spacer, and a 2mm silver bead.

Finish the ends

[1] String a crimp bead and a 4mm fire-polished bead. Go through the first link of the silver chain. Go through the 4mm bead and the crimp bead, and pull the wire gently to tighten. Crimp the crimp bead and trim the tail.

[2] To make the optional two dangles at the end of the chain, stack an 8mm pearl and a rondelle on a head pin. Stack a 4mm pearl, two spacers, and an 8mm fire-polished bead on a head pin. Attach both dangles to the last link in the chain with wrapped loops (**photo j**). ◗

Write to Christine Strube at 33 Frederick Lane, Glendale, Missouri 63122, or via email at chstrube@earthlink.net.

Tips & Techniques

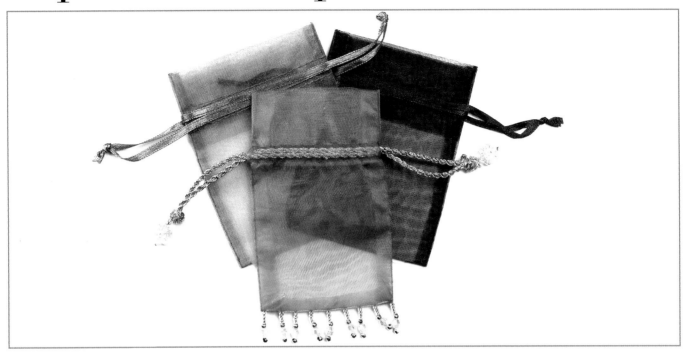

Beaded drawstring bags

Add beaded fringe to the bottom of a drawstring bag for the perfect gift bag. They also make great sachets filled with potpourri.

Tie a knot at the end of a length of thread and sew through from the inside of the bag to a bottom corner. String seed beads, a 4-6mm crystal or Czech glass bead, and a seed bead. Skip the last seed and sew back through the beads and the bag. Position the needle so it exits the bottom of the bag where you want to add the next dangle. Repeat across the bottom of the bag. I also like to embellish the drawstrings with beads.

– Mardi Callahan, Glendale, Wisconsin

Clean beads

It's always fun to find beads at estate sales, on ebay, or even between the cushions of the couch, although such finds are usually coated in dust or mixed with lint and other foreign objects. To easily clean and separate the beads, place them in a bucket and fill it to the top with water. Twirl your hand in the water and the small foreign particles, such as lint and hair, will float to the top and flow over the sides of the bucket. Scoop out the beads and dry them on a towel.

– Betsy Youngquist, Rockford, Illinois

Hide thread ends

When knotting two threads together, at least two (four, if doubled) ends of string remain near the knot. I used to pull the ends through several beads to hide them, but sooner or later, a short end or two would protrude in the middle of the beadwork. To solve this problem, put a twisted wire needle through several beads and thread one short end through the eye. Before pulling it inside the beads, dab some glue on the thread. The short end becomes glued to the main thread inside the bead and will never come out. Repeat with the other ends, but go through several beads in the opposite direction. When the glue dries, trim the ends with a razor.

– Evelina Kolchinsky
Andover, Massachusetts

Wir

ework

Jump Start

Create a
colorful bracelet
with furnace glass
and jump rings
while learning
basic jump-ring
assembly

by **Catherine
Hansen-VandenBerg**

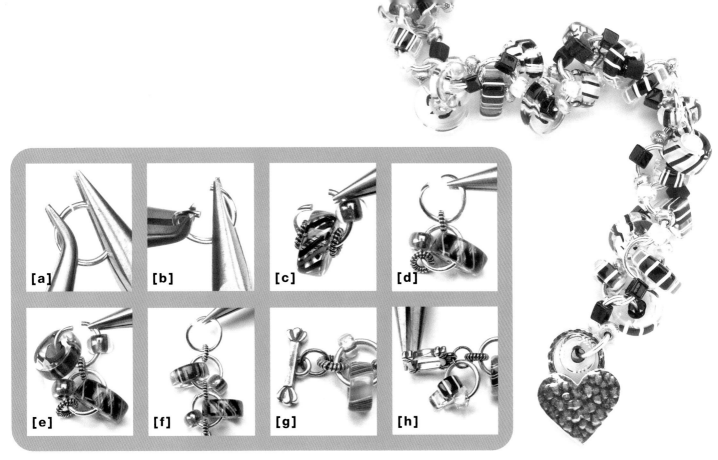

stepbystep

Multicolor bracelet

[1] Open a large jump ring with two pairs of pliers (Basics and **photos a** and **b**).

[2] String a coiled ring, a furnace glass bead, a coiled ring, and an accent bead on the jump ring (photo c). Close the jump ring.

[3] Open a second large jump ring. Slide it through one of the coiled rings on the first jump ring (photo d).

[4] String a furnace glass bead on one side of the open jump ring, so it falls on the opposite side of the furnace glass on the first jump ring. Then string an accent bead on the other side of the jump ring (photo e). String a coiled ring and close the jump ring.

[5] Open a large jump ring and slide it through the coiled ring strung in the previous step (photo f). Repeat step 4.

[6] Repeat steps 3–5 until you have one large jump ring remaining.

[7] Open a small jump ring and slide it through the loop on one clasp component and an end coiled ring. Close the jump ring (photo g). Repeat at the other end of the bracelet with the remaining clasp half.

[8] Open the last large jump ring and string an accent bead and a furnace glass bead. Slide the large jump ring onto the small jump ring that connects to the loop on the round half of the clasp. Close the jump ring (photo h).

[i]

Black-and-white bracelet

[1] Open a large jump ring, following step 1 for the multicolor bracelet.

[2] String a silver bead, a furnace glass bead, and an accent bead. Close the jump ring.

[3] Open a large jump ring and slide it through the previous jump ring (photo i).

[4] Repeat step 2.

[5] Repeat steps 3–4 and connect the remaining large jump rings. Alternate the placement of the furnace glass bead on each jump ring as you did in step 4 for the multicolor bracelet.

[6] Use small jump rings to connect the clasp to the end jump rings on the bracelet. ●

Kits are available for the multicolor and black-and-white bracelets. Contact Cathy at (248) 348-4926.

MATERIALS

bracelets 7½ in. (19cm)

both projects
- 2 5mm jump rings
- toggle clasp
- 2 pair chainnose pliers or 1 pair chainnose and 1 pair bent chainnose

multicolor bracelet
- 17 furnace glass beads
- 16 jump rings, 7–8.5mm inside diameter, 16- or 18-gauge wire
- 17 5mm coiled rings
- 17 accent beads: size 8º or 6º seed beads, size 5º triangles, or 4mm cubes

black-and-white bracelet
- 23 jump rings, 7–8.5mm inside diameter, 16- or 18-gauge wire
- 23 4–5mm silver beads with a large hole
- 23–34 accent beads: size 8º or 6º seed beads, size 5º triangles, or 4mm cubes
- 23 furnace glass beads

Diamond Delights

Combine crystal bicones, wire, and chain for a pair of sparkling earrings that can keep up with all your last-minute accessorizing

by **Molli Schultz**

step*by*step

Dangles

[1] Cut two 3-in. (7.6cm) pieces of wire. Cut two pieces of chain with three attached links each.

[2] Slide a teardrop crystal to 1 in. (2.5cm) from the end of a 3-in. length of wire. Bend the wire ends up next to the point of the crystal and cross the wires above it **(photo a)**. Make two wraps with the short end of the wire and trim the excess **(photo b)**. Flatten the end of the wire against the wraps with chainnose pliers.

[3] Make a 90-degree bend ⅛ in. (3mm) from the first set of wraps and start a wrapped loop **(photo c** and Basics, p. 10). Slide an end link of one chain link set into the loop and finish with two wraps **(photo d)**. Cut off any excess wire and flatten the end with chainnose pliers.

[4] Repeat to make a second dangle and set both aside.

Hoop

[1] Cut two 8-in. (20cm) pieces of wire. Make a wrapped loop at the end of one 8-in. length of wire. String a spacer, a 4mm crystal, and a spacer. Bend the wire at a 45-degree angle ⅛ in. (3mm) away from the last spacer **(photo e)**.

[2] String eight 4mm crystals on the wire. Carefully make a 90-degree bend with your fingers just past the last crystal **(photo f)**.

[3] Repeat step 2 three more times **(photo g)**.

[4] String the dangle on the wire. Wrap the wire end twice under the spacer **(photo h)**.

[5] Trim any excess wire and flatten the end with chainnose pliers.

[6] Make a second earring to match. Open the loop (Basics) on each earring finding and attach a hoop. Close the loops. ◗

Contact Molli at otelias jewelrybox@yahoo.com.

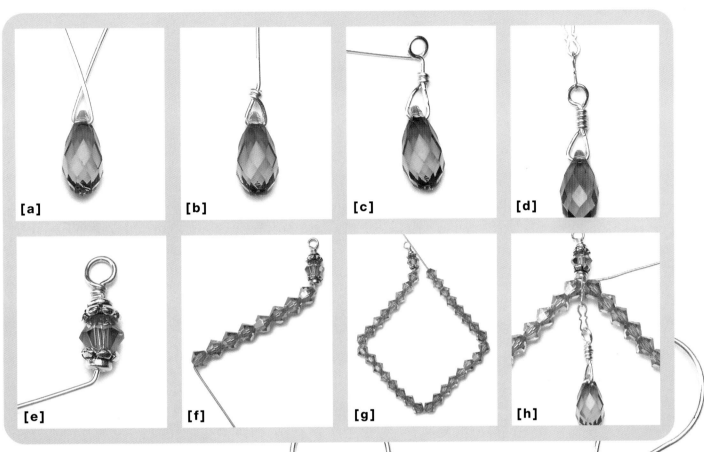

[a]

[b]

[c]

[d]

[e]

[f]

[g]

[h]

EDITOR'S NOTE: Make a smaller earring by reducing the number of crystals strung in step 2 of the hoop and attaching a shorter dangle.

MATERIALS

one pair of earrings

- **66** 4mm bicone crystals
- **2** 5 x 7mm top-drilled teardrop crystals
- **4** 3mm spacers
- **7** links or 1½ in. (3.8cm) of fine chain
- 22 in. (56cm) 22–24-gauge wire
- **2** earring findings
- chainnose pliers
- roundnose pliers
- wire cutters

Ancient Rings

by **Anne Mitchell**

The design known as ancient and Italian link is the most delicate-looking chain mail pattern. But its complex appearance is extremely deceptive, as it is one of the easiest techniques to learn. I'm sure you'll fall in love with the flowing links of this necklace and bracelet, just as I have.

step*by*step

Bracelet

[1] Start with 30 closed jump rings (Basics, p. 10).

[2] Open 28 jump rings (Basics), for a total of 58.

[3] Connect pairs of closed jump rings with pairs of open jump rings **(photo a)**. This is a basic 2+2+2 chain **(photo b)**.

[4] Repeat steps 1–3 to make a second chain.

[5] Open 30 jump rings.

[6] Start at one end of the first chain and attach two jump rings to the first pair of rings. Skip the next pair of rings and add two jump rings, one on each side, to the third pair **(photo c)**.

[7] Continue adding two jump rings, one on each side, to every other pair of rings on the chain.

[8] Repeat steps 5–7 with the second chain.

[9] Open a 4mm jump ring and attach a clasp loop to the end pair of rings on one chain between the two floating rings **(photo d)**. Repeat with the second chain and the clasp's second loop. Connect the other end of the chains to the remaining clasp half.

MATERIALS
both projects
- **4** 4mm jump rings
- 2-strand silver clasp (pacificsilverworks.com)
- **2** pair chainnose pliers or **1** pair chainnose and **1** pair bent chainnose

bracelet 7¾ in. (20cm)
- 1.5 troy oz. (see p.71) sterling silver jump rings, 6.5mm inside diameter, 18-gauge wire (Beadissimo code SS)

necklace 17½ in. (44cm)
- 3 troy oz. sterling silver jump rings, 6.5mm inside diameter, 18-gauge wire

Necklace
Follow the steps for the bracelet, using 68 closed and 64 open jump rings to make a necklace 17½-in. (44cm) long. ◉

Contact Anne at anne@annemitchell.net or annemitchell.net. Kits for this and other chain designs are available on her website.

EDITOR'S NOTE: For an anklet variation, make a single chain (steps 1–3 and 5–7) 9½ in. (24cm) long and attach a large lobster claw clasp with a 4mm jump ring. Add silver charms to the floating rings on one side of the chain for an anklet that dances with every step.

[a]

[b]

[c]

[d]

Out
of the

LOOP

An all-occasion pair of earrings starts with these easy wire loops.
Make daisy-shaped findings and hang a trio of crystal dangles.
In a flash, you'll have something wonderful to wear.

by **Wendy Witchner**

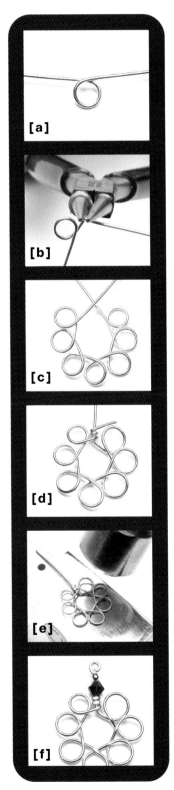

[a]

[b]

[c]

[d]

[e]

[f]

step*by*step

[1] Cut an 8-in. (20cm) piece of 22-gauge wire.
[2] Grip the wire 1 in. (2.5cm) from the end with the larger part of the round-nose pliers. Wrap the long end of the wire around one jaw of the pliers. Reposition the pliers and continue wrapping the wire until it forms a loop **(photo a)**.
[3] Hold the long end of the wire next to the loop and form a second loop the same size as the first **(photo b)**.
[4] Refer to the template below right and make five more loops **(photo c)**.
[5] Bring the first and last loops side by side and wrap the short wire end around the long wire a few times **(photo d)**. Trim the excess wire as close to the long wire as possible.
[6] Place the wire finding on an anvil or steel block and flatten it slightly with a hammer **(photo e)** to stiffen it.
[7] String a 4mm crystal and a round 2mm bead on the wire and against the wrap. Then make a plain loop

(Basics, p. 10) above the beads **(photo f)**.
[8] To make the center dangle, cut a 1½-in. (3.8cm) piece of wire and make a plain loop at one end. String a 2mm bead, 6mm bead, 2mm bead, crystal, and 2mm bead. Make a loop at the other end in the same plane as the first loop **(photo g)**.
[9] Open the loop (Basics) closest to the 6mm bead and slide a charm into the loop. Close the loop.
[10] Connect the top loop of the dangle to the center loop on the wire finding.
[11] Cut a 1½-in. piece of wire. Trim the end of the wire so it is straight, as shown in **photo h**, left.
[12] Place the end of the wire on an anvil or steel block and hammer the end until it is large enough to keep a 2mm bead from sliding off **(photo h**, right). Use a metal file to round the edges and remove any sharp points.
[13] String a 2mm bead, crystal, 2mm bead, crystal, and 2mm bead on the wire. Make a plain loop above the

beads **(photo i)**.
[14] Connect the dangle to the finding's third loop.
[15] Repeat steps 11–13 to make another dangle and attach it to the fifth loop on the wire shape.
[16] Attach the earring wire to the loop at the top of the wire finding.
[17] Make a second earring to match the first. **◗**

Wendy is a contributing editor to Bead&Button *magazine. Contact her at editor@beadandbutton.com.*

MATERIALS
one pair of earrings

- **25 in.** (64cm) 22-gauge wire
- **20** 2mm round spacers
- **6** 4mm bicone crystals
- **2** 6mm beads
- **2** charms
- **2** earring findings
- roundnose pliers
- chainnose pliers
- wire cutters
- metal file
- hammer
- anvil or steel block

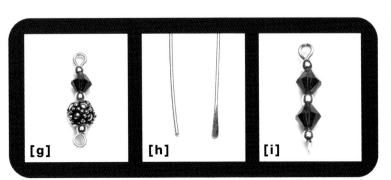

[g]   [h]   [i]

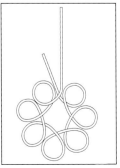

Trading Spacers

by **Lisa Niven Kelly**

Spirals and coils make versatile spacer
bars in a whimsical bracelet

I developed a technique to create my
own spacers when I couldn't find
exactly what I needed. I liked them
so much, I made several pieces using
just the bars! When forming the coils,
it's best to make them as long as you
can. If you antique your silver, leave
them on the mandrels while you
blacken them in liver of sulfur and
buff with steel wool. After polishing,
they can then be removed from the
mandrel and cut to any length.

stepbystep

Spacer bars

[1] Cut a length of 20-gauge
wire 2 in. (5cm) longer than
the desired length of your
spacer. My spacers range
from ¾ in. (2cm) to 3 in.
(7.6cm) long.

[2] Use the 18-gauge wire
as a mandrel or straighten
out a large paper clip. Bend
the 20-gauge wire 1½ in.
(3.8cm) from the end. Wrap
it around the mandrel once
(photo a).

[3] Use the tip of your
chainnose pliers to pinch the
loop together (photo b).

[4] Stack the desired beads
on the wire. (See photo g for
several examples of beaded

spacers.) Trim the wire 1½ in.
past the top of the end bead.
Line the mandrel up just past
the top of the end bead
(photo c).

[5] Wrap the wire around
the mandrel once (photo d).
Pinch the loop together as in
step 3.

[6] Bend the end of the wire
above the beaded section at
a 90-degree angle (photo e).
Bend the end of the wire
below the beaded section at
a 90-degree angle in the
opposite direction.

[7] Use chainnose pliers to
form the spirals. Cover the
jaws of the pliers with
painter's tape to prevent
marring. Turn a small loop at
the tip of the wire and pinch it

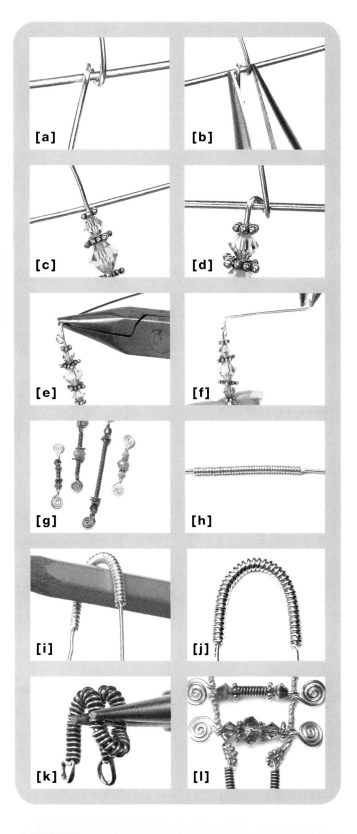

MATERIALS
bracelet 7 in. (17.8cm)

- 4–13mm Swarovski bicone crystals, rondelles, and accent beads
- assortment of silver daisy and star-shaped spacers
- 16-in. (41cm) strand 1mm Hill Tribes silver beads (Fire Mountain Gems, 800-355-2137, firemountaingems.com), or 10g seed beads size 15º, silver
- 10 ft. (3m) 20-gauge sterling silver wire, dead soft
- 30 ft. (9.1m) 24-gauge sterling silver wire, dead soft
- 4 in. (10cm) 18-gauge wire, half hard, or large paper clip
- flexible beading wire, .014
- **4** crimp beads
- chainnose pliers
- roundnose pliers
- crimping pliers
- wire cutters
- painter's tape (optional)
- liver of sulfur (optional)
- steel wool, extra fine (optional)
- polishing pad (optional)
- safety glasses (optional)

closed **(photo f)**. Grab the loop flat in the jaws of the pliers and turn. Reposition the pliers after every turn. Keep turning until the spiral is centered above the spacer. Repeat to form a spiral below the beaded section **(photo g)**.

[8] To make coils, use a 16-in. (41cm) length of 20-gauge wire as a mandrel. Wrap 1 ft. (30cm) of 24-gauge wire around it **(photo h)**. Cut the coils to the desired length.

Coiled clasp
[1] To make the coil-covered loop, cut a 3-in. length of 20-gauge wire. Using this piece as a mandrel, coil 1 in. (2.5cm) of 24-gauge wire around it.
[2] Center the coil on the mandrel. Place a pencil in the middle of the coil and bend it into a U-shape **(photo i)**.
[3] Trim the excess mandrel wire to ½ in. on both ends **(photo j)**. Turn a small loop at each end of the wire. (You will attach the beading wire to these loops in step 2 of the bracelet assembly.)
[4] To make the hook, double the measurements in step 1.

Shape the coil over the pencil, then make loops on both ends as in step 3. Gently pinch the U-shaped coil. Use roundnose pliers to fold the coil into a hook **(photo k)**.

Bracelet assembly
[1] Cut two lengths of flexible beading wire 2 in. longer than your wrist measurement.
[2] String a crimp bead and eight 15º seed beads. Go through the loop on one end of the clasp and back through the crimp bead. Tighten the wire. Crimp the crimp bead (Basics, p. 10) and trim the tail. Repeat on the other clasp loop.
[3] String beads and spacer bars as desired. My bracelet starts with one silver bead, a spacer, and eight silver beads between subsequent spacers **(photo l)**.
[4] Attach both wires to the other end of the clasp as in step 2. ◉

Contact Lisa at Lisa@leelabeads.com, and see her work at leelabeads.com.

EDITOR'S NOTE: These bracelets are made entirely of two-hole spacers, but Lisa says the sky's the limit when planning your own project. It's easy to make additional holes at any point on the spacer by making a loop as in photo d and pinching it closed.

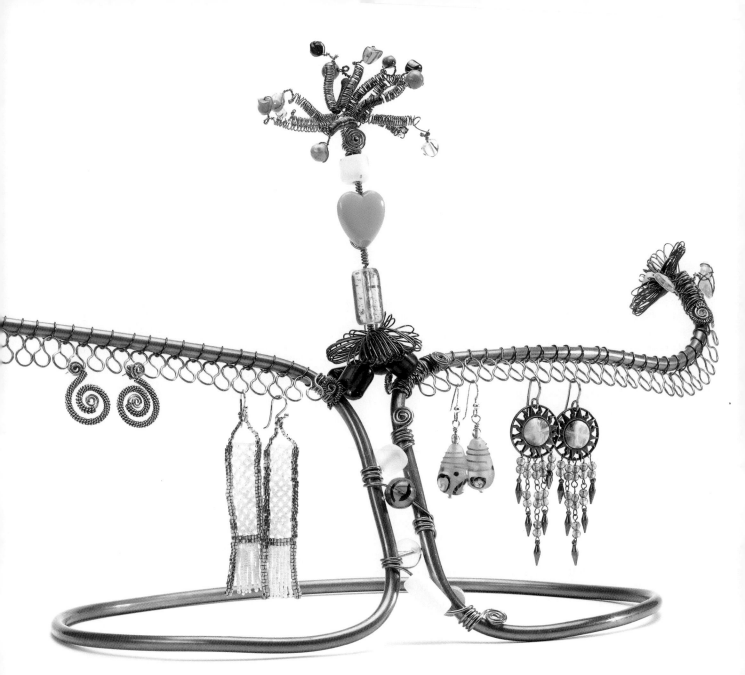

Earring Tree

Use your imagination and wire-wrapping skills to create eclectic earring trees. Add color and texture by making shapes and figures with glass beads and colored craft wire. These trees are so easy to make, they'll leave you plenty of time to fill them up with your own earring creations.

by **Erica Morris**

step*by*step

Bend copper tubing to create the tree. Make a series of loops out of colored wire and attach them by wire wrapping. Embellish with beads and more wire for a fun, funky tree.

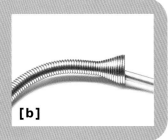

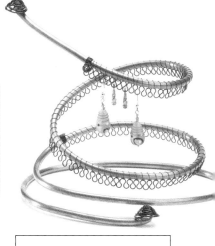

Form the tree
[1] Insert the copper tubing into the bending coil (photo b). Form the large curves of the tree base by bending the coil gently and moving it up the tubing as you go. Keep going until you reach the desired shape.
[2] Cut the copper tubing using the tube-cutting tool (photo c). Gently hammer the ends until the tube is circular again (photo d).

Make the loops
[1] Leaving a 10-in. (25cm) tail, place the wire in roundnose pliers and bend it down (photo e).
[2] Grab the wire on one side of the newly formed loop and bend the wire over the top of the pliers (photo f). Make a second bend the same height as the first.
[3] Place the pliers inside the two loops and squeeze them

together (photo g) to make uniform shapes. Repeat until you've made enough loops to embellish the copper tubing. Leave another 10-in. tail and cut the wire.

Attach the loops
[1] Starting 1 in. (2.5cm) from the end of the tail on the 20-gauge wire loops, wrap the next several inches with 24-gauge wire. Do not cut the 24-gauge wire.
[2] Make a coil with the wire-wrapped portion then wrap both the 20- and 24-gauge wire around the tube where you want the loops to begin. Secure the loops to the tube by wrapping 24-gauge wire through them (photo h). When you reach the end, finish off the other tail as you did the first.
[3] To make the coils for the ends (photo i), insert a 1-ft. (30cm) length of 16-gauge

wire approximately 3 in. (7.6cm) into the end of the tube. Gently flatten the end of the tube with a hammer and bend the end up by hammering it over the edge of the anvil or steel block.
[4] Make a coil with the protruding 16-gauge wire and bend it over the end (photo j). Embellish your tree by wire wrapping more beads to the tubing to create a variety of colorful and imaginative shapes. ●

Erica is from Moreno Valley, California. Email her at moonbeams113@hotmail.com.

MATERIALS
- ¼-in. (6mm) copper tubing (home improvement stores)
- spool of 16-, 20-, and 24-gauge colored wire
- assortment of beads for embellishing
- roundnose pliers
- wire cutters
- tube cutter
- tube-bending coil
- hammer
- anvil (Rio Grande, 800-545-6566, riogrande.com) or steel block

EDITOR'S NOTE: This tree requires a trip to your garage or hardware store for the following items: copper tubing, a tube-bending coil, tube-cutter, and hammer (photo a). The bending coil allows you to manipulate the tubing without kinks. Small anvils are available from Rio Grande, or you can use any steel surface.

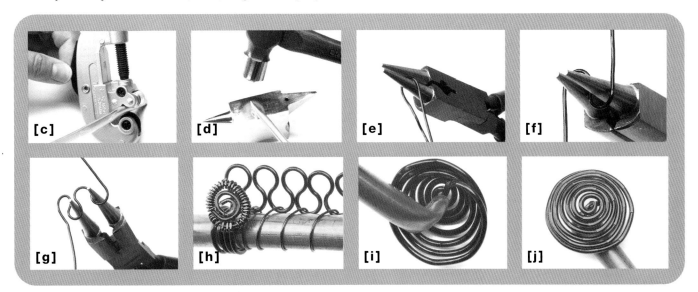

Angel Pendant

Not everyone spends the holidays thinking about snow — this graceful pendant, with its shimmering abalone shell and pearls, takes us back to the beach

by **Anna Lemons**

stepbystep

[1] Cut five lengths of 22-gauge square wire 4 in. (10cm) longer than the circumference of the abalone shell.

[2] Hold one of the wires with your flatnose pliers and pull it through a polishing cloth to clean and straighten it. Repeat with the remaining four wires.

[3] Working with one wire, center the bottom of the shell on the wire and mark the wire where each of the four bindings will be (photo a).

[4] Place the five wires side by side and bundle them together with a three-wrap bind using 22-gauge half-round wire (photo b).

[5] Shape the bundled wires around the shell so the wire ends cross at the top (photo c). Remove the shell and place a three-wrap binding on each side just below the cross.

[6] Use flatnose pliers to bend the wires up where they cross so they are parallel to each other (photo d). Check the fit again and make any adjustments necessary. Then bind all ten wires together above the bend (photo e).

[7] Separate the wires above the bind into five pairs (photo f). String the pearl on one of the center wires and make a large wrapped loop (Basics, p. 10) above the pearl. Trim the excess wire.

[8] Bring the remaining center wire up the back of the pearl and wrap it around the top of the pearl a few times to form the halo (photo g). Trim the excess wire and tuck the wire end in under the halo.

[9] Set the shell in the wire frame. Use flatnose pliers to bend the edge wire on the front of the frame to hold the shell in place (photo h). Repeat on the back of the frame.

[10] To form the arms and hands, bring the bottom two wire pairs down so they cross in a heart shape. End the wires decoratively with flat coils and loops (photo i).

[11] Twist the remaining wires with a pin vise (photo j). Shape the wires to form the wings and attach the wires to the back of the frame (photo k). Tuck in the wire ends.

[12] Make a wrapped loop at the end of a piece of 22-gauge half-round wire. String the small pearl and crystal and make a loop. Slide the wrapped loop onto one of the loops forming the angel's hands.

[13] Attach the snap bail to the large wrapped loop above the halo. ●

Anna's work can be found at annalemonsjewelry. com. Email her at anna@ annalemonsjewelry.com.

MATERIALS

- 45 in. (1.1m) 22-gauge square wire, dead soft
- 10 in. (25cm) 22-gauge half-round wire, half hard
- 1–1½ in. (2.5-3.8cm) abalone shell, triangular shape (Fire Mountain Gems, 800-355-2137, firemountaingems.com)
- 10–12mm pearl
- 4–6mm pearl
- 4mm bicone crystal
- snap bail
- roundnose pliers
- flatnose pliers
- fine-point marker
- wire cutters
- pin vise
- polishing cloth

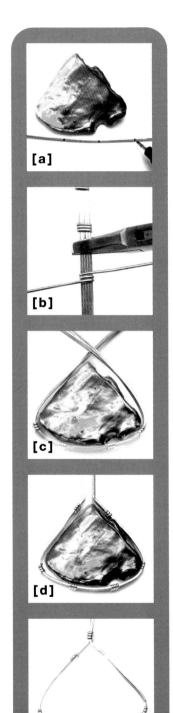

[a]

[b]

[c]

[d]

[e]

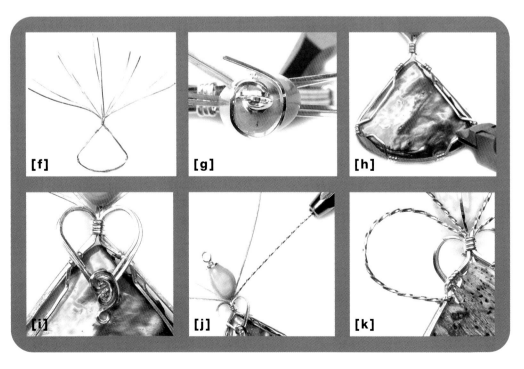

[f]

[g]

[h]

[i]

[j]

[k]

Tryzantine

Simple jump rings combine for an intricate bracelet

by **Anne E. Mitchell**

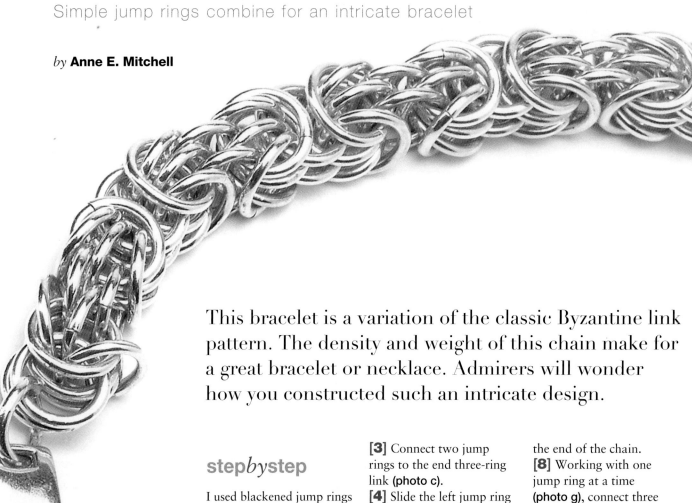

This bracelet is a variation of the classic Byzantine link pattern. The density and weight of this chain make for a great bracelet or necklace. Admirers will wonder how you constructed such an intricate design.

step*by*step

I used blackened jump rings in the following photos for clarity in distinguishing which rings to add in each step. Refer to Basics, p. 10, for instructions on how to open and close jump rings.

[1] Open three jump rings and connect them to three closed jump rings **(photo a)**.

[2] Slide the outer two jump rings onto a paper clip **(photo b)**.

[3] Connect two jump rings to the end three-ring link **(photo c)**.

[4] Slide the left jump ring to the left so it rests against the jump rings on the paper clip. Repeat on the right with the right jump ring **(photo d)**.

[5] Turn the assembly on its side **(photo e)**.

[6] Open two jump rings and connect them to the center three rings **(photo f)**.

[7] Place a closed ring between the two rings at the end of the chain.

[8] Working with one jump ring at a time **(photo g)**, connect three jump rings through the two end rings and the closed center ring just added **(photo h)**.

[9] Connect two jump rings to the end three-ring link and slide them to the sides as before **(photo i)**.

[10] Repeat steps 5-9 until the chain is the desired length.

[11] Attach a lobster claw

Bracelet

EDITOR'S NOTE:
Troy weight is an ancient system of measuring precious metals and gemstones. It is derived from the troy system, which predates the eleventh century. The name comes from the city of Troyes in France, an important trading city in the Middle Ages. One troy oz. equals 31.10 grams. A standard ounce weighs 28.35 grams.

clasp to the end two-ring link with a jump ring. Connect a jump ring to the two-ring link at the other end of the chain. ○

Anne has kits for this and other chain designs available on her website annemitchell.net. E-mail her at anne@annemitchell.net.

MATERIALS

- 1.5 troy oz. sterling silver jump rings, 6.5mm inside diameter, 16-gauge wire
- lobster claw clasp
- paper clip
- **2** pair chainnose pliers or **1** pair chainnose and **1** pair bent chainnose

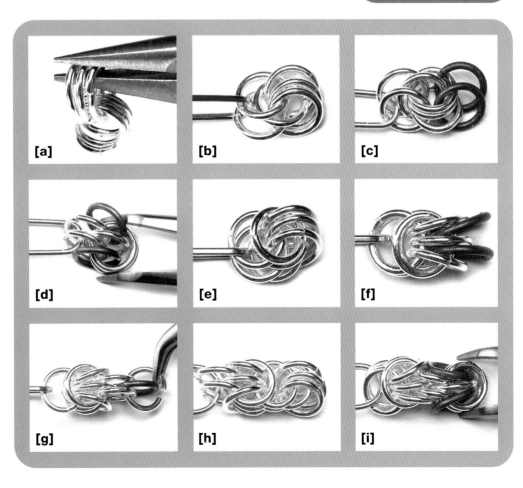

[a]   [b]   [c]

[d]   [e]   [f]

[g]   [h]   [i]

Flower Formation

Wrap semi-precious stones into flowery shapes using sterling silver wire. Once you're familiar with the technique, make a bracelet to match.

by **Lisa Claxton**

step*by*step

Large flower

[1] String six main color (MC) beads on a 10-in. (25cm) piece of wire and leave a 2-in. (5cm) tail.

[2] Cross the wire ends to form the beads into a circle **(photo a)**. Wrap the long end around the tail to secure the beads. Position the working wire so it points across the center of the circle **(photo b)**.

[3] String an accent color (AC) bead on the wire and center it in the circle. Bring the wire through the circle and under the wire between the third and fourth beads **(photo c)**.

[4] Bring the wire to the

[a] **[b]** **[c]** **[d]**

front of the circle and wrap it around the inside curve of a bead on one side of the wire **(photo d)**. Turn the flower over and wrap the wire around the inside curve of the next bead **(photo e)**.

[5] Continue wrapping the wire around the beads, alternating from the front to the back so each bead has one wrap **(photo f)**.

[6] Change directions by wrapping around the last bead on the circle **(photo g)**. Now wrap the opposite side of the beads. End with the wire on the opposite side of the circle as the tail **(photo h)**.

[7] Use your fingernail to reposition any wire wraps that have slipped. Secure the flower by wrapping the working wire around the circle's wire as shown in **photo i**. Pull the wrap tight.

[8] String an AC bead and make a wrapped loop (Basics, p. 10), but don't trim the wire. Keep wrapping the wire over the wraps back toward the loop **(photo j)**. Trim the wire and squeeze the wire's end against the wraps with chainnose pliers.

[9] String an AC bead on the tail and make a double-wrapped loop in the same plane as the first **(photo k)**.

[10] Make three more large flowers.

Small flower

[1] String four AC beads on an 8-in. (20cm) piece of wire and leave a 1½-in. (3.8cm) tail. Form the beads into a circle as you did for the

MATERIALS

necklace 15 in. (38cm)
- **24** 4mm round semi-precious stones (large flower, main color)
- **28** 4–5mm round semi-precious stones (small flower, accent color)
- **12** 6mm semi-precious stones, any shape
- **7** 3–4mm sterling silver rondelles
- **6** 4mm round sterling silver beads
- **10** ft. (3m) 26-gauge sterling silver wire
- clasp
- chainnose pliers
- roundnose pliers
- wire cutters

large flower.

[2] Follow steps 3–9 for the six-petal flower, but instead of an AC, string a rondelle to the center of the circle in step 3, and string a 4mm silver bead as in steps 8–9.

[3] Make two more small flowers.

Bead links

[1] Cut a 4 in. (10cm) piece of wire. Make the first half of a wrapped loop about 1½ in. from one end.

[2] Slide the loop through a loop on a large flower **(photo l)** and complete a double wrap.

[3] String a 6mm bead on the wire and make the first half of a wrapped loop in the same plane as the first. Slide the loop through a loop on a small flower and complete a double wrap.

[4] Repeat steps 1–3 to

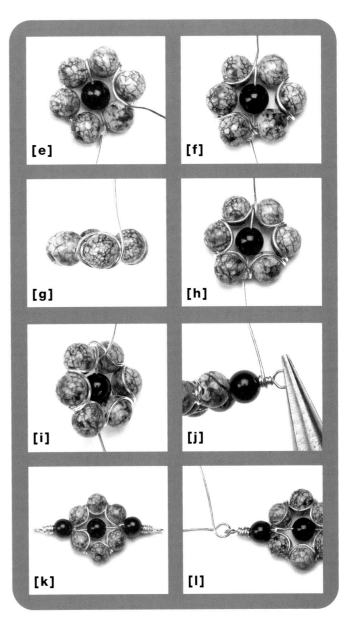

connect the large and small flowers in an alternating pattern. End with a 6mm bead link but don't finish the second loop.

[5] Check the length. If you need to make the necklace longer, add a bead link to each side of the necklace using the following bead pattern: an AC, a rondelle, a 6mm bead, a rondelle, and

an AC. End with a 6mm bead link as in step 4.

[6] Attach a clasp half to each end 6mm bead link. ●

Contact Lisa in care of editor@beadandbutton.com.

Sparkling Loops

These quick earrings use only a small number of beads, making them a perfect project for leftovers

by **Anna Nehs**

step*by*step

Both projects

[1] Cut the chain in half, making sure an equal number of links are on each chain (14 links for the blue earrings and 12 for the pink). Open the loop (Basics, p. 10) on a post earring finding, attach the end link of one of the chains, and close the loop **(photo a)**.
[2] String a crystal on a head pin and make a plain loop (Basics) above the crystal. Repeat with the remaining crystals and pearls.

Blue earrings

[1] Open the loop on one 4mm bicone crystal dangle and attach it to the loop on the post earring finding **(photo b)**.
[2] Attach the remaining dangles as follows: two 4mm bicones to the second link; a 4mm round pearl and a 5mm bicone crystal to the third link; and a 6mm faceted pearl to the fourth link **(photo c)**. Continue with this bead sequence, ending with a 4mm round pearl and a 5mm

bicone crystal on the last link.
[3] Open a jump ring (Basics) and connect the last link to the ear nut **(photo d)**.
[4] Make a second matching earring.

Pink earrings

[1] Open the loop on one 4mm round pearl unit and attach it to the loop on the post earring finding.
[2] Attach the remaining dangles as follows: a 4mm bicone crystal, a 6mm bicone crystal, and a 4mm rice pearl on the second link. Skip a link and attach a 4mm round pearl and a 6mm faceted pearl to the fourth link **(photo e)**. Repeat the bead sequence, ending with a 4mm round pearl on the last link.
[3] Open a jump ring (Basics) and connect the last link to the ear nut.
[4] Make a second earring to match the first. ●

Contact Anna at editor@beadandbutton.com.

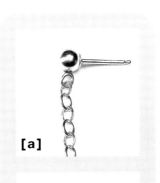

[a]

[b]

MATERIALS

both projects

- wire cutters
- chainnose pliers
- roundnose pliers

blue earrings

- **6** 6mm faceted pearls
- **8** 5mm bicone crystals
- **30** 4mm bicone crystals
- **8** 4mm round pearls
- **52** 1-in. (2.5cm) 22-gauge head pins
- **3** in. (7.6cm) cable chain
- **2** post earring findings with loop
- **2** ear nuts
- **2** 3mm jump rings

pink earrings

- **6** 6mm bicone crystals
- **4** 6mm faceted pearls
- **8** 4mm round pearls
- **6** 4mm rice pearls
- **6** 4mm bicone crystals
- **30** 1-in. head pins
- **2** in. (5cm) cable chain
- **2** post earring findings with loop
- **2** ear nuts
- **2** 3mm jump rings

[c]

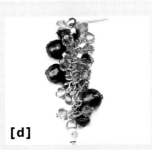

[d]

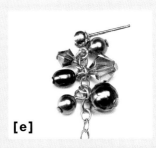

[e]

Wrapped Rings

We think you'll adore the chic look of this wire ring. It's an easy way to showcase buttons and art beads and to accessorize your favorite outfits.

by **Jeannette Coons**

step*by*step

[1] Determine the finished ring size.

[2] Working two sizes larger than the finished size, hold a 24-in. (61cm) piece of wire against the mandrel. Position the wire with 10 in. (25cm) on the left of the mandrel and 14 in. (36cm) on the right.

[3] Hold the wire in place with your left hand and wrap the 14-in. length around the mandrel three times with your right hand.

[4] Cross the wires on the front of the mandrel and adjust them, if necessary, so they are the same length.

[5] Bend both wires away from the mandrel using chainnose pliers **(photo a)**.

[6] Slide the bead over both wires and against the mandrel **(photo b)**. If you are using a button, position one wire in each buttonhole.

[7] Hold the bead and the mandrel in your left hand and hold the wires together just above the bead or button with your right. Twist the wires together by turning the mandrel and bead halfway around.

[8] Place your thumb on the hole of the bead and bend the wires against the bead **(photo c)**. Gently apply pressure with your thumb to hold the wires snugly against the bead. Turn the bead and mandrel with your left hand three or four times to form the wires into a coil at the center of the bead **(photo d)**. Repeat until the coil is the desired size.

[9] Bring the wires down the side of the bead individually or together (depending on the shape of your bead) and wrap them around the wires below the bead **(photo e)**. Make two to three wraps.

[10] Position the wires so they are on opposite sides of the bead above the band.

[11] Remove the ring from the mandrel. Working one side at a time, wrap a wire around the band three to four times **(photo f)**.

[12] Use roundnose pliers to make a small coil with the end of the wire against the wraps if desired, or trim the wire on the inside of the band and squeeze it flush against the band with chainnose pliers.

[13] Finish the remaining wire the same way. ◉

Jeannette is the owner of Girly Girl World – The Artsy Bead and Jewelry Boutique in Independence, Missouri. Contact her by e-mail at girlygirlworld@sbcglobal.net or visit girlygirlworld.com.

MATERIALS
one ring
- 24 in. (61cm) 18-gauge wire, dead soft
- 1–3 12–20mm disk-shaped beads or buttons with 2mm holes (flower bead by Stephanie Sersich, sssbeads.com)
- ring mandrel
- wire cutters
- chainnose pliers
- roundnose pliers

[a]

[b]

[c]

[d]

[e]

[f]

Harlequin Romance

by **Elizabeth Larsen**

Black onyx and white "jade" give my *Harlequin* necklace a bold presence that earned it the second-place award for finished jewelry in the 2004 Bead Dreams competition. The beaded cluster is surprisingly lightweight and smooth to the touch. All the wire is looped at the ends, offering rich texture with no sharp edges. Echo the sleek design by making a pair of complementary earrings.

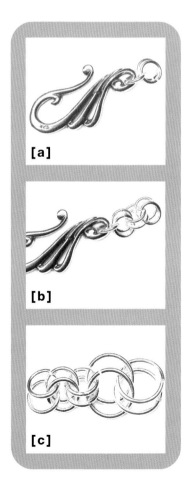

[a]

[b]

[c]

step*by*step

Assemble the chain

[1] Open one 5mm jump ring (Basics, p. 10) and connect it to a clasp loop and two closed 5mm jump rings (photo a).

[2] Open two 5mm jump rings and connect them to the last two rings and two closed 5mm jump rings (photo b). Continue for 6 in. (15cm) of links or 35 jump ring pairs.

[3] Open two 7mm jump rings and connect them to the last two rings and two closed 7mm jump rings (photo c). Continue for 3 in. (7.6cm) of links for a total of 26 jump-ring pairs.

[4] Repeat steps 1–2 in reverse order to complete the chain.

Wrap the beads

[1] Cut a 6-in. strip of silver wire. Make a wrapped loop (Basics) at the end of the wire, string a black bead, then make a wrapped loop at the other end but don't cut the wire (photo d, p. 80).

[2] Hold this loop with chainnose pliers and wrap the wire around the bead with your other hand (photo e).

[3] Wrap the wire around the base of the first loop's wraps then cut the wire flush against the wraps (photo f).

[4] Repeat steps 1–3 with the remaining black beads.

[5] Repeat steps 1–3 using black wire and all the white beads.

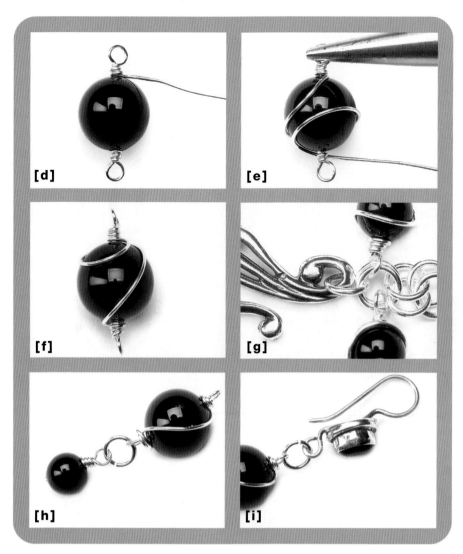

[d]

[e]

[f]

[g]

[h]

[i]

MATERIALS

both projects
• wire cutters
• chainnose pliers
• roundnose pliers

necklace 16½ in. (42cm)
• black onyx
  70 6mm beads
  52 8mm beads
  16 10mm beads
• white "jade" (dolomite marble)
  70 6mm beads
  52 8mm beads
  16 10mm beads
• **132** 5mm jump rings, silver
• **44** 7mm jump rings, silver
• 23 yd. (21m) 24-gauge wire, sterling silver
• spool of 24-gauge black wire
• clasp

earring pair
• black onyx
  2 6mm beads
  2 10mm beads
• **4** 5mm jump rings, silver
• **2** head pins, silver
• 6 in. (15cm) 24-gauge wire, sterling silver
• ear wires with black onyx
  (Fire Mountain Gems, 800-355-2137,
  firemountaingems.com)

Build the necklace

[1] At one end of the chain, open two of the double-linked jump rings and attach the loop from a 6mm black bead. On the other side of the links, attach a second 6mm black bead (photo g).

[2] Repeat step 1 using the remaining 6mm black beads for 3½ in. (8.9cm).

[3] Repeat step 1 using 8mm black beads for 2½ in. (6.4cm).

[4] Repeat step 1 using 10mm black beads for 1½ in. (3.8cm).

[5] Repeat steps 1–4 in reverse order using the wrapped white beads.

Make matching earrings

[1] String a 6mm black bead on a head pin, make a wrapped loop, then trim the wire.

[2] Repeat steps 1–3 of "Wrap the beads" using a 10mm black bead.

[3] Open a 5mm jump ring and attach the loop from the 6mm wrapped bead

to one of the 10mm bead's loops (photo h). Close the ring.

[4] Open a 5mm jump ring and attach the other loop from the 10mm bead to the ear wire's loop. Close the ring (photo i).

[5] Make a second earring to match the first. ○

Contact Elizabeth at elarsen2003@ yahoo.com.

EDITOR'S NOTE:
If you feel comfortable manipulating jump rings, consider wrapping your beads first, then attaching them as you assemble your chain. Or you can purchase large-linked chain with unsoldered rings. If you go this route, adjust your bead count to accommodate the ring sizes.

by **Dorothy Bonitz**

Passion Flower

Exotic blooms grace the holiday table

The *Passiflora*, or passion flower, is an exotic climbing plant native to South America. In the early 1600s, Christian missionaries saw the flower as a religious symbol of the crucifixion and gave this large, complex bloom its name. Today, there are more than 400 species found worldwide. Unlike the beaded version, passion flowers last just one day, closing forever at night.

stepbystep

Refer to the flower illustration on p. 83 as you work.

Petals and leaves

[1] Transfer one strand of pearl white beads onto the spool of 26-gauge white or gold wire.

[2] Working 3 in. (7.6cm) from the end of the wire, form 3¾ in. (10cm) of beads into a loop and twist the wires together a few times to secure them (photo a).

[3] Position the working wire lengthwise through the center of the petal and slide enough beads down to fill the space between the base and tip of the petal (photo b).

[4] Wrap the wire over the tip between the end beads, and slide down enough beads to fill the space between the tip and the base. Twist the wires together at the base to secure them.

[5] Cut the working wire from the spool so it is flush with the 3-in. tail.

[6] Cut the end of the green floral tape at an angle and in half lengthwise. Place the tapered end at the base of the petal and wrap it around the wires for ¼ in. (6mm) (photo c).

[7] Make a total of ten pearl-white, four-row crossover petals.

[8] Make five four-row crossover leaves using 26-gauge green wire and dark green seed beads.

Corona filaments

[1] Cut a 10-in. (25cm) piece of 28-gauge gold wire and fold it in half.

[2] Place the corsage pin in the fold and wrap one end of the wire around the pin eight to ten times (photo d).

[3] Remove the coil from the pin and cut it in half through the coil.

[4] On one wire, string 1 in. (2.5cm) of purple beads, one dark purple bead, two white crystal beads, one dark purple bead, and ½ in. (1.3cm) of purple beads (photo e).

[5] Repeat step 4 with the remaining wire. Then twist the straight ends of the wires together just below the beads.

[6] Make a total of 35 corona filaments (17 pairs and one single).

[7] Cut a piece of floral tape as you did for the petals. Tape together two pairs by wrapping the tape around the wires just under the beads for ¼ in.

[8] Repeat step 7 with the remaining wires. You will have eight groups of four and one with three.

Stamens

[1] Cut an 8-in. (20cm) piece of 28-gauge gold wire.

[2] String seven lime green beads to the center of the wire. Form them into a loop by twisting the wires together beneath the beads.

[3] Position the wire ends side by side and string six lime green beads over both wires (photo f). Secure the beads in place with a ¼-in. wrap of floral tape.

[4] Make five.

Stigmas

[1] Transfer the crystal white beads onto the spool of 28-gauge gold wire.

[2] Slide the beads 3 in. from the end of the wire, skip the end bead, and bring the wire back through 1 in. of beads. Push the beads up against the end bead and cut the spool wire flush with the short wire (photo g).

[3] Make three.

Tendrils

[1] Cut three pieces of 28-gauge gold wire to the following lengths: 7 in. (18cm), 9 in. (23cm), and 11 in. (28cm).

[2] Wrap each wire with brown floral tape. Coil the wires around a skewer.

[3] Shape the wires as desired (photo h).

Assembly

[1] Hold the three stigmas together and slide the 8mm bead over all three wires and against the seed beads.

[2] Arrange the five stamen parts below the 8mm bead. Wrap the wires together with 28-gauge gold wire.

[3] Start just below the stamens and wrap about 1 in. of the wires with green floral tape to hold the parts in place.

[4] Arrange the corona filaments ½ in. below the stamen so some tape shows on the stem (photo i). Wire a couple groups to the stem at a time, then secure with floral tape as before. I wrap the stem with floral tape several times at this point to give it a wider base.

[5] Arrange the flower petals, leaves, and tendrils next. At this point you can start to cut some of the stem wires to form the stalk into the desired shape.

[6] Wrap the entire stem with floral tape.

[7] Shape the flower as shown in the illustration. ●

Email Dorothy at rosemary@swva.net.

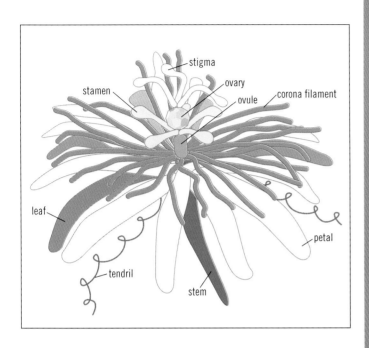

stigma

stamen

ovary

ovule

corona filament

leaf

petal

tendril

stem

MATERIALS

one flower

- seed beads size 11º
  5 strands pearl white
  2 strands medium to dark green
  2 strands purple
  strand dark purple
  strand white in crystal or
    transparent white-lined
  strand lime green
- 8mm glass bead, pale green or
  white
- 26-gauge craft wire, green and
  white or gold
- 28-gauge craft wire, gold
- corsage pin
- floral tape, brown and green
- wood barbecue skewer or mandrel
  with 2–3mm diameter
- wire cutters
- chainnose pliers

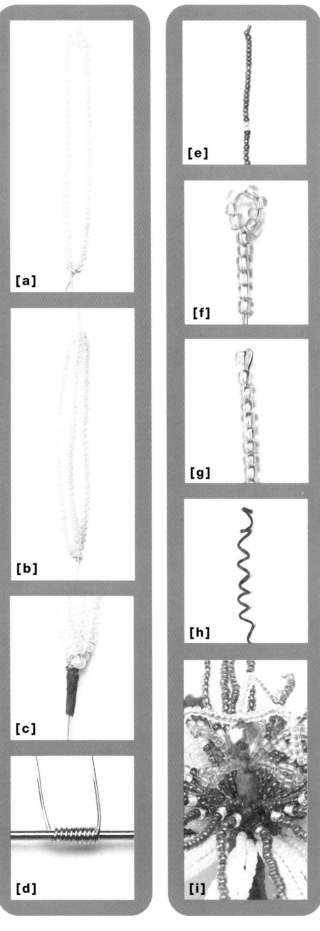

[a]

[b]

[c]

[d]

[e]

[f]

[g]

[h]

[i]

Cotillion

Step back in time and recall the grace and elegance of a bygone era. Create a necklace that is as stylish today as it was at its debut.

by **Terri Torbeck**

step*by*step

Necklace

[1] Measure your neck to determine the finished length of the necklace, subtract 1 in. (2.5cm) for the clasp, and cut two pieces of chain to this length.

[2] Cut a 3-in. (7.6cm) piece of wire. Start a wrapped loop (Basics, p. 10) near one end. Slide the loop into one of the two long links at the center of one chain. Complete the wraps **(photo a)**.

[3] String a seed bead, a teardrop, and a seed bead on

the wire. Start a wrapped loop in the same plane as the first. Slide the loop into a long link on the second chain as before **(photo b)**. Make sure there are no twists in the chain and that the component lies flat. Finish the wraps **(photo c)**.

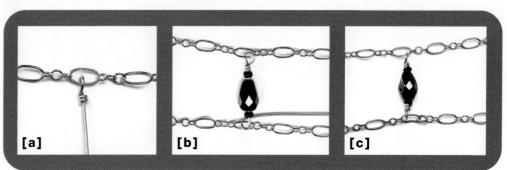

[a]   [b]   [c]

Choker

EDITOR'S NOTE:
To add a more authentic quality to this necklace, consider using vintage beads. For online bead sources, check our links at beadandbutton.com/bnb/community/links/.

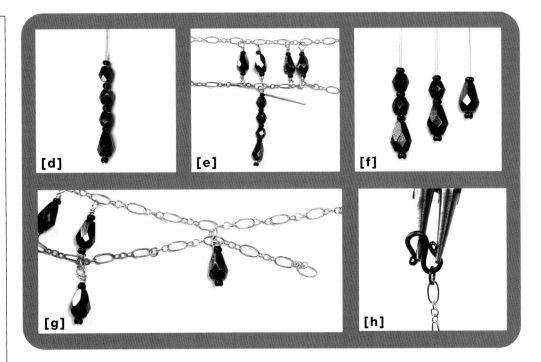

[4] Repeat steps 2-3 three times, working toward one end of the chains. Keep teardrops oriented in the same direction and connect each new wrapped loop in the next long link.
[5] Attach four more components as above, working from the center to the opposite end.

Dangles
[1] String a seed bead, a teardrop, and a seed bead on a head pin.
[2] String a 4mm and a seed bead three times **(photo d)**.
[3] Start a wrapped loop. Slide it into one of the center links on the lower chain **(photo e)**. Finish the wraps.

[4] Repeat steps 1-3 three more times. As you work along the chain toward one end, use one fewer 4mm bead for each successive dangle **(photo f)**.
[5] Attach four additional dangles, working from the center toward the opposite end.

Finishing
[1] String a seed, a teardrop, and a seed on a head pin and start a wrapped loop. To make a swag in the chain, slide the loop into a long link on the upper chain 1 in. from the last component. On the lower chain, slide the loop into a long link about 1½ in. (3cm) from the last

component **(photo g)**. Finish the wraps. Repeat on the other end of the necklace. Cut off the remaining lower chain.
[2] Open a pair of jump rings (Basics) and slide each into an end chain link. Close the rings.

Clasp
[1] Slide one end of the S-hook clasp into one of the jump rings and lightly compress that end with chainnose pliers so it won't fall off **(photo h)**. ❂

Contact Terri in care of editor@beadandbutton.com

Tiered Drops

Combine pearls and crystals with a novel new wrap

by **Annie Corkill**

Queen Elizabeth inspired this choker. No, it wasn't the monarch herself but a necklace worn by actress Cate Blanchett in the historical drama *Elizabeth*. While Blanchett's jewelry incorporated intricate metalsmithing, this choker requires uncomplicated wirework. Simple wraps secure dangling pearls and crystals. The project is quick and easy, perfect for the beginner beader or anyone desiring an elegant necklace.

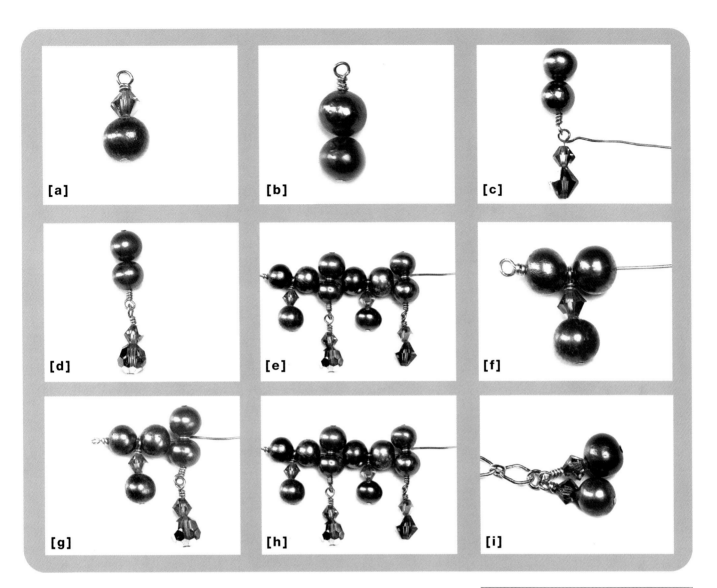

[a] [b] [c]

[d] [e] [f]

[g] [h] [i]

step*by*step

Dangles

[1] On one head pin, string a pearl and a 4mm bicone crystal, then make a wrapped loop (Basics, p. 10, and **photo a**). Make 16 more dangles and set aside.

[2] String two pearls on a head pin and make a wrapped loop (**photo b**). Make 15 more pearl components.

[3] String a 6mm bicone crystal and a 4mm bicone on a head pin. Start a wrapped loop, slide a pearl component into the loop (**photo c**), then finish the wraps. Make five more dangles.

[4] Repeat step 3 using a 6mm round crystal instead of a 6mm bicone (**photo d**). Make five more dangles.

Necklace base

[1] Using 2 ft. (61cm) of 24-gauge wire, make a wrapped loop at one end.

[2] String a pearl, the loop on one of the short dangles from step 1 of Dangles, and a pearl (**photo e**).

[3] Wrap the wire around a 6mm round crystal dangle from step 4 of Dangles, with the wire wraping between the two pearls (**photo f**).

[4] Repeat step 2.

[5] Repeat step 3 using a 6mm bicone crystal dangle (**photo g**).

[6] Repeat steps 2–5 seven times.

[7] Make a wrapped loop at the other end of the wire.

Adjustable chain ends

[1] Open a jump ring (Basics) and attach it to a wrapped loop at the end of the wire and 1 in. (2.5cm) of chain (**photo h**). Close the ring.

[2] Open a jump ring and attach the clasp to the other end of the chain. Close the ring.

[3] Repeat step 1 at the other end of the necklace using 3 in. (7.6cm) of chain.

[4] String a pearl and a 4mm bicone crystal on a head pin and make a wrapped loop. Make a second dangle.

[5] Use a jump ring to attach the two dangles to the chain (**photo i**). ●

Contact Annie in care of editor@beadandbutton.com.

MATERIALS

choker (12½–15 in./32–38cm)

- **90** 6mm round pearls
- Swarovski crystals
  33 4mm bicones
  8 6mm bicones
  8 6mm rounds
- **54** head pins, fine
- 4 in. (10cm) chain with 4mm links
- **4** 4mm jump rings
- lobster claw clasp
- 2 ft. (61cm) 24-gauge wire
- roundnose pliers
- chainnose pliers
- diagonal wire cutters

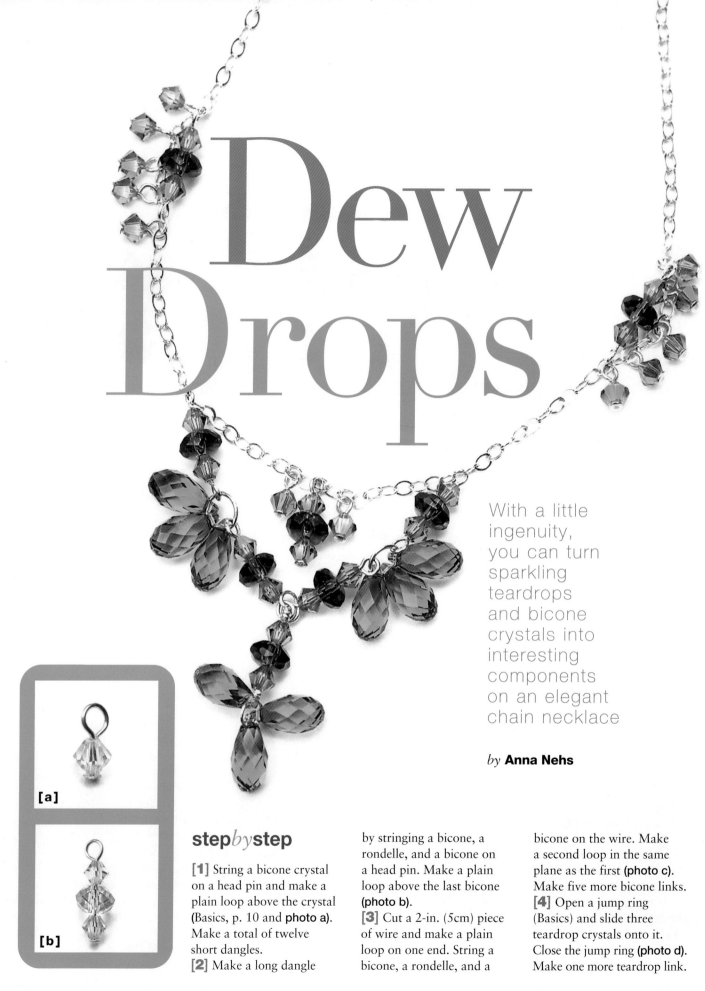

Dew Drops

With a little ingenuity, you can turn sparkling teardrops and bicone crystals into interesting components on an elegant chain necklace

by **Anna Nehs**

[a]

[b]

step*by*step

[1] String a bicone crystal on a head pin and make a plain loop above the crystal (Basics, p. 10 and **photo a**). Make a total of twelve short dangles.
[2] Make a long dangle by stringing a bicone, a rondelle, and a bicone on a head pin. Make a plain loop above the last bicone **(photo b)**.
[3] Cut a 2-in. (5cm) piece of wire and make a plain loop on one end. String a bicone, a rondelle, and a bicone on the wire. Make a second loop in the same plane as the first **(photo c)**. Make five more bicone links.
[4] Open a jump ring (Basics) and slide three teardrop crystals onto it. Close the jump ring **(photo d)**. Make one more teardrop link.

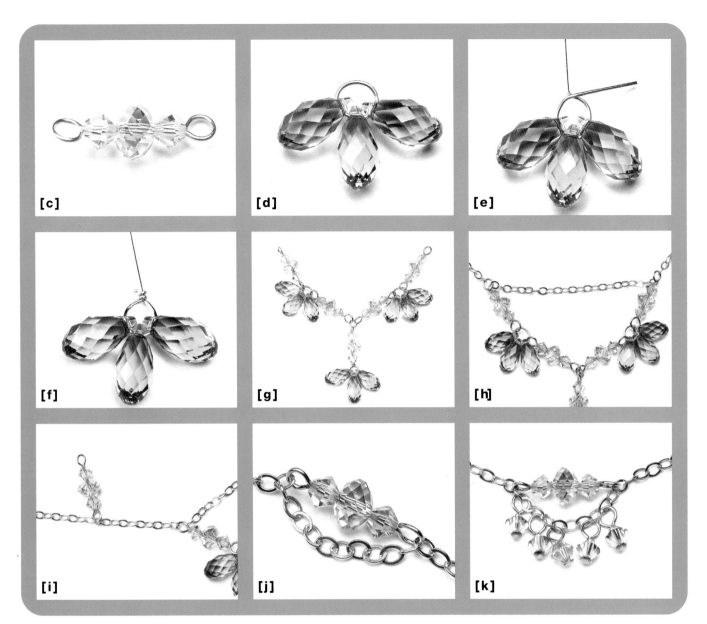

[c]

[d]

[e]

[f]

[g]

[h]

[i]

[j]

[k]

[5] To make the focal dangle, make half of a wrapped loop (Basics) on a 3-in. (7.6cm) piece of wire. Slide three teardrops into the loop (photo e). Finish with two wraps (photo f). Flatten the cut end with chainnose pliers. String a bicone, a rondelle, and a bicone on the long end. Make a wrapped loop above the bicone.

[6] Open one loop on two bicone links. Connect the bicone links to a teardrop link. Close the loops. Repeat to make a second set. Open the loops at one end of each set and connect them to the focal dangle from step 5

(photo g). Close the loops.

[7] Cut a 2-in. length of chain. Cut the remaining chain into two 9-in. (23cm) lengths. Open the loops at the ends of the unit made in step 6 and connect them with the 2-in. chain. Then attach a 9-in. chain to each loop (photo h). Close the loops.

[8] Open both loops on a bicone link. Attach one loop to the tenth chain link, working from the connection made in step 7 (photo i). Skip ten chain links and attach the other loop to the next link (photo j). Close the loops. Repeat on the other end of the necklace.

[9] On the chains that parallel the bicone links, attach a short dangle to every other link (photo k).

[10] On the 2-in. chain from step 7, attach the long dangle to the center link and connect a short dangle on each side. (Shorten the 2-in. chain if the dangles overlap the bicone links below it when you wear the necklace.)

[11] Attach a jump ring to each end chain link and a lobster clasp to either of the rings. ●

Contact Anna at editor@beadandbutton.com.

MATERIALS

necklace 17 in. (43cm)

- **9** 11 x 5.5mm teardrop crystals
- **28** 4mm bicone crystals
- **8** 6mm rondelles
- **20** in. (51cm) fine chain
- **12** in. (31cm) 22-gauge wire
- **13** head pins, 22-gauge
- lobster clasp
- **4** 6mm jump rings
- wire cutters
- roundnose pliers
- chainnose pliers

Foxtail pearl float

Suspend pearls in a chain of jump rings

by **Anne Mitchell**

Add drama to the medieval allure of linked rings by caging pearls or glass beads in a ropelike chain called a Full Persian. The open weave of this intricate chain creates chambers that just beg to be filled. Once I envisioned beads suspended in the chain, there was no turning back. I had to make it happen.

step*by*step

For clarity, the instructions refer to the position of each jump ring as north (away from you), south (toward you), east (to your right), and west (to your left).

Assemble the chain
[1] Close four 10mm jump rings and open the remaining large rings (Basics, p. 10).
[2] Connect the closed jump rings with a pair of open jump rings for a 2+2+2 section of chain (photo a).
[3] Attach a paper clip to one end of the chain as shown in **photo b.** Tape it to your work surface so the chain points away from you.

   The two rings attached to the paper clip are rings 1 and 2, the two middle rings are rings 3 and 4, and the top rings are 5 and 6.
[4] Hold rings 5 and 6 with pliers and drop ring 6 to the east of the chain (photo c). Then drop ring 5 to the west (photo d).
[5] Separate rings 3 and 4, bringing one ring to the north and one to the south (photo e). Arrange the rings so that they are positioned as shown. Rings 3 and 4 (north and south) should be slightly raised, and rings 5 and 6 (east and west) should be

pointing down toward your work surface.
[6] Connect an open jump ring to rings 1 and 2 (photo f). Don't close the jump ring.
[7] Hold the open jump ring (ring 7) with one pair of pliers, grasp ring 6 (on the right) with a second pair of pliers, and place it onto the open ring (photo g).
[8] Continue holding ring 7.

Grasp ring 5 (on the left) with the second pair of pliers and place it onto the open ring (photo h). Close the jump ring.
[9] Connect a jump ring to rings 5, 1, 2, and 6 so it sits next to ring 7 (photo i). This is ring 8.
[10] Connect two rings (9 and 10) to rings 7 and 8 (photo j, p. 92).

EDITOR'S NOTE: When you tape the paper clip to your work surface, tape the top of it just below the rings. This will hold the rings in place and keep the chain from shifting as you work.

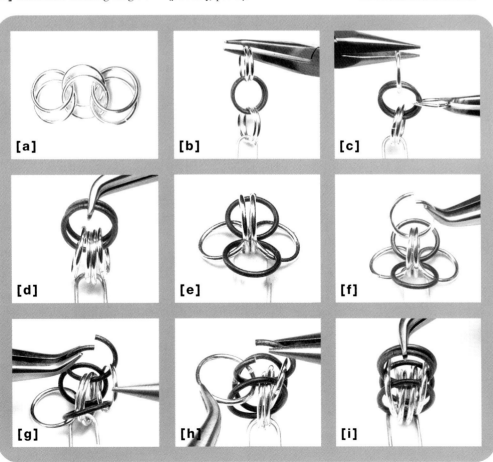

[a]

[b]

[c]

[d]

[e]

[f]

[g]

[h]

[i]

[11] Bring ring 10 to the east and grab rings 7 and 8 with your pliers, so ring 9 falls to the west of the chain (photo k).

[12] Separate rings 7 and 8, as you did in step 5, and slide a jump ring (ring 11) onto rings 5 and 6, which will pop up slightly on the sides of rings 1 and 2 (photo l). Don't close the jump ring.

[13] Bring ring 10 up from the right of the chain and slide it onto ring 11. Then bring ring 9 up from the left of the chain and slide it onto ring 11 (photo m). Close the jump ring.

[14] Connect ring 12, as you did in step 9, through the four center rings so it sits next to ring 11 (photo n).

[15] Repeat steps 10–14 until you reach the desired length. Now that the pattern is established, you can remove the chain from the paper clip.

[16] Attach three 5mm jump rings to each end of the chain as shown in photo o.

[17] Attach the lobster claw clasp to the end 5mm jump ring at one end of the chain.

String the pearls

[1] Crimp a crimp bead (Basics) at the end of a 24-in. (61cm) piece of flexible beading wire and trim the wire as close to the crimp as possible. When crimping one strand, I like to squeeze the crimp with chainnose pliers after I crimp it to make sure it is secure.

[2] Position the awl through the center intersection of the first and second chambers so it intersects all four rings (photo p).

[3] Using the awl as a guide, slide the uncrimped end of the beading wire through the center of these rings. Pull the wire about halfway through, lay the chain down on your work surface, and string a pearl on the wire. Don't let the bead go into the chain chamber.

[4] Carefully pick up the chain and reposition the awl through the intersection of the second and third chambers (photo q).

[5] Feed a few inches of the wire through the center of these jump rings, using the awl as a guide. Place the chain on your work surface, remove the awl, and gently pull on each end of the wire (photo r) and pop the pearl into the chamber (photo s).

[6] String a pearl on the wire and repeat steps 4–5. Repeat until you reach the second-to-last chamber. The first and last chambers of the chain remain empty.

[7] After all the pearls are in place, pull the wire all the way through the chain and form the chain into a circle. Use a fine-point marker to mark the wire just past the intersection of the last two chambers.

[8] Pull on the unfinished end of the wire so the chain collapses on itself and exposes the mark you just made. String a crimp over the mark and crimp it in place.

[9] Trim the excess wire. When you straighten the chain, the crimps will tuck inside the end chambers. ●

Contact Anne at anne@annemitchell.net. Kits are available for this and other chain designs on her website annemitchell.net.

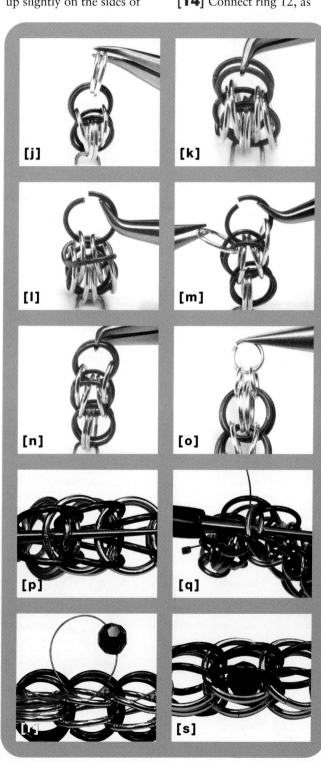

[j]

[k]

[l]

[m]

[n]

[o]

[p]

[q]

[r]

[s]

MATERIALS
- 2 troy oz. (64g) sterling silver jump rings, 10mm inside diameter, 16-gauge wire
- **6** sterling silver jump rings, 5mm inside diameter, 18-gauge wire
- 24 in. (61cm) flexible beading wire, .014–.015
- **2** crimp beads
- 16-in. (40cm) strand 4–5mm pearls or beads
- lobster claw clasp
- paper clip
- beading awl
- chainnose pliers
- bent chainnose pliers
- crimping pliers
- wire cutters

Tips & Techniques

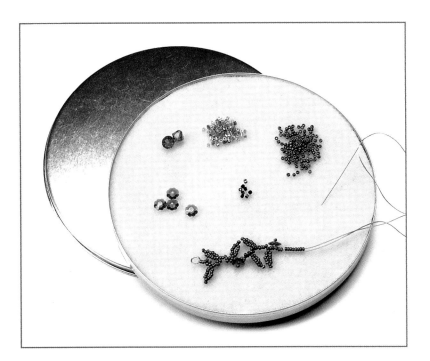

Portable bead tray

I work on several projects at one time, so finding a way to keep my projects separated, organized, and portable is critical. CD tins are a great size for a single project, and since they have lids, I can keep all the components needed for a project together.

Line the lid and bottom of the tin with Vellux or a similar material and work on the bottom half. When you need to put the project aside or take it with you, cover the bottom with the lid and secure it with a rubber band. When you open the tin, the beads will be where you left them. CD tins are available in two shapes, round and rectangular. Check the bridal section at your local craft store, where they are sold as party favors, or order tins from www.effectuality.com.
– *Alyssa Draeger,*
Dousman, Wisconsin

Consistent loops

When making a project that has multiple wire-wrapped loops, such as chandelier earrings, make the first loop, then use a permanent marker to mark that place on the jaw of your roundnose pliers. Use this mark as a guide for making the rest of the loops the same size. Since the jaws of the pliers are metal, the mark wears off.
– *Jamie Cloud Eakin,*
Modesto, California

Website bookmarks

I have visited hundreds of bead-related websites (thanks to *Bead & Button*) and bookmarked the ones I like the best. Unfortunately, when I needed to find a specific product, I couldn't remember which website I saw it on. Now, I edit the bookmarks so instead of keeping just the web address, I also have the reason why I bookmarked it (great price on crystals). My personalized bookmarks make it easy for me to find what I am looking for and why I saved the website in the first place.
– *Glenda Blakemore,*
Aurora, Illinois

Hole-punching pliers

I love my split ring pliers! Not only are they invaluable for their intended use, they are perfect for pre-punching needle holes in suede and leather for bead embroidery. It's easier than using an awl, and you don't need a padded work surface.
– *Ali Dean, Arlington, Texas*

Photo backgrounds

For about $1 each, I can buy a variety of professional-looking backgrounds to photograph my beadwork on. Scrapbook papers (12 x 12 in./31 x 31cm) come in a variety of colors and textures at most craft stores, and they are easy to store in a folder. When it comes to lighting my beadwork, I find that natural light works the best.
– *Kimberly Szalkiewicz,*
Escondido, California ●

Stitching

Stitch a lacy wildflower choker
to enjoy throughout the seasons

Running Wild

by **Erin Robinson**

I've been doing beadwork since I was a ten-year-old with
my first loom. Now, at the ripe old age of seventeen, I'm
putting my passion to good use designing jewelry that has
served me well at proms, parties, and graduations. This
lacy choker was a big hit at a spring dance. With a few
color variations, it will be just as beautiful when the leaves,
or even the snow, starts to fall.

step*by*step

Make this necklace from end to end, starting and ending with a picot flower. Although the finished necklace shows three connections between flowers, you only stitch one connection as you make the flowers. You'll work the other two connections in the last step before attaching the clasp.

Picot flower

[1] Using a comfortable length of Fireline, pick up 12 color A seed beads. Leaving a 10-in. (25cm) tail, tie the working thread and tail together with a square knot (Basics, p. 10) to form the beads into a ring. Sew through the first bead again.
[2] Pick up a 4mm round crystal and go through bead 7 on the ring **(figure 1, a–b)**.
[3] Pick up a color C bugle and six A 11°s. Cross through the third seed bead strung to form a picot **(b–c)**.
[4] Pick up two A 11°s and a C bugle and go through bead 8 on the center ring **(figure 2, a–b)**. Go back up through the bugle just added **(b–c)**.
[5] Pick up six A 11°s and make a picot as in step 3 **(figure 3, a–b)**. Pick up two A 11°s and a C bugle **(b–c)**.
[6] Working in the same direction, go through the next bead on the center ring and back through the bugle just added **(c–d)**.
[7] Repeat steps 5–6 until you have 12 bugles and 12 picots **(d–e)**.
[8] Go through the first bugle, bead 7 on the ring, the bugle, and continue through the five beads on the first picot **(e–f)**. Don't end the thread.

Accent flower

[1] Pick up a D bugle and 12 B 11°s. Go through the first bead again in the same direction **(figure 4, a–b)**. Pick up a 4mm round crystal and go through bead 7 on the ring **(b–c)**.
[2] Go through beads 8–12 on the ring and the bugle. Exit the right side of the top picot bead **(c–d)**.
[3] Pick up a B 11°, a 4mm E bicone, a B 11°, and a D bugle **(figure 5, a–b)**. Go through

bead 2 on the ring and back through the D bugle **(b–c)**.
[4] Pick up a B 11°, a color E bicone, a B 11°, and a D bugle. Go through bead 4 on the ring and back through the bugle **(c–d)**. Continue around the circle, skipping beads 3, 6, 9, and 12 on the ring. There should be eight bugles in place **(d–e)**.
[5] Pick up a B 11°, an E bicone, and a B 11°. Go through the first D bugle and exit bead 1 on the ring **(e–f)**.

[6] Go through beads 2–5 on the ring and exit bugle 4 **(figure 6, a–b)**.
[7] Go through the B 11°, E bicone, and B 11°. Pick up an A 11° **(b–c)**. This is the top picot bead of the next flower. Go through the next B 11°, E bicone, and B 11° **(c–d)**.
[8] Go down through bugle 6 and the adjacent two B 11°s on the ring. Come back up through bugle 5 and exit through the new picot bead **(d–e)**.

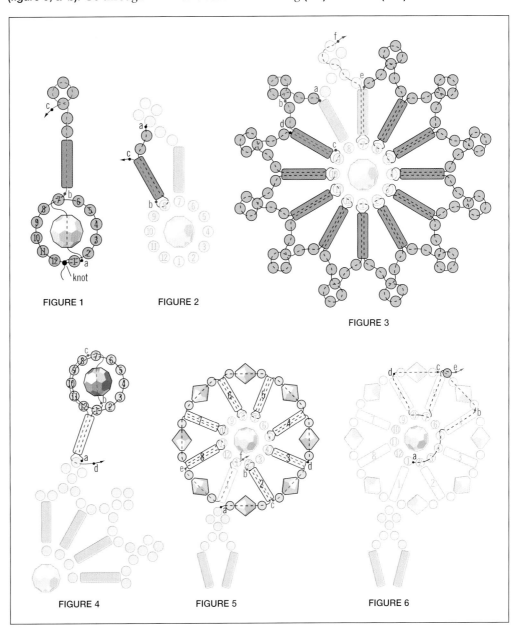

FIGURE 1

FIGURE 2

FIGURE 3

FIGURE 4

FIGURE 5

FIGURE 6

Second picot flower

[1] Pick up four A 11°s and a C bugle (figure 7, a–b). Pick up 12 A 11°s and go through the first bead on the ring again (b–c).

[2] Pick up a 4mm round crystal and go through bead 7 on the ring (c–d). Go through beads 8–12 on the ring and exit the bugle (d–e).

[3] Go through the four A 11°s and the tip of the picot on the accent flower (e–f).

[4] Pick up an A 11° and go through the second 11° picked up in step 1 (f–g).

[5] Pick up two A 11°s and a C bugle (figure 8, a–b). Go through the next A 11° in the ring and the new bugle (b–c).

[6] Repeat steps 5–7 of the first picot flower to continue the petals. Keep going until you've made three picot flowers and three accent flowers, ending with step 8 of the accent flower. Don't end the thread.

Center picot flower

The center flower is a larger version of the first picot flower with a crystal on every other picot.

[1] Pick up four A 11°s and a C bugle (figure 9, a–b). Pick up 15 A 11°s and go through the first bead again (b–c).

[2] Pick up a 6mm coin crystal. Go through bead 8 on the ring (c–d). Go through beads 9–15 on the ring and exit the bugle (d–e).

[3] Repeat steps 3–5 from the second picot flower (e–f).

[4] Pick up three A 11°s, a 4mm F bicone, and an A 11° (f–g). Skip the last A 11° and go back through the F bicone, and one A 11°. Pick up two A 11°s and a C bugle (g–h).

[5] Go through the adjacent 11° on the ring and back through the new C bugle (h–i).

[6] As you continue making petals, skip beads 4, 10, and 15 on the center ring. Continue until there are 12 bugles in place, alternating between picots and bicones.

[7] After completing the petals, go through the beads on the ring and exit the top of the fourth picot. Make three accent flowers and three picot flowers as before.

Reinforce the joins

[1] Anchor a new thread in the first picot flower near its connection to the accent flower. Join one picot tip next to the connection to the closest point on the accent flower with an F bicone (figure 10, a–b).

[2] Weave through the accent flower and exit the closest point between the two flowers on the other side of the primary connection. Join the two with an F bicone as before (b–c).

[3] Repeat across the necklace, adding a crystal on each side of each connection until every pair of flowers is connected at three points. When connecting picot points of the center flower, don't add a bicone. Just sew through the bicone picots.

Attach the clasp

[1] Thread a needle on the tail at one end of the choker.

[2] Go through the loop on the lobster claw clasp and the picot opening several times.

[3] Secure the thread with half-hitch knots between a few adjacent beads and trim the tail.

[4] Repeat on the other end to add the soldered ring. ●

Erin is from Ontario, Canada. Send her an email at beadthesystem@hotmail.com.

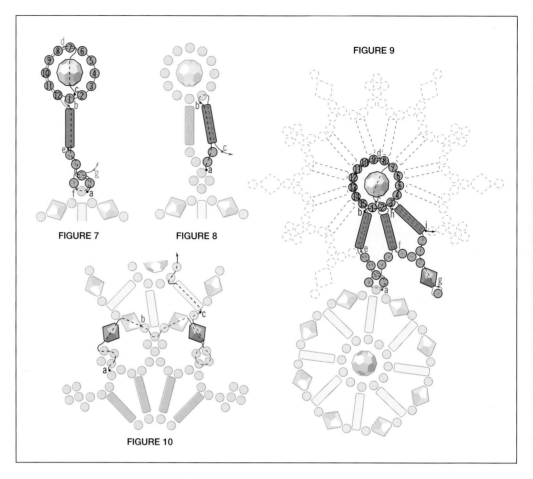

FIGURE 9

FIGURE 7

FIGURE 8

FIGURE 10

MATERIALS

choker 14 in. (35.6cm)
- seed beads, size 11°
  15g color A
  15g color B
- bugle beads, size 2 (6mm)
  7g color C
  7g color D
- Swarovski crystals
  6 4mm faceted round for picot flowers
  6 4mm faceted round for accent wheels

54 4mm faceted color E bicones for accent flowers
26 4mm faceted color F bicones for center flower and connections
6mm faceted coin crystal for center flower
- small lobster claw clasp with soldered jump ring
- Fireline 6 lb. test
- beading needles, #12

Staggered by Daggers

Colorful hanks of dagger beads inspire an easy, embellished bracelet in square stitch

by **Judy Saye-Willis**

step*by*step

Base

[1] Determine the desired finished length of your bracelet. This one is 7 in. (18cm). Subtract the length of the button or toggle clasp to determine the length of the beaded section.

[2] Pick up four 6º seed beads and slide them to 12 in. (30cm) from the end of a 2-yd. (1.8m) length of doubled thread. Sew back through the first two 6ºs **(figure 1, a–b)**.

[3] Pick up two 6ºs and sew back through two 6ºs on the previous row and the first new 6º **(b–c)**. Continue in square stitch (Basics, p. 10) until you reach the length determined in step 1.

[4] To make a button clasp, pick up five 11ºs, the button, and five 11ºs. Sew back into the end row of square stitch **(figure 2, a–b)**. Reinforce the loop by retracing the thread path through the 11ºs and the button several times. Secure the thread with half-hitch knots (Basics) between beads and trim the tails.

Using the thread tails left in step 2, pick up enough 11ºs to fit around the button and sew back through the end row of 6ºs **(figure 3, a–b)**. Secure the tail as before.

[5] For a toggle clasp, pick up a 6º and the loop half of the clasp. Sew back through the 6º and into the end row of square stitch **(figure 4, a–b)**. Secure the tail as before.

Using the thread tails left in step 2, pick up two 6ºs and the bar half of the clasp. Sew back through the two 6ºs and into the end row of square stitch **(c–d)**. Secure the tails.

Daggers

[1] Secure a 3-yd. (2.7m) length of thread in the first few square-stitch rows and exit the second bead on either side **(figure 5, point a)**. Pick up five daggers and sew through the third bead on the opposite side **(a–b)**.

[2] Continue adding daggers in the same manner along the square stitch base. Secure the thread and trim the tails. ●

Contact Judy Saye-Willis in care of Bead&Button *magazine at* editor@beadandbutton.com.

MATERIALS

bracelet 7 in. (18cm)
- **350–375** dagger beads
- Japanese seed beads
  20g size 6º
  2g size 11º
- Nymo D or Silamide to match bead color
- 12mm button with shank or toggle clasp
- beading needles, #12

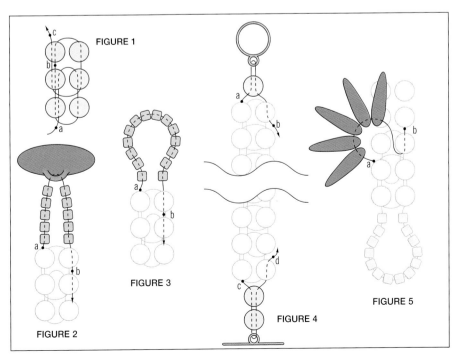

FIGURE 1

FIGURE 2

FIGURE 3

FIGURE 4

FIGURE 5

Heart's Desire

Cover a mesh heart with pearls and crystals for a romantic pin or pendant with a whisper of times past

by **Anne Nikolai Kloss**

MATERIALS

one pin or pendant

- heart-shaped mesh pin or pendant (Designer's Findings, 262-574-1324)
- **40** (approx.) small rice pearls
- crystals:
  heart-shaped crystal
  48 4mm bicone crystals, dark
  32 (approx.) 4mm bicone crystals, light
- seed beads, size 15º
  3g to match pearl color
  3g to match dark crystal
- Fireline 6 lb. test
- beading needles, #12
- chainnose pliers
- clear nail polish
- permanent marker

step*by*step

[1] Separate the mesh top from its bottom. Draw a heart on the mesh dome with a permanent marker **(photo a** and **figure 1)**. Cover the outside of the bottom piece with tape to prevent it from getting scratched and set it aside.

[2] Using 1–2 yd. (.9–1.8m) of Fireline, sew in and out of two adjacent holes in the center of the dome to secure the thread. Tie the tail and working thread together on the back of the dome with a square knot (Basics, p. 10). Come through to the front of the dome near the center.

[3] To start the fringe, pick up a pearl and a 15º and slide them against the dome. Go back through the pearl and dome **(photo b)**.

[4] To make a second style of fringe, come out through a

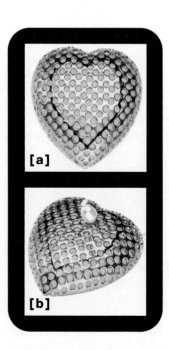

[a]

[b]

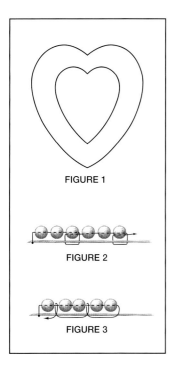

FIGURE 1

FIGURE 2

FIGURE 3

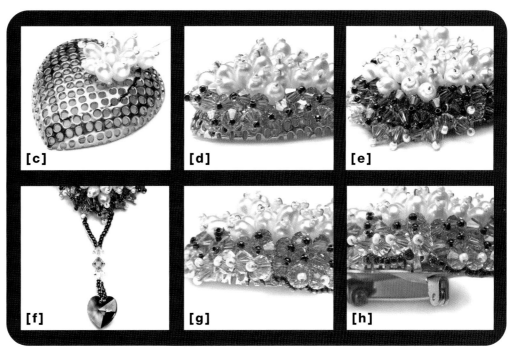

[c]

[d]

[e]

[f]

[g]

[h]

hole close to the first fringe. Pick up a 15º, pearl, and 15º. (Changing the fringe beads slightly helps them fit closer together.) Go back through the pearl, 15º, and dome.

[5] Repeat steps 3–4 to fill in the outlined section (photo c). You may not use every hole on the mesh or you may use a hole more than once. Some pearls will flop over as you work, but they'll stand up once you finish the surrounding area.

[6] Sew two rows of dark crystal fringe around the pearl section (photo d), keeping the heart shape as defined as possible. As you fill in different areas, run the thread through the holes; don't leave long threads running across the back of the dome.

[7] Sew one row of light crystal fringe around the dark crystals (photo e).

[8] Exit a hole one row from the bottom edge and two holes from the point. Pick up

⅝ in. (1.6cm) of 15ºs, a light crystal, dark crystal, light crystal, five 15ºs, and the heart-shaped crystal. Pick up five 15ºs, go back through the three crystals, and pick up ⅝ in. of 15ºs. Go through the corresponding hole on the opposite side of the point. The dangle should hang evenly below the point (photo f). Secure the thread by sewing through two holes several times.

[9] Place the dome on the base and outline the prongs with the marker. Remove the dome.

[10] Stitch 15ºs to the dome to cover the exposed metal (photo g), but don't fill in the marked areas for the prongs and don't end the thread. You may use a mix of beaded backstitch (figure 2) and a variation of couching (figure 3) to work around the crystals.

[11] Coat the underside of the dome with clear nail polish or glue to seal the

knots and secure the threads.

[12] Set the dome on the base. Using chainnose pliers, gently squeeze the prongs onto the dome to hold the dome in place (photo h).

[13] Finish stitching the 15ºs over the prongs and secure the thread.

[14] Remove the tape from the base. ○

Anne is a contributing editor at BeadStyle *magazine. Contact Anne at annekloss@mac.com.*

EDITOR'S NOTE: When you stitch over metal, use Fireline or another high-tech material that can take the abrasion of being pulled against a metal edge. Nylon threads are durable in most beading applications, but we don't recommend using them for this type of project.

Dutch Treat

Make easy
crystal earrings
using the Dutch
spiral technique

by **Cyndy Klein**

If you enjoy special-occasion jewelry, treat yourself to this pair of sparkling earrings. Worked in an easy variation of tubular peyote that yields the distinctive curves known as Dutch spiral, these earrings can be finished in an evening of leisurely beading.

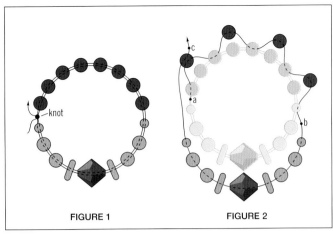

FIGURE 1   FIGURE 2

step*by*step

[1] On 24 in. (61cm) of thread, string eight main color (MC) 11ºs, a 14º, two accent color (AC) 11ºs, a heishi, a 4mm crystal, a heishi, two ACs, and a 14º. Go through the beads again to form a circle, leaving a 6-in. (15cm) tail. Tie the tail and working thread together with a surgeon's knot (Basics, p.10 and **figure 1**).

[2] Work in peyote stitch (Basics): Go through the first MC, pick up an MC, skip the next MC on the circle, and go through the third MC. Repeat three times, going through the 14º to complete the last stitch (**figure 2, a–b**). Keep the tension tight.

[3] Pick up a 14º, two ACs, a heishi, a 4mm crystal, a heishi, two ACs, and a 14º. (These are the floating beads.) Go through the first MC added in step 2 (**b–c**).

[4] Repeat steps 2–3 until you've used 11 4mm crystals. Finish with a four-bead peyote row of MCs, but don't end the thread.

[5] To make the dangle at the bottom of the earring, string a 14º, a 5mm crystal, and a 14º on a head pin. Trim the wire to ⅜ in. (1cm) above the end bead and turn a small plain loop (Basics and **photo a**).

[6] Attach the head pin's loop to an eye pin (**photo b**). Slide a heishi onto the eye pin, and insert the eye pin through the spiral between the first and second rows of floating beads. Exit between the last two rows (**photo c**).

[7] Trim the wire to ⅜ in. above the spiral and make a loop as before. Attach this loop to the earwire (**photo d**).

[8] To align the floating beads, use the thread from step 4 and sew back and forth through the 14ºs on each side of the spiral, working from end to end. Tighten the thread and secure the tails in the beadwork.

[9] Make a second earring to match the first. ◉

Contact Cyndy at dualaspects@cox.net or visit her website, dualaspects.com.

MATERIALS

- bicone crystals
  22 4mm
  2 5mm
- **46** 4mm hex heishi or 4mm flat spacer beads
- seed beads
  3g size 11º, each of two colors (main color and accent color)
  2g size 14º
- Power Pro 10 lb. or Fireline 6 lb. test
- beading needles, #12
- **2** 3-in. (7.6cm) eye pins
- **2** 2-in. (5cm) head pins
- pair earwires
- chainnose and roundnose pliers
- wire cutters

[a]   [b]   [c]   [d]

EDITOR'S NOTE: The beadwork will feel flimsy as you stitch, but don't worry about the finished piece. Once you sew through the 14ºs in step 8, the tension changes considerably, and you'll have a firm, well-defined spiral.

by **Debbie Nishihara**

Lemon Twist

Marcasite and gemstone beads spice up a spiral rope

Gemstone distributors are finally offering a wider variety of beautiful, and beader-friendly, focal beads. This necklace features fancy spiral-cut and checkerboard-faceted gems.

step*by*step

[1] String a stop bead on 1 yd. (91cm) of Fireline and leave a 10-in. (25cm) tail. Go through the stop bead again in the same direction.

[2] Pick up seven seed beads and slide them down to the stop bead **(figure 1)**.

[3] Working from bottom to top, come back through the first four beads. These four beads are considered the core. The three seeds now parallel to it are the spiral loops **(figure 2)**.

[4] To do a basic spiral rope, pick up four seeds. Go through the end three core seeds and the first new seed. You should now have five seeds on the core and two sets of three seeds parallel to it **(figure 3)**. Repeat this step until you reach the desired length.

[5] To do an embellished version, pick up two seeds, a crystal, and one seed. Go through the end three core beads and the first new seed. I started adding crystals with every fourth spiral loop **(photo a)** and increased as I got nearer to an accent bead. I added a crystal on every spiral loop between the briolettes in rope 2.

[6] When adding accent beads with larger holes, string the bead, then pick up enough seeds to slide down into it. Resume the rope from as far inside the bead as possible. For example, if you restart the rope from two seeds inside the lip of the marcasite, you need to pick up five seeds to continue

steps 2 and 3. The first stitch after the accent bead will tend to move away from it. Push the beads inside the marcasite together with a needle file **(photo b,** p. 106). The faceted gemstone beads **(photo c)** have a small hole and don't require any filler. Simply string a

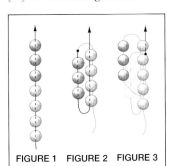

FIGURE 1   FIGURE 2   FIGURE 3

[a]

MATERIALS

- marcasite beads (Eclectica, 262-641-0910, eclecticabeads.com)
  2 26mm cones
  2 20mm tubes
  17mm round
  2 15mm barrels
- gemstone beads:
  strand dark amethyst spiral-cut briolettes
  strand amethyst/lemon quartz faceted briolettes
  2 sets checkerboard-faceted lemon quartz
- 36g seed beads, size 11º, purple-lined teal
- **100** (approx.) 3mm bicone crystals, olivine
- assorted beads for toggle (optional)
- Fireline 6 lb. test
- beading needles, #12
- 6 in. (15cm) 22-gauge wire, sterling silver
- silver toggle clasp
- chainnose pliers
- roundnose pliers
- wire cutters

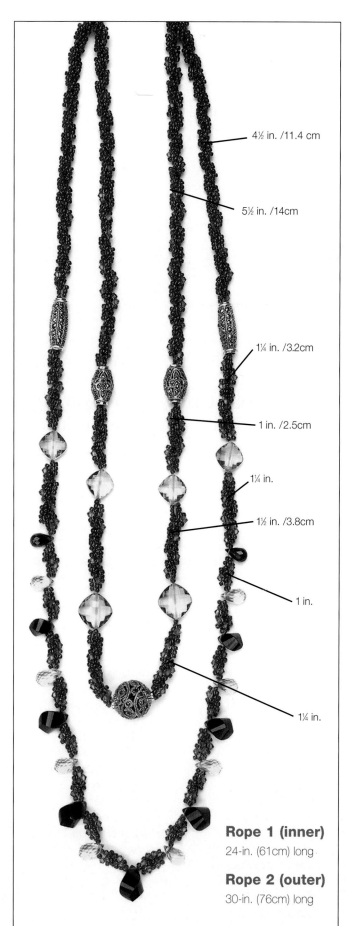

4½ in. /11.4 cm

5½ in. /14cm

1¼ in. /3.2cm

1 in. /2.5cm

1¼ in.

1½ in. /3.8cm

1 in.

1¼ in.

Rope 1 (inner)
24-in. (61cm) long

Rope 2 (outer)
30-in. (76cm) long

[b]

[c]

[d]

[e]

[f]

gemstone and restart the rope from step 2, keeping the seeds pushed firmly against the gemstone.

[7] To end rope 1, go back through several seeds, make a few half-hitch knots (Basics, p. 10), come back up through a few seeds, and exit the last core bead (photo d). Leave a 10-in. (25.4cm) tail.

[8] Rope 2 is the longer, outer rope and is the same as rope 1 but with a different gemstone configuration. When rope 2 is complete, attach it to the tip of rope 1 by sewing through nearby seeds, making several half-hitch knots and exiting near the last core bead on rope 1.

[9] Cut two lengths of silver wire 3 in. (7.6cm) longer than your cones. Make a small wrapped loop (Basics)

on one end of both wires. Bring the tails from both ropes together and tie them to a wrapped loop using an overhand knot (Basics). Sew both tails back through a few beads, make a half-hitch knot, go through a few more beads, and trim the tails.

[10] Pull the wire through the cone until the ropes are snug inside it (photo e). I added a few seeds and crystals to the wire before attaching it to one half of the toggle clasp with a wrapped loop (photo f).

[11] Remove the stop beads from the necklace's other end. Finish the same way. ❍

Debbie is an associate editor at Bead&Button *magazine. Contact her at editor@ beadandbutton.com.*

New Spin on Spiral

by **Anna Nehs**

Harmonize pearl and crystal loops using a spiral rope variation

Adding bead loops to embellish an existing base never yields the results I'm after, so I developed a variation on the traditional approach. Instead of working a single row of loops – as in spiral rope, for example – I make a second pass to hold the first round of loops in place. The result is a thick, rich-looking rope with great body.

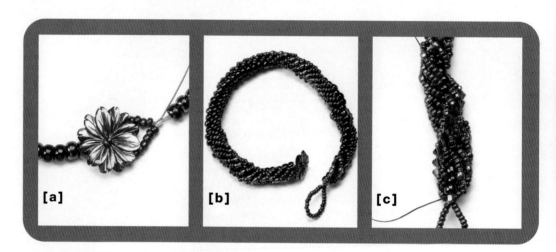

step*by*step

Base

[1] String a crimp bead, an 11º seed bead, the flower or button clasp, and an 11º to 1½ in. (3.8cm) from the end of a 12-in. (31cm) piece of beading wire. Go back through the flower, the 11º, and the crimp bead. Crimp the crimp bead (Basics, p. 10). Trim the tail.
[2] String enough size 6º seed beads to fit loosely around your wrist.
[3] String a crimp bead and enough 11ºs to encircle the widest part of the flower. Go back through the crimp bead and crimp it, leaving ⅛ in. (3mm) of space between the 6º and the crimp **(photo a)**.

Pearl loops

[1] Start a 3-yd. (2.7m) length of thread through the first four 6ºs on either end, leaving a 6-in. (15cm) tail.

[2] Pick up four 11ºs, a 15º, a pearl, a 15º, and four 11ºs. Sew through beads one through five on the base **(figure 1, a–b)**. This completes the first loop and positions the needle for the next loop. Push the first loop to one side.
[3] Pick up four 11ºs, a 15º, a pearl, a 15º, and four 11ºs. Sew through beads two through six on the base **(b–c)**. Push this loop on top of the previous loop. Make sure the loops stack on top of each other and don't flop around.
[4] Repeat step 2, moving up one bead along the base for each loop added until you exit the last 6º. The spiral doesn't take shape until the crystal loops are added **(photo b)**.
[5] Secure the thread by sewing back through the last few loops added and tying half-hitch knots (Basics) between a few of the beads. Repeat on the other end and trim the tails.

Crystal loops

[1] Start a new 3-yd. thread. Sew through the first three 6ºs on the same end you started the pearl loops. Leave a 6-in. (15cm) tail.
[2] Pick up two 11ºs, a 15º, a crystal, a 15º, and two 11ºs. Sew back through base beads one through four **(figure 2, a–b)**. This completes the first loop and positions the needle for the next loop. Push the crystal loop to the same side as the pearl loops.
[3] Pick up two 11ºs, a 15º, a crystal, a 15º, and two 11ºs. Sew through base beads two through five **(b–c)**. Push this loop on top of the previous crystal loop **(photo c)**.
[4] Repeat step 2 until you exit the last 6º. Remember to work in the same direction as the pearl loops, pushing all the loops to one side.
[5] Secure the tails with half-hitch knots and trim. ●

*Anna is an associate editor
at Bead&Button magazine.
Contact her at
editor@beadandbutton.com.*

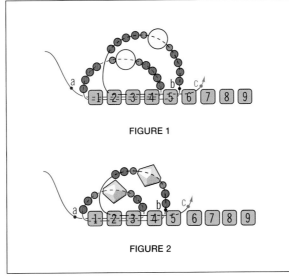

FIGURE 1

FIGURE 2

EDITOR'S NOTE:
**The only tricky part is
to make sure you
follow the path
defined by the pearl
loops, to avoid
splitting the loops
down the middle.**

MATERIALS

bracelet 8 in. (20cm)

- **58** 4mm Swarovski
  bicone crystals
- **57** seed pearls
- Japanese seed beads
  10g size 15º
  10g size 11º
  5g size 6º
- ⅞-in. (2.2cm) flower or
  button for clasp
- flexible beading wire, .014
- **2** crimp beads
- Silamide or Fireline 6 lb. test
- beading needles, #13
- crimping pliers
- wire cutters

Layered

Ladders

Stitch a handsome collar overflowing with beads

by **Jean Disrud**

Beads dangle from waves of bugles on this delicately stitched necklace. To start, make bugle ladders, connect them with a modified right-angle weave, then string everything together with beaded bridges. Crystal closures provide alternate settings so you can adjust the collar length to go with the flow.

step*by*step

Ladder sections

[1] Stitch four bugle beads into a tight ladder (Basics, p. 10, and **figure 1, a–b**), leaving an 8-in. (20cm) tail.

[2] Start the picot edging by picking up three 11º seed beads. Sew through the next to the last bugle on the ladder, pick up three 11ºs, then sew through the last bugle **(b–c)**.

[3] Stitch three bugles onto the ladder, as before **(c–d)**.

[4] Repeat steps 2–3 twice, but only attach two bugles to finish **(d–e)**.

[5] Pick up five 11ºs **(e–f)**.

[6] Sew through the last two bugles, then make a half-hitch knot (Basics) between the bugle and 11º seed bead. Make a second knot. Go through the next few beads and trim the thread.

[7] Thread a needle on the 8-in. tail. Pick up five 11ºs, then sew through the bugle and first two 11ºs **(figure 2, a–b)**. Pick up an 11º, an 8º, a 4mm bead, a flower bead, and an 11º. Turn, skip the 11º, then sew back through the flower, the 4mm, the 8º, and one 11º **(b–c)**. Skip the center 11º on the five-bead row and sew through the next two 11ºs **(c–d)**. End the thread as in step 6.

[8] Repeat steps 1–7, making 29 more ladder sections **(photo a, p. 113)**.

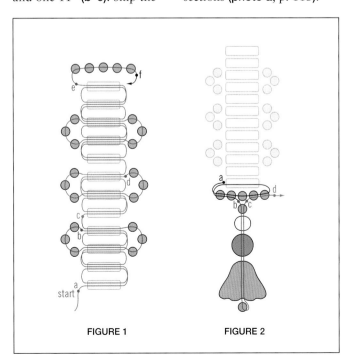

FIGURE 1   FIGURE 2

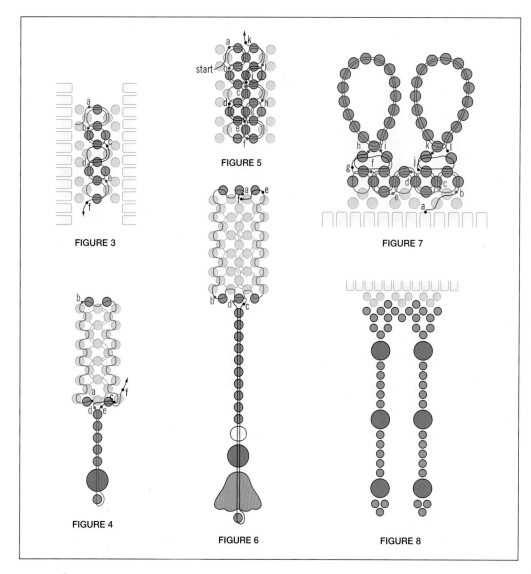

FIGURE 3

FIGURE 5

FIGURE 7

FIGURE 4

FIGURE 6

FIGURE 8

MATERIALS

16-in. (41cm) necklace

- 10g 7mm bugle beads
- Czech seed beads
  15g size 11º
  2g size 8º
- **105** 4mm beads, round
- **30** 6x8mm flower beads
- **6** 6mm fire-polished
  beads
- SoNo or Nymo
  conditioned with
  beeswax
- beading needles, #12

step*by*step

Connecting ladders

[1] Place two ladder sections next to each other **(photo b)**.
[2] Start a new thread and stitch the ladders together using a modified right-angle weave (Basics) as follows: Pick up an 11º, go through an 11º on the second ladder, pick up an 11º, then go through an 11º on the first ladder. Sew through the next three 11ºs again **(figure 3, a–b)**.
[3] Pick up three 11ºs and go through the second 11º added in the last step. Sew through the next two 11ºs again **(b–c)**.
[4] Go through an 11º on the second ladder, pick up an 11º, go through an 11º on the first ladder, then go

through the 11º from the last step. Sew through the next two 11ºs again **(c–d)**.
[5] Repeat step 3 **(d–e)**.
[6] Repeat step 4 **(e–f)**.
[7] Pick up an 11º, then turn and sew back through the edge beads **(figure 4, a–b)**.
[8] Pick up an 11º, go through the first 11º added in step 1, pick up an 11º, then sew through the seed beads on the other edge **(b–c)**. Pick up an 11º and go through the next 11º **(c–d)**.
[9] Pick up five 11ºs, a 4mm bead, and an 11º. Turn, skip the 11º, then sew back through the 4mm and the five 11ºs **(d–e)**. Go through two 11ºs **(e–f)**. End the thread as before.
[10] Repeat steps 1–9 to

make 13 more connected ladder pairs **(photo c)**.
[11] Set two ladders aside.

Center section

[1] Start a new thread in one of the two remaining ladder sections and position the thread so it exits the center bead on the top picot.
[2] Pick up three 11ºs, then go through the 11º on the first ladder again. Sew through the three new 11ºs again **(figure 5, a–b)**.
[3] Pick up three 11ºs, then go through the last 11º added in step 2. Sew through the next two 11ºs again **(b–c)**.
[4] Pick up two 11ºs, go through an 11º on the first ladder, then go through the 11º from step 3. Sew through

the next two 11ºs **(c–d)**.
[5] Repeat step 3 **(d–e)**.
[6] Repeat step 4, but sew through one bead instead of two **(e–f)**.
[7] Place the remaining ladder section next to the one you've been stitching.
[8] Pick up an 11º, go through an 11º on the second ladder, pick up an 11º, then go through the 11º from step 6. Sew through the next three 11ºs **(f–g)**.
[9] Go through an 11º, pick up two 11ºs, then go through the 11º from the last step. Sew through the next two 11ºs again **(g–h)**.
[10] Go through the 11º on the second ladder, pick up an 11º, go through an 11º, then go through the 11º from the last step. Sew through the next two beads **(h–i)**.
[11] Repeat step 9 **(i–j)**.
[12] Repeat step 10 **(j–k)**.
[13] Pick up an 11º, go through an 11º, pick up an 11º, then turn and sew through the edge beads **(figure 6, a–b)**.
[14] Pick up an 11º, go through an 11º, then pick up an 11º **(b–c)**.
[15] Pick up ten 11ºs, an 8º, a 4mm bead, a flower bead, and an 11º. Turn, skip the 11º, and sew through the flower, 4mm, 8º, and ten 11ºs **(c–d)**.

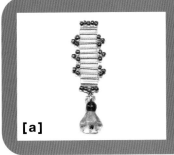

[a]

[b]

[c]

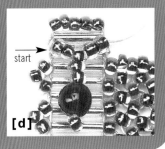

start

[d]

[16] Go through the next two 11°s, pick up an 11°, then turn and sew through the edge beads (d–e).

[17] Pick up an 11° and go through an 11° (e–f).

[18] Sew back to the nearest bugle, then end the thread.

Embellishments and bridges

[1] Arrange your 15 ladder pairs in a row with the center section in the eighth position.

[2] Start a 3-yd. (2.7m) length of thread in the first ladder and exit the second bugle from the top.

[3] To start the first bridge, pick up a bugle, five 11°s, a 4mm bead, and an 11°. Turn, skip the 11°, and sew back through the 4mm bead and three 11°s. Pick up two 11°s. Go back through the new bugle, through the second bugle from the top, then through the first bugle in the ladder (photo d).

[4] Pick up an 11°, a 4mm bead, and an 11°.

[5] Go through the first bugle in the next ladder, then through the second bugle (photo e).

[6] Repeat step 3.

[7] Pick up three 11°s. Go through the adjacent top bugle on the next ladder, then down through the second bugle (photo f).

[8] Repeat steps 3–7, joining and embellishing all the ladder sections. When stringing the bridge between the center connection, pick up two 4mm beads instead of one.

[9] Secure the last bridge by weaving through the ladder below it.

[10] To embellish the top edge, go back through the three-bead bridge and up through the next two 11°s. Pick up an 11°, an 8°, a 4mm bead, an 8°, and an 11° (photo g).

[11] For reinforcement, sew back through two 11°s on the edge of the end ladder, then retrace your path.

[12] Go through two 11°s on top of the ladder and the next three-bead bridge.

[13] Repeat steps 10–12 until reaching the last bridge. Do not tie off the thread.

Finishing the ends

[1] Weave through the ladder, then exit the fifth bugle from the top.

[2] Go through two 11°s (figure 7, a–b).

[3] Pick up three 11°s, then go back through the 11° from step 2. Sew through the next three 11°s again (b–c).

[4] Pick up three 11°s, then go through the second 11° from the last step. Sew through the next two beads again (c–d).

[5] Pick up two 11°s, go through an 11°, then go through the 11° from the last step. Sew through the next two seeds again (d–e).

[6] Repeat step 4 (e–f).

[7] Repeat step 5, but sew through only one bead again instead of two (f–g).

[8] Pick up two 11°s, then go through three 11°s (g–h).

[9] Pick up 16 11°s. Sew through the first 11° and retrace the thread path a second or third time for security (h–i).

[10] Weave through the beads and exit at j.

[11] Pick up two 11°s, then go through three 11°s (j–k).

[12] Repeat step 9 (k–l).

[13] Sew through the 11°s to reach the bugles, then end the thread.

[14] At the other end of the necklace, repeat steps 1–8. Then pick up an 11°, a 6mm bead, five 11°s, a 6mm bead, five 11°s, a 6mm bead, and three 11°s. Turn and sew back through these beads.

[15] Repeat steps 10, 11, and 14 to make the second clasp dangle (figure 8). ●

Contact Jean at jedisrud@aol.com.

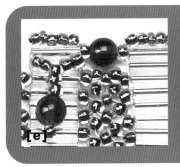

[e]

[f]

[g]

Interlaced Loops

by **Dottie Hoeschen**

Bracelets come together in a variety of ways. In this version, two strips of cube beads are connected with graceful loops that create a focal point along the bracelet's length. Smaller loops form a low-key fringe that embellishes the long edges.

step*by*step

Bracelet band

[1] To determine the length of the stitched portion of your bracelet, measure your wrist, subtract the length of your clasp, and add ½ in. (1.3cm) for ease.

[2] Using doubled thread and 4mm cubes, stitch a ladder (Basics, p. 10 and **figure 1, a–b**) to the length determined above. Use an even number of cube beads and keep the tension moderately loose. Secure the thread in the ladder

and trim. Make a second ladder the same length and set it aside.

[3] Start a thread in the ladder (not doubled this time) and exit an end cube (**figure 2, point a**). Pick up an 8º, two triangles, seven 15ºs, two triangles, and an 8º. Skip the second cube and go through the third (**a–b**).

[4] Reverse direction and come up through the second cube (**b–c**). Pick up the same sequence of beads as in step 3. Go down through the fourth cube (**c–d**) and come back up through the third cube. Continue through the 8º above the third cube (**d–e**). Keep each loop in front of the previous one as you work.

[5] Pick up two triangles, seven 15ºs, two triangles, and an 8º. (You no longer need to pick up the first 8º in the sequence.) Continue as in step 4, adding loops across the row (**photo a**). Secure the thread in the beadwork and trim.

[6] Place the finished strip on your work surface with the bead loops facing right (lefties, reverse these directions). Using the ladder set aside in step 2, start a new thread as before and exit the end cube bead. Lay this strip parallel to the first so the thread exits at the end closest to you, pointing toward the finished strip.

[7] Pick up an 8º, two triangles, seven 15ºs, two triangles, and an 8º. Go under

and through the end loop of beads on the first ladder. Go down through the third cube (**photo b**). The first loops on both strips are now connected.

[8] Come up through the second cube, picking up the same sequence of beads as in step 7. Go under and through the second loop, then go down through the fourth cube, back up the third, and through the 8º.

[9] You won't need to pick up the first 8º in the sequence for the remaining loops. Continue adding and connecting loops until you reach the end of the ladder. Secure the thread and trim.

[10] Start a thread and exit the end cube on the outside edge of either ladder (**figure 3, point a**). Pick up five 11ºs and go through the third cube. Change direction and come up through the second cube (**a–b**). Pick up five 11ºs (**photo c**) and repeat. Add loops to both edges of the bracelet. Secure the thread and trim.

Clasp

This bracelet works equally well with a toggle clasp or a button-and-loop closure. Vary these bead counts as necessary to suit the specific size and style of your clasp or button.

[1] Start a doubled thread and come

out on the inside edge of the second to last cube on one end of the bracelet (**figure 4, point a**). Pick up four or more 11ºs, an 8º, and three 11ºs. Go through the loop on the loop half of the clasp and pick up three more 11ºs. Go through the 8º again (**a–b**). Pick up four or more 11ºs as before and go through the corresponding cube on the other edge (**b–c**). The clasp loop should be centered and slightly past the end of the bracelet.

[**2**] Come back through the end cube (**c–d**), pick up enough seed beads to reach the 8º strung in step 1, and go through it. Then string an equal number of seed beads and go through the end cube on the other edge (**d–e**).

[**3**] Go through all these beads a second time to reinforce them. Secure the thread and trim.

[**4**] Repeat these steps to attach the toggle half of the clasp to the other end of the bracelet.

[**5**] For a button-and-loop closure, start a doubled thread and come out at the inside edge of the second to last cube on one end of the bracelet as in **figure 4, point a**. Pick up eight or more 11ºs (adjust the number of beads based on the size of your button) and go through the button's shank. Continue through the corresponding bead on the other edge. Go through the end cube, pick up four or more 11ºs, and go through the shank again. Pick up four or more 11ºs and go through the end cube (**photo d**).

[**6**] For the loop, start a doubled thread at the opposite end of the bracelet and exit the second to last cube as before. Pick up five 11ºs, a cube bead, and enough beads to form a loop that will go over the button. Go back through the cube, pick up five 11ºs, and go through the corresponding cube on the other edge. Go through the end cube, pick up four 11ºs, and go through the cube and loop beads. Pick up four 11ºs, go through the corresponding cube bead on the other edge, and secure the thread (**photo e**). ❂

Contact Dottie via email at stonebrash@juno.com.

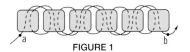

FIGURE 1

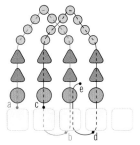

FIGURE 2

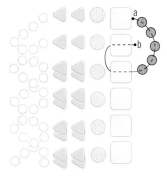

FIGURE 3

FIGURE 4

MATERIALS

- **80–100** 4mm cube beads, color A
- 15g size 10º triangle beads, color B
- seed beads
  15g size 11º, color A
  5g size 8º, color B
  5g size 15º, color C
- Fireline 6 lb. test or Nymo D
- beeswax for Nymo
- beading needles, #12
- toggle clasp or small button

[a]

[b]

[c]

[d]

[e]

EDITOR'S NOTE:

As you stitch the cube beads, keep the tension fairly loose, as noted in the instructions. Without some ease between the flat edges of the cubes, the bracelet will be too rigid to curve around your wrist.

Fringed Earring Duo

Two dynamic earring variations spring from a brick-stitch base.

by **Dragon**

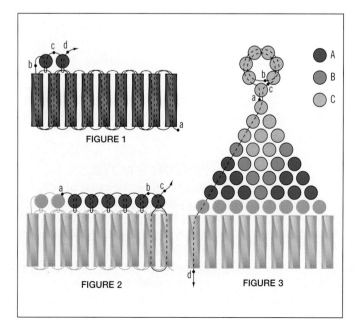

FIGURE 1

A
B
C

FIGURE 2

FIGURE 3

stepbystep

Brick-stitch base

Refer to the color chart for each pattern in the materials list before you start.

[1] Using a 2-yd. (1.8m) length of conditioned Nymo, stitch a nine-bead ladder (Basics, p. 10) with bugle beads (figure 1, a–b).

[2] Position the ladder so the working thread exits

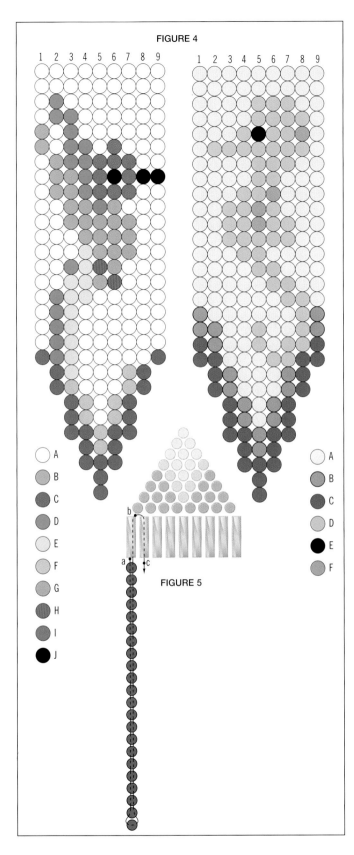

FIGURE 4

FIGURE 5

A
B
C
D
E
F
G
H
I
J

A
B
C
D
E
F

[4] To complete the row, pick up an A, go down the ninth bugle, come up the eighth bugle, and exit the last A (b–c).

[5] Turn your work after each row and continue in brick stitch following the pattern in **figure 3**.

Earring loop

[1] Pick up seven Cs (**figure 3, a–b**). Skip the first C and go back through the remaining Cs in the same direction (**b–c**). Go through the beads again and pull them into a tight circle.

[2] Go through the skipped C in the previous step, and sew down through the first bead on each row and the first bugle (**c–d**).

Fringe

Follow either pattern in **figure 4**.

[1] Pick up the bead sequence for the first fringe. Skip the last bead, go back up through the rest of the fringe beads, and exit the first bugle (**figure 5, a–b**). Go down through the next bugle (**b–c**).

[2] Repeat, stringing a total of nine fringes.

Finishing

[1] After completing the fringe, exit the last bugle in the ladder and make several half-hitch knots (Basics) between beads.

[2] Dot the knots with glue and let them dry. Hide the tail in nearby beads.

[3] Make a second earring to match the first.

[4] Use chainnose pliers to open the loop on an earring finding (Basics). Attach the earring to the finding and close the loop. Repeat with the other earring and finding so the hummingbirds or seahorses will face each other when worn. ●

MATERIALS

both projects
- Nymo B conditioned with beeswax
- beading needles, #12
- chainnose pliers
- G-S Hypo Cement

seahorse earrings
- **18** 7mm bugle beads, light blue
- seed beads, size 11º
  8g light blue, color A
  1g royal blue, color B
  1g cobalt blue, color C
  1g gold, color D
  1g black, color E
  1g amber, color F
- pair of earring findings

hummingbird earrings
- **18** 7mm bugle beads, silver
- seed beads, size 11º
  8g silver, color A
  1g turquoise, color B
  1g cobalt blue, color C
  1g forest green, color D
  1g lime, color E
  1g light blue, color F
  1g amber, color G
  1g brown, color H
  1g purple, color I
  1g black, color J
- pair of earring findings

You can write to Dragon at 3189 Cedonia-Addy Road, Hunters, Washington 99137. She has several imaginative kits available on her website, uniquebeadedjewelry.com.

from the top of the left bugle (**point b**). Work in brick stitch as follows: Pick up one color A, sew under the thread bridge between the first and second bugle, and go back through the A (**b–c**).

[3] Pick up an A, sew under the next thread bridge, and go back up through the new A (**c–d**). Repeat five more times (**figure 2, a–b**).

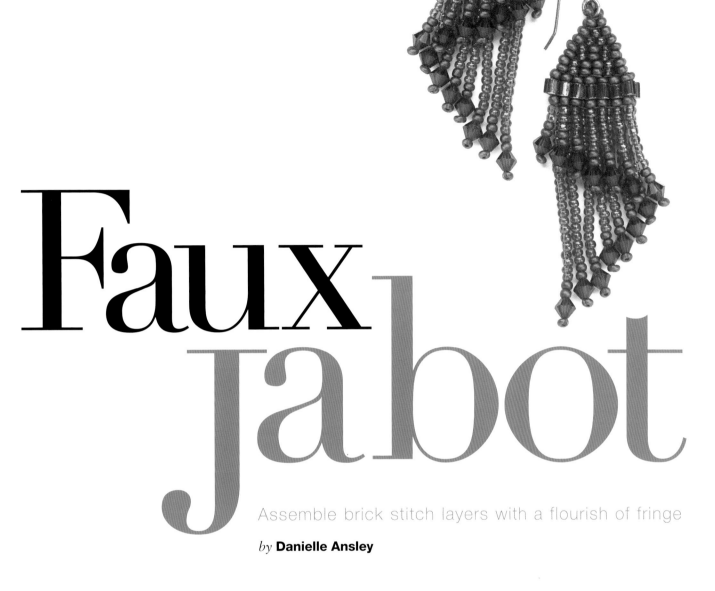

Faux Jabot

Assemble brick stitch layers with a flourish of fringe

by **Danielle Ansley**

To re-create the look of the soft pleats of a ruffled jabot, I sewed together several layers of brick-stitch triangles. This made a base for a fringe of crystals, giving the illusion of gently folded fabric.

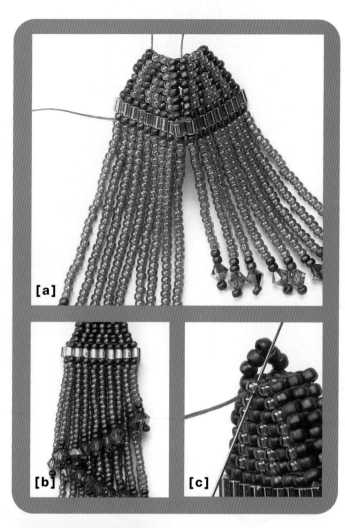

[a]

[b]

[c]

(MC), 2AC, 2MC, 2MC, 2AC, 2MC, 2AC (d–e).
Row 3: 2AC, 2MC, 2AC, 2MC, 2AC, 2MC, 2AC (e–f).
Row 4: AC, MC, AC, AC, MC, AC (f–g).
Row 5: AC, MC, AC, MC, AC (g–h).
Row 6: AC, MC, MC, AC (h–i).

[4] Thread a needle onto the tail. Pick up 42 MCs, two ACs, a 4mm crystal, and an AC. Sew back through to **point j.** Continue through the first three beads of the ladder then through the fourth through sixth beads **(j-k).**
[5] String the rest of the fringe as in step 4, decreasing two MCs per fringe. The shortest fringe will be 26 MCs long.
[6] Secure the tails in the beadwork with half-hitch knots (Basics), staying away from the edge beads. Trim the tails.

Middle triangle

[1] Start the middle triangle by repeating steps 1–3 of the back triangle. Make the longest fringe as in step 4, but use 24 MCs. Then decrease each fringe by one MC. The last fringe will have 16 MCs.
[2] Square stitch (Basics) the edge beads of the middle triangle with the shortest fringe to the edge beads of the back triangle with the longest fringe **(photo a).** Repeat on the other edge.
[3] Secure the tails and trim.

Front triangle

[1] Make the front triangle the same way as the other two. String the longest fringe with 14 MCs and the shortest with 6 MCs. Square stitch the front triangle to the middle one. Line up the shortest fringe from the front with the longest fringe of the

step*by*step

Centerpiece
Back triangle
[1] String an accent color (AC), an 8º, two ACs, an 8º, and an AC to the middle of a 3-yd. (2.7m) length of thread. Go back through all the beads strung **(figure 1, a–b).** Exit at **point b.**
[2] Work in ladder stitch (Basics, p. 10) until you have nine sets **(a–c).** Weave back through the beads to the first set to reinforce the ladder **(c–d).**
[3] Work rows 2–3 in double brick stitch (pick up two beads for every one bead of standard, single brick stitch) and rows 4–6 in single brick stitch (Basics) using the following bead counts:
Row 2: 2AC, two main color

middle triangle **(photo b).**
[2] Weave along the edge beads to exit the shortest row of brick stitch on the front triangle. Pick up five ACs and sew through the corresponding bead on the back triangle. Go up through the next bead on the back triangle **(photo c).** Pick up five ACs and sew through the next bead on the front triangle.
[3] Repeat, adding five ACs across the top of the three triangles.
[4] Secure the tails and trim.

Neck strap

[1] Center a needle on a 6-yd. (5.5m) length of thread. String a stop bead to 10 in. (25cm) from the end of the doubled thread and go through the bead again.

[2] Pick up a 4mm, an AC, an 8°, an AC, a 4mm, three MCs, a 4mm, an AC, an 8°, and an AC. Sew back through the first 4mm strung (**figure 2, a–b**).

[3] Pick up three MCs, a 4mm, an AC, an 8°, and an AC. Sew back through the 4mm on the previous loop (**b–c**).

[4] Repeat step 3 for about 8 in. (20cm), then begin to decrease the MCs along one edge of the neck strap (**d–e**).

[5] Sew the neck strap to the middle triangle, adding an MC on each edge (**e–f**). Secure the tails and trim.

[6] Remove the stop bead and thread the needle on the tail. Pick up 12 MCs and one half of the clasp. Sew through the opposite crystal, AC, 8°, and AC, and back through the crystal the thread was exiting (**figure 3**). Reinforce with a second thread path, secure the tails, and trim.

[7] Repeat steps 1–6 to finish the second side of the neck strap.

Earrings

Make the earrings similar to the centerpiece and refer to **figure 4** for the bead counts. The earrings consist of only two layers. Make the back triangle as shown in **figure 4**. To make the front triangle, shorten the first fringe by two MCs, then each fringe by one MC. Assemble the two triangles using square stitch, as you did for the centerpiece. Then make a three-AC loop at the top of the earring and attach the ear wire. Secure the tails and trim. Repeat for the other earring. ●

Contact Danielle at crystalmavin@att.net.

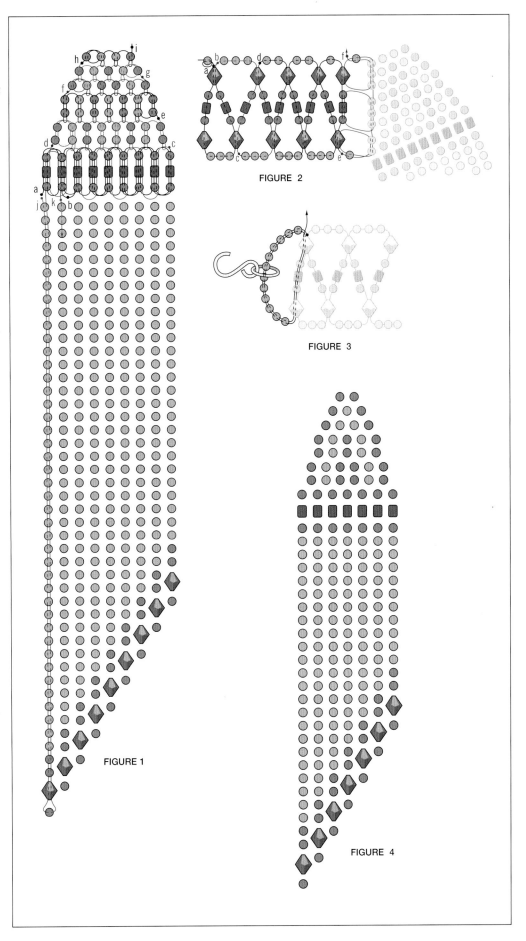

FIGURE 1

FIGURE 2

FIGURE 3

FIGURE 4

Catching
cabs

Highlight an elegant
brick-stitch bracelet
with bezeled cabochons

by **Glenda Payseno**

After working with individual cabochons as the
focal point of necklaces and bracelets, I wanted to
incorporate multiple cabs into a single piece.
Keeping the sections symmetrical was a challenge,
but I found that bugle beads solved the problem.
They are twice the length of seed beads, require
fewer rows, and provide symmetry on each side of
the cabochon.

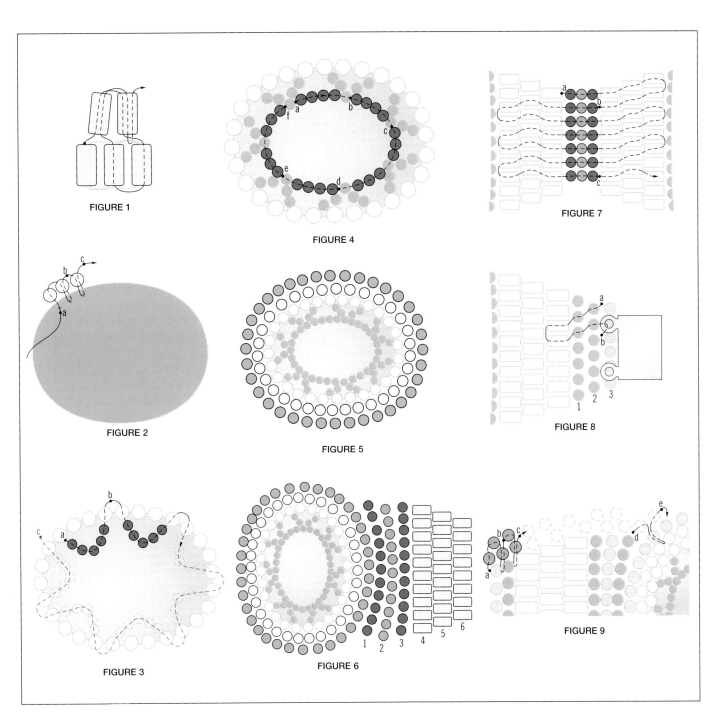

FIGURE 1

FIGURE 4

FIGURE 7

FIGURE 2

FIGURE 5

FIGURE 8

FIGURE 3

FIGURE 6

FIGURE 9

step*by*step

Sort through the bugles and discard any that have sharp or broken edges or are not uniform in size and shape.

To help keep the edge beads straight on the rows between cabochons, work the first and last stitches with a modified stitch that locks the beads in place **(figure 1)**.

Preparing the cabochons

[1] Place a cabochon on the faux suede and draw around it. Cut out the shape, working slightly inside the cutting line so the fabric is exactly the same size as the cabochon.

[2] Thread a needle with Nymo and knot one end, leaving a 6-in. (15cm) tail. Go through the fabric from front to back anywhere

along the edge. Pick up two accent color A beads and go through the fabric from back to front exactly two bead-lengths away from the starting point. Go back through the last bead added **(figure 2, a–b)**.

[3] Pick up another A and go through the fabric from back to front. Go through the last bead added as before **(b–c)**. Keep the beads snug, but don't stretch the fabric

by crowding the beads.

[4] Continue adding beads around the edge, stitching a total of 28 beads into place for the base row. Go back through the first bead, fabric, and first bead again. Then go through the second bead (your needle will be pointing toward the center) to start the netting **(figure 3, a)**.

[5] Pick up five silver-lined beads, skip two beads along the edge, and go through the

next bead **(a–b)**. Come out through the next bead. Repeat, ending at **point c.**

[6] Go through the next bead along the base row and continue through the next three beads of the netting, exiting the center bead **(figure 4, a)**. Slip the cabochon under the netting.

[7] Pick up four beads and go through the middle bead of the second five-bead net **(a–b)**. Pick up four beads between the second and third nets **(b–c)**; three beads between the third, fourth, and fifth nets **(c–d)**; four beads between the fifth and sixth nets **(d–e)**; and three beads between each of the remaining nets **(e–f)**.

[8] Go through this round of beads again. Tighten the beads and weave the thread back to the base row. Secure the thread in the beads and trim the tails.

[9] Prepare a total of three cabochons.

Stitching the sides

[1] Start a new thread near the base row of one cabochon and exit any bead along that row. Using accent color A, work one row of brick stitch (see Basics, p. 10 and **figure 5**) around the edge. Increase by four evenly spaced beads.

[2] Work a second row in accent color B, adding four beads as before **(figure 5)**.

[3] Work the next six rows in brick stitch as described below **(figure 6)**:

Row 1: Find the center bead on one long side of the cabochon. Count five beads in either direction from the center to find your starting point. Attach 11 silver-lined beads to the edge row.

Row 2: Work another 11-bead row using the B-color beads.

Row 3: Work an 11-bead row using silver-lined beads.

Rows 4–6: Work a ten-bead, a nine-bead, and an eight-bead row using bugles.

[4] Repeat these steps on the other edge of the cabochon. Then stitch the remaining two cabochons to match. Don't cut the thread tails.

Joining the sections

[1] Using the tail, pick up a silver-lined bead, a B, and a silver-lined bead. Go through the end bugle on another cabochon and continue through several rows of beads. Weave back to the edge **(figure 7, a–b)**.

[2] Pick up three beads as in step 1. Go through the corresponding bead on the first cabochon and continue through several rows. Work back and forth between cabochons, adding three beads each time, until the sections are securely joined **(b–c)**.

[3] Repeat steps 1–2 to join the third cabochon to the second.

Stitching sides to clasp

[1] Secure a new thread in the beads near the last row of bugles and exit the edge bead. Work the next three or four rows in brick stitch as described below **(figure 8)**:

Rows 1–2: Work a seven-bead row followed by a six-bead row using silver-lined beads.

Row 3: Work a six-bead row using Bs. Repeat this row one or more times if you need the extra length.

[2] If your thread is short, start a new piece. Exit an end bead in the last row of silver-lined beads, position the clasp behind the beadwork, and go through a clasp loop **(figure 8, a–b)**. Work through several rows of beads and go back through to the edge. Retrace the thread path several times, then repeat to attach the other clasp loop. Knot and bury the thread.

[3] Repeat to finish the other end of the bracelet.

Finishing the edges

[1] Start a thread along the edge at one end. Pick up three Bs and go under the thread at the edge of the next row. Go back through the last bead added to form a picot **(figure 9, a–b)**.

[2] Pick up two beads and go under the thread at the edge of the next row. Go back through the last bead added as before **(b–c)**.

[3] When you reach the outer row surrounding the cabochon, add one bead to make a picot, as follows: pick up a bead and go through the existing bead. Go around the thread below it and exit that bead **(d–e)**. Repeat along the cab's edge.

[4] Resume making three-bead picots once you pass the cabochon. ●

Contact Glenda via email at glendapayseno@comcast.net.

MATERIALS

- 3 18x13mm cabochons
- seed beads
  5g silver-lined, size 11º
  5g silver-plate, size 11º, accent color A
  5g size 10º or Japanese size 11º, accent color B
- 10g 3mm silver bugle beads
- Ultrasuede or Sensuede
- Nymo D with beeswax or thread conditioner
- beading needles, #10 or 12 or quilting needles, #12 betweens
- 2-hole box clasp

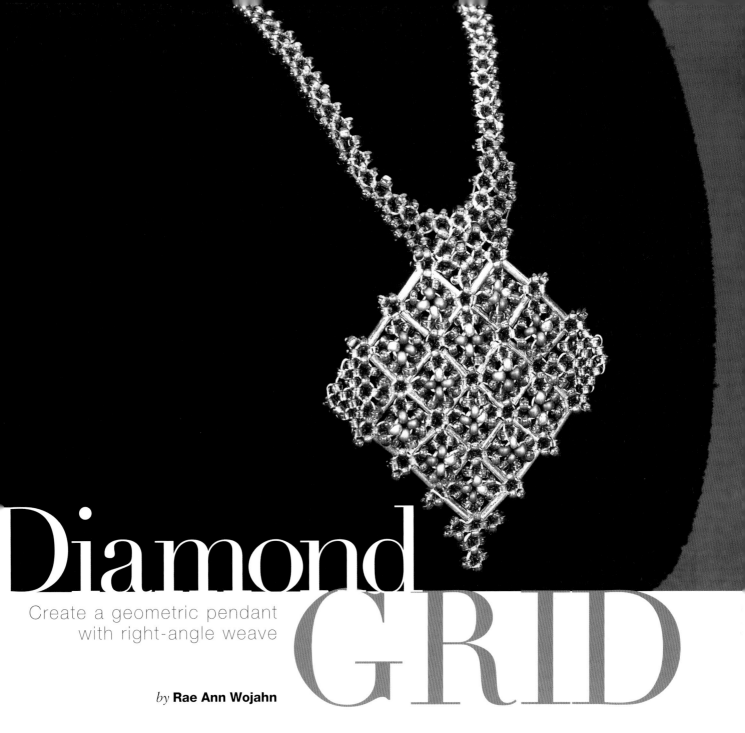

Diamond
GRID

Create a geometric pendant
with right-angle weave

by **Rae Ann Wojahn**

Working in right-angle weave creates an open, geometric design much like a square-holed net. To make the stitch, you sew rings of beads in a figure-8 pattern and alternate direction with each ring.

My pendant takes the stitch a step beyond the basics. Use bugles and seed beads to create a diamond-shaped framework, then fill in the open spaces with two colors of seed beads. Once the first base unit is in place, simply repeat the shape to build a grid of beaded diamonds. Once you've mastered the technique, enjoy adapting the idea to your own design.

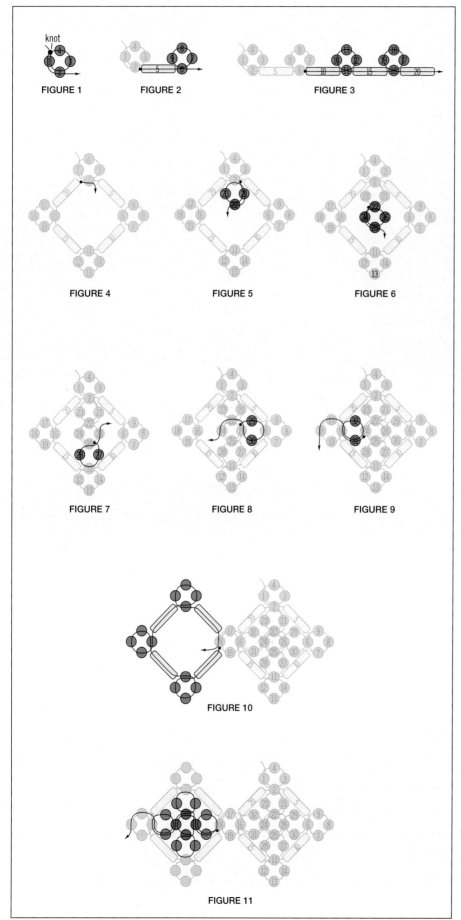

FIGURE 1

FIGURE 2

FIGURE 3

FIGURE 4

FIGURE 5

FIGURE 6

FIGURE 7

FIGURE 8

FIGURE 9

FIGURE 10

FIGURE 11

MATERIALS

- 30-40 6 or 7mm silver bugle beads, (BeadCats, 503-625-2323, beadcats.com)
- PowerPro, 10 lb. test
- beading needles, #10
- seed beads, size 11º
  12g main color
  5g accent color
- lobster claw clasp
- 6 in. (15cm) chain
- 2 5mm split rings

step*by*step

Diamond outline

[1] Pick up four main-color (MC) seed beads. Tie them into a circle with a surgeon's knot (Basics, p. 10). Sew through beads 1 and 2 again **(figure 1)**.

[2] Pick up a bugle bead and four MCs. Go through the first new MC (bead 6) in the same direction **(figure 2)**.

[3] Repeat step 2 twice and end with a bugle **(figure 3)**.

[4] Go back through bead 2 to form the diamond outline **(figure 4)**.

Center

[1] Pick up an MC, an accent-color (AC) bead, and an MC. Go through bead 2 and through beads 21 and 22 again **(figure 5)**.

[2] Pick up three ACs and go through beads 22, 24, and 25 **(figure 6)**.

[3] Pick up an MC and go through bead 11. Pick up an MC and go through beads 25 and 26 **(figure 7)**.

[4] Pick up an MC and go through bead 6. Pick up an MC and go through beads 26, 22, and 24 **(figure 8)**.

[5] Pick up an MC and go through bead 16. Pick up an MC and go through beads 24, 31, 16, 17, and 18 **(figure 9)**. This completes the basic diamond unit.

Horizontal units

[1] Starting at bead 18, repeat step 2 of the diamond outline three times. Pick up a bugle and go through bead 18 to form a diamond **(figure 10)**.

[2] Fill the center of the diamond with right-angle weave as in **figure 11**.

[3] Repeat steps 1–2 as desired to

determine the widest row of your pendant. (My pendant's widest row is four diamonds across.)

[4] When working the last unit, exit as shown in **figure 12** to begin the next row.

Additional rows

[1] Work as in step 2 of the diamond outline. Pick up a bugle and go through the corresponding seed bead on the adjacent diamond (**figure 13, a–b**).

[2] Fill in the center of the diamond as before and exit as shown to start the next unit (**b–c**).

[3] Build the pendant design by adding rows of units as desired.

[4] Go through the bugles and beads along the edge, adding a bead to each group of four seed beads to make a picot around the outside of the pendant (**figure 14**).

Necklace

[1] Cut the chain in half. With a new thread, sew through an end link of chain, pick up four MC beads, and knot them around the link. Stitch 11 in. (28cm) of four-bead right-angle weave (**figure 15**).

[2] When you work the last stitch, go through the end link on the other piece of chain. Weave each tail back through several beads. Tie a half-hitch knot (Basics) between beads and dot with glue. Go through several more beads and trim the thread.

[3] Sew an AC bead along one edge of the strap (**figure 16**). This becomes the top edge of the necklace.

[4] Center the pendant along the bottom edge of the necklace and stitch it in place.

[5] Attach a split ring to each end of the chain.

[6] Attach a lobster claw clasp to one of the split rings. ●

Contact Rae at rawojo@juno.com.

EDITOR'S NOTE: Bugle beads are sold by length or by a number designation. This pendant calls for ¼-in. (6–7mm) bugle beads, which are Czech size 3. If you buy Japanese bugles, ask for size 7.

FIGURE 12

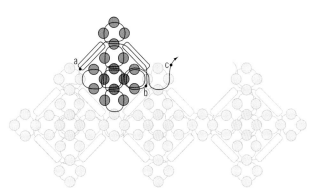

FIGURE 13

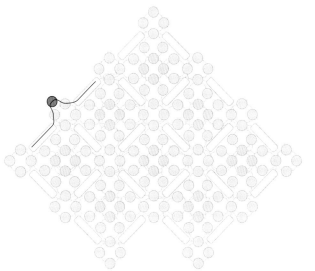

FIGURE 14

FIGURE 15

FIGURE 16

Creative twist

by **Diane S. Hertzler**

After taking a class with Rachel Cotugno at the 2003 *Bead&Button* Show on making decorative shapes from herringbone tubes, I designed this easy pretzel. Add salt to your pretzel with silver-lined crystal beads and add a pinback to wear it as a brooch. Attach a colorful ribbon and it becomes an ornament.

MATERIALS

- Japanese seed beads
  8g size 11º, in one or two
  topaz colors (pretzel)
  4g size 10º, clear silver-
  lined (salt)
- 8 in. (20cm) 18- or
  16-gauge wire
- Nymo B conditioned with
  beeswax
- beading needles,
  #10 or 12

step*by*step

If you are using two colors of 11º seed beads, mix them together so you pick up the colors randomly as you stitch. **[1]** Working with a comfortable length of conditioned thread (Basics, p. 10), pick up three 11ºs and sew through the beads again, leaving a 6-in. (15cm) tail. **[2]** Pull the beads into a snug circle, tie the tail and working thread together with a square knot (Basics), and sew through the next bead on the circle (figure 1). **[3]** Pick up two 11ºs and sew through the next bead on the circle (figure 2, a–b). Repeat two more times (b-c). Then sew through the first bead added on this round (c-d). **[4]** Work in tubular herringbone (Basics and figure 3) until the tube is about 8 in. (20cm) long. Keep the tension tight as

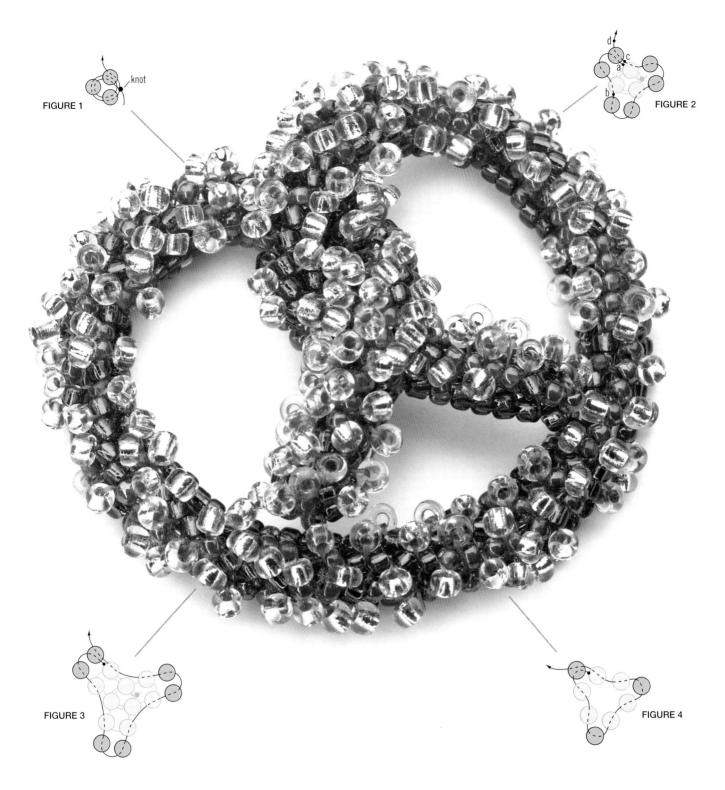

FIGURE 1

FIGURE 2

FIGURE 3

FIGURE 4

you work. Pull the beads together so they stack above the previous round. The beads will start to form a tube after the fourth round. **[5]** Slide an 8-in. (20cm) piece of wire into the tube. **[6]** Work one more row, adding one bead per stitch **(figure 4)**. Sew through the

three beads just added and cinch them together to close the end of the tube. Tie several half-hitch knots (Basics) between beads. Don't cut the thread. **[7]** Form the tube into the shape of a pretzel. **[8]** To add the salt, position the thread so it exits a bead

on the front of the pretzel. Embellish the surface with size 10º seed beads, stitching beads randomly and in different directions. Weave through the herringbone tube as you add the salt beads to make sure your thread doesn't show between beads. ●

Contact Diane at
PO Box 611,
Mt. Gretna, Pennsylvania
17064-0611,
(717) 964-3071, or
dianehertzler@dejazzed.com.

Graceful Companions

Combine herringbone stitch and right-angle weave
to showcase gemstone rondelles

by **Mindy Brooks**

A latticework of beads and gemstones plays the central role in
this elegant bracelet. Created with right-angle weave, it dovetails
nicely at each end with a panel of Ndebele herringbone. Blending
these two stitches, while unusual, produces an openwork grid that
showcases a collection of attractive gemstones. You can readily
substitute small pearls or crystals for the gemstones in your version
of this design.

step*by*step

Band

[1] Measure your wrist to
determine the finished length
of your bracelet. (Mine is
7in./18cm.) To change the
length, adjust the number of
herringbone rows near each
end (steps 3–5 and 16).
[2] Work in right-angle
weave as follows: On 1 yd.
(.9m) or more of Fireline,
pick up two 10º seed beads
and two 11ºs twice, leaving
a 6-in. (15cm) tail. Go
through the first six beads
again **(figure 1, a–b)**. Pick up
two 11ºs, two 10ºs, and two
11ºs. Go through the two
10ºs your thread is exiting in
the same direction as before
and continue through the
next four beads on the ring
(b–c). Make a total of eight
rings. Continue around the
end ring and exit at **point d**.
[3] To begin stitching in
herringbone, pick up four
10ºs and go down through
the next 11º on the end ring
(figure 2, a–b). Come up
through the neighboring 11º

on the next ring **(b–c)**.
Repeat across the row **(c–d)**.
[4] To turn after the last
stitch, continue around the
right-angle-weave ring and
exit through the second-to-
last 11º **(d–e)**. Go up through
the two 10ºs on the edge of
the beadwork **(e–f)**. Pick up
four 10ºs as before and work
in herringbone across the
row **(f–g)**. To turn, go through
the 10º one stack in from the
edge and the two 10ºs on the
edge **(g–h)**.
[5] On the next row, pick up
a 10º, two 11ºs, and a 10º for
each stitch **(h–i)**. Turn by
going back up through the
two 10ºs and an 11º one
stack in from the edge. Exit
at **point j**.
[6] To return to right-angle
weave, pick up two 10ºs, two
11ºs, and two 10ºs. Go back
through the two 11ºs on the
herringbone row and the first
two new 10ºs **(figure 3, a–b)**.
Pick up two 11ºs and two
10ºs and go back through the
11ºs on the herringbone row
and the next six beads on
this ring **(b–c)**.

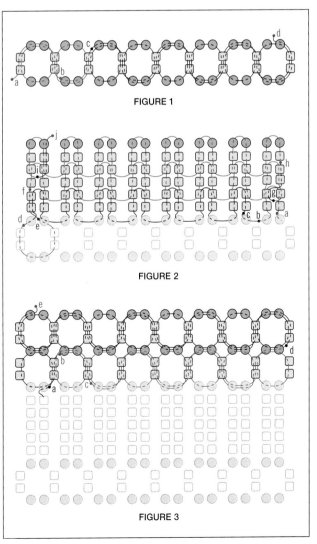

FIGURE 1

FIGURE 2

FIGURE 3

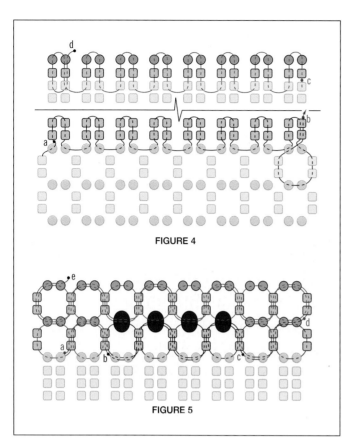

FIGURE 4

FIGURE 5

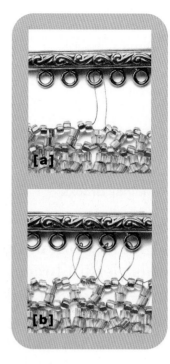

[a]

[b]

[14] Work six rows of herringbone as in step 8.
[15] Work two rows of right-angle weave as in steps 6 and 7.
[16] Work six herringbone rows as in step 3–5.
[17] Work one row of right-angle weave as in step 6. Secure the thread.

Clasp

[1] Start a new thread at either end of the bracelet and exit through an edge bead between the fourth and fifth right-angle-weave rings. Sew through the center loop on half the clasp (photo a).
[2] Weave through two edge beads and sew through the next clasp loop. Repeat (photo b), then turn and work back across the edge to connect the remaining loops.
[3] Work across the edge several times to reinforce the connection between the clasp and the stitches, then repeat at the other end of the bracelet.

Edges

Secure a new thread at any corner of the band and stitch through the beads along the long edge to reinforce it. Repeat on the other edge. o

MATERIALS

bracelet 7 in. (18cm)

- seed beads
  10g size 10º 2-cuts (also known as square cuts)
  10g size 11º
- **34** 4mm faceted gemstones, rondelles or button-shaped
- Fireline 6 lb. test
- beading needles, #12
- 5-strand slide clasp (Fire Mountain Gems, 800-355-2137, firemountaingems.com)

Continue in right-angle weave across the row (c–d).
[7] Work a second row of right-angle weave, exiting through the edge 11º at the top of the end ring (d–e).
[8] Change to herringbone as in step 3. Pick up four 10ºs for each stitch across the row. Turn as in step 4 (figure 4, a–b). Work a total of five rows. For the sixth row, pick up a 10º, two 11ºs, and a 10º for each stitch. To turn, continue through the second to last stack and exit through the 11º (c–d).
[9] Change to right-angle

weave. Make the first two rings using 10ºs and 11ºs as before (figure 5, a–b). For the next four rings, substitute a gemstone for the 11ºs (b–c). Work the last two rings using 10ºs and 11ºs (c–d).
[10] Work another row of right-angle weave using only 10ºs and 11ºs. Go through the gemstones as shown (d–e).
[11] Repeat steps 9 and 10.
[12] For the next six rows, repeat steps 9 and 10 three times, but increase the number of gemstones to six.
[13] Repeat steps 9 and 10 twice.

Mindy is the editor of Bead&Button *magazine. Contact her at editor@beadandbutton.com*

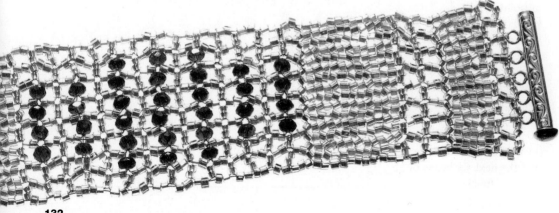

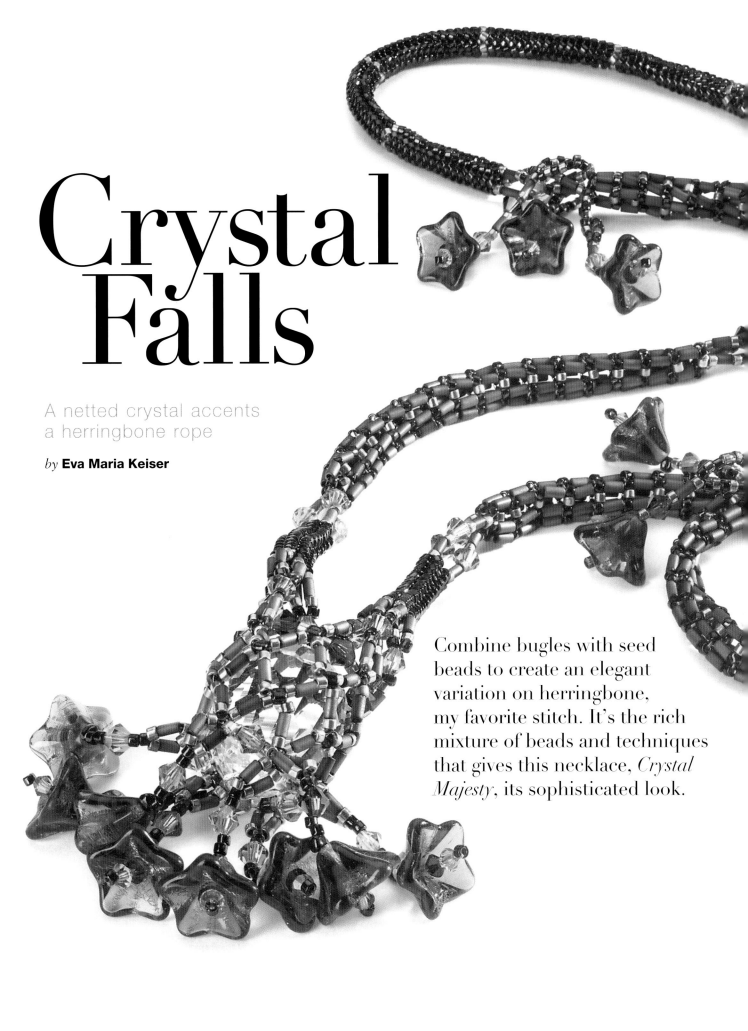

Crystal Falls

A netted crystal accents
a herringbone rope

by **Eva Maria Keiser**

Combine bugles with seed
beads to create an elegant
variation on herringbone,
my favorite stitch. It's the rich
mixture of beads and techniques
that gives this necklace, *Crystal
Majesty*, its sophisticated look.

step*by*step

Netted centerpiece

[1] Using a 3-yd. (2.7m) length of Fireline, pick up an accent color (AC) cylinder, a 4mm main color (MC) crystal, an AC cylinder, and a triangle, leaving a 2-ft. (61cm) tail. Repeat the sequence five more times and tie the tail and working thread together with a surgeon's knot (Basics, p. 10). Go through the beads again, then exit a triangle **(figure 1, a–b)**. This circle of beads is the bottom ring, and it supports the fringe, which is added in step 7.

[2] Pick up an AC cylinder, a bugle, an AC cylinder, a triangle, an AC cylinder, a bugle, and an AC cylinder. Sew through the next triangle on the circle **(b–c)**. Repeat five more times. Sew through the first AC cylinder, bugle, AC cylinder, and triangle added **(c–d)**.

[3] Pick up an AC cylinder, a bugle, an AC cylinder, a triangle, an AC cylinder, a bugle, and an AC cylinder. Sew through the next triangle on round 2 **(d–e)**. Repeat five more times. Then sew through the first AC cylinder, bugle, AC cylinder, and triangle in this round **(e–f)**.

[4] Repeat step 3 to add the third round of netting, sewing through the triangles on round 2 **(f–g)**.

[5] Pick up an AC cylinder, a 4mm AC crystal, and an AC cylinder. Then sew through the next triangle. Repeat five more times, but before sewing through the last triangle, slip the centerpiece crystal into the netting, so the point with the top-drilled hole goes into the bottom ring **(photo a)**. Go

through the last round again, pull the beads into a tight circle, then tie half-hitch knots (Basics) between beads. Weave down to the bottom row of netting and exit through a triangle.

Flower fringe

[1] Pick up an AC cylinder, a bugle, an AC cylinder, two MC cylinders, a 4mm MC crystal, two MC cylinders, a triangle, a flower, a 3mm AC crystal, a 3mm MC crystal, and an MC cylinder. Skip the last MC cylinder and sew back through to the first MC cylinder **(figure 2, a–b)**. Pick up an AC cylinder, a bugle, and an AC cylinder. Sew back through the triangle and the next four beads, exiting the next triangle on the circle **(b–c)**. Repeat five more times.

[2] To add two more fringes on top of the existing fringes on opposite sides of the circle of beads, repeat step 1 with these changes: Pick up a 4mm MC crystal instead of an AC, and after the flower, pick up a 3mm AC crystal and a 3mm MC crystal **(photo b)**.

[3] Secure the working thread with half-hitch knots and trim.

Making the spokes

[1] Thread a needle on the tail and make sure it exits a triangle. Pick up an AC cylinder, a bugle, an AC cylinder, an MC cylinder, a 4mm MC crystal, an MC cylinder, an AC cylinder, a bugle, an AC cylinder, two MC cylinders, an AC cylinder, a bugle, an AC cylinder, and an MC cylinder **(figure 3, a–b)**. Sew back through the 4mm MC crystal and pick up an MC cylinder, an AC cylinder, a bugle, and

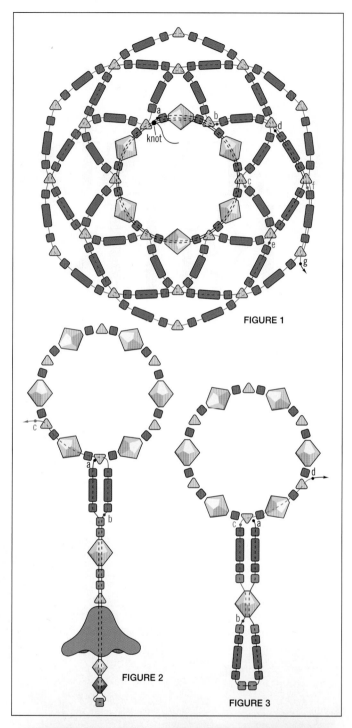

FIGURE 1

FIGURE 2

FIGURE 3

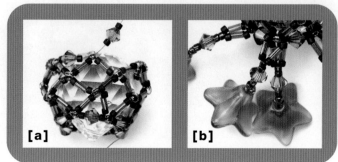

[a]

[b]

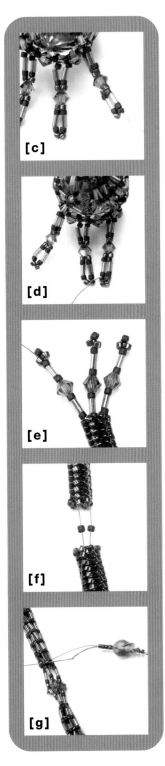

[c]

[d]

[e]

[f]

[g]

an AC cylinder (b–c). Sew through the triangle again and through to the next triangle on the ring (c–d).
[2] Repeat step 1 five more times. Sew through one of the spokes and exit an MC cylinder (photo c).

Neck strap

[1] Work in tubular herringbone (Basics) to connect three adjacent spokes as follows: Pick up two MC cylinders and sew down through the next MC cylinder in the same spoke. Go up through the MC cylinder in the next spoke (photo d). Repeat using the next two spokes. Connect these beads into a tube by sewing through the first two MCs on the first spoke. Continue in herringbone stitch for 16 rounds, stepping up after each one.
[2] Pick up an AC cylinder, a bugle, an AC cylinder, a 4mm MC crystal, an AC cylinder, a bugle, an AC cylinder, an MC cylinder, an AC cylinder, and an MC cylinder. Skip the last three beads and sew back to the first AC cylinder strung. Sew down through the next MC, then up through the next MC in the same row (figure 4, a–b). Repeat two more times, then sew through the first spoke, and exit the MC cylinder as shown (photo e and figure 5, point a).
[3] Pick up a bugle, an AC cylinder, an MC cylinder, an AC cylinder, and a bugle. Sew down through the next MC cylinder on the spoke, and up through the MC cylinder on the next spoke (a–b). Repeat twice more. Exit the first bugle and MC added in this step. Continue picking up this sequence of

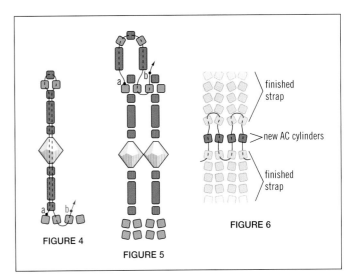

FIGURE 4

FIGURE 5

finished strap

new AC cylinders

finished strap

FIGURE 6

five beads to work 16 rows of herringbone. Remember to step up at the end of each row by sewing up through the bugle and MC cylinder.
[4] Repeat step 2, but use an AC crystal instead of an MC crystal.
[5] Repeat step 3.
[6] Repeat step 2, omitting the sixth AC and skipping the last two beads instead of three.
[7] Work in tubular herringbone using MC cylinders for 16 rows, then switch to AC cylinders for one row. Repeat five more times.
[8] Repeat steps 1–7 with the three remaining spokes.
[9] Weave the ends of the strap together (photo f and figure 6).

Floral embellishment

[1] Secure a 1-yd (91cm) length of thread in the

herringbone strap between the last bugle and herringbone sections and sew through an MC cylinder. Pick up three AC cylinders, a triangle, a flower bead, a 3mm MC crystal, and an MC cylinder.
[2] Skip the last bead and sew back through the beads. Sew through the next MC cylinder, AC cylinder, and MC cylinder on the strap (photo g). Repeat two more times, varying the length of the fringe if desired by changing the number of MCs added in step 1.
[3] Secure the tails with half-hitch knots and trim. Repeat the flower embellishment on the other half of the strap. ◓

Contact Eva Maria at keiserdesigns.com, eknow@ msn.com, or 877-372-5218.

MATERIALS
necklace 36 in. (91cm)
- Swarovski bicone crystals
  24 4mm, main color
  18 4mm, accent color
  18 3mm, main color
  12 3mm, accent color
- 23x18mm Swarovski pendant, round
- Japanese cylinder beads
  30g main color
  5g accent color
- 14g size 10º Japanese triangle beads
- 30g 3mm Japanese bugles
- **14** glass flower beads
- Fireline 6 lb. test
- beading needles, #10

Social Butterflies

Work a bracelet of adorable butterflies in Ndebele herringbone stitch

by **Stacey M. Summerhill**

The butterfly house at the Detroit zoo is one of my favorite places to spend the afternoon. I love how the butterflies fly around me, landing gracefully on my arm or my hair. I designed this bracelet to capture those relaxing afternoons and to honor the pageant of fluttering wings.

stepbystep

Butterflies

Body

[**1**] On a 1-yd (90cm) length of Fireline, work a four-bead ladder (Basics, p. 10) using seed beads (**figure 1, p. 138**).

[**2**] Stitch the first and fourth beads together to connect them into a ring (**figure 2, a–b**).

[**3**] Tie the working thread and tail together with a square knot (Basics). Sew up through the first bead (**b–c** and **photo a**).

[**4**] Work row 2 in tubular herringbone stitch (Basics). Pick up two beads and sew down through the next bead on the previous row (**figure 3, a–b**). Sew up through the third bead. Pick up two beads and sew down through the fourth bead (**b–c**). Then sew up through the first bead on the previous row and the bead above it on the row just added (**c–d**).

[**5**] Repeat step 4 until you have a total of nine rows (**photo b**).

Antennae

[**1**] Pick up six beads. Skip the end bead and sew back through five beads and all the herringbone body beads (**photo c**).

[**2**] Sew up through the adjacent stack of body beads (**photo d**).

[**3**] Make the antenna the same way.

MATERIALS

bracelet 7½–8½ in. (19–21.6cm)
- **24** 10 x 8mm teardrop glass beads vertically drilled (Fire Mountain Gems, firemountain.com)
- 5g seed beads, size 11º
- toggle clasp
- Fireline 6 lb. test
- beading needles, #12

Wings

Working one side at a time, add the wings to the herringbone body.

[**1**] Sew under a thread bridge next to the bead the needle exits and tie a half-hitch knot (Basics). Then sew back up through the end three beads in the stack.

[**2**] Pick up a seed, a teardrop bead narrow end first, and a seed and position the beads against the body. Sew back through the drop, pick up a seed, and sew through the next two beads on the stack (**photo e, p. 138**).

[**3**] Repeat step 2 to add the top half of the wing and exit the ninth bead on the stack.

[**4**] Sew down through beads nine and eight on the stack (no antenna) at the back of the body (**photo f**). Pick up nine seeds and sew through the bead at the tip of the top half of the wing (**figure 4, a–b**).

[**5**] Pick up ten seeds and sew down through bead five on the stack (**b–c**). Sew back through six of the ten

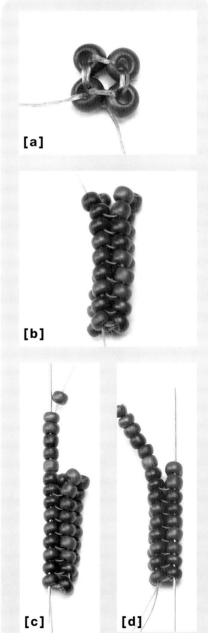

[a]

[b]

[c]   **[d]**

[e]

[f]

[g]

[h]

[i]

beads just added (c–d).

[6] Pick up four seeds and sew through the bead at the tip of the bottom half of the wing (d–e). Pick up nine seeds and sew down through bead two and bead one on the stack (e–f and **photo g**).

[7] Now add seed beads around the wing on the front of the butterfly. Sew up through beads one and two on the front stack. Pick up nine seeds and sew through the bead at the tip of the bottom half of the wing.

[8] Pick up ten seeds and sew up through bead five on the stack. Sew back through the first six beads just added, pick up four seeds, and sew through the bead at the tip on the top half of the wing. Pick up nine seeds and sew through beads eight and nine on the stack.

[9] Sew down the other stack on the front of the body and repeat steps 1–8 to add a wing on the other side of the butterfly.

[10] Secure the working thread and tail with half-hitch knots between a few beads and trim.

[11] Make five butterflies for a 7½-in. (19cm) bracelet and six for an 8½ in. (22cm).

Connections

[1] Secure a comfortable length of Fireline in the top right wing of a butterfly so it exits the bead at the tip (figure 5, point a).

[2] Pick up a seed (a–b) and sew through the corresponding bead on a second butterfly. Sew back through the bead and the tip bead on the first wing (b–c). Reinforce the thread path with a few more passes.

[3] Weave down through the beads on the wing of the first butterfly and exit the bead at the tip on the bottom half of the wing. Repeat step 2 and connect the the bottom half of the wings (photo h).

[4] Secure the thread in the beadwork with half-hitch knots between a few beads and trim.

[5] Repeat steps 1–4 to connect the remaining butterflies.

Clasp

[1] Secure a comfortable length of Fireline in the wing of one of the end butterflies and exit the bead at the tip of a wing.

[2] Pick up four seed beads, sew through the loop on the round end of the toggle, and pick up four seed beads. Sew through the bead at the tip of the other wing (photo i).

[3] Reinforce the thread path with a second pass and end the thread.

[4] Repeat steps 1–3 with the other end of the bracelet, stringing seven beads to attach the bar end of the toggle clasp. ●

Contact Stacey via email at staceysummerhill@earthlink.net.

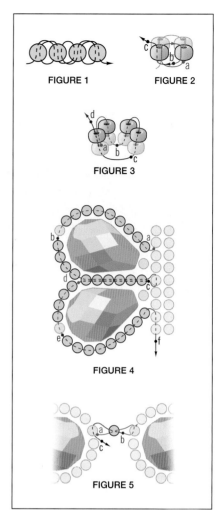

FIGURE 1   FIGURE 2

FIGURE 3

FIGURE 4

FIGURE 5

An exotic flower
explodes with color
on a herringbone cuff

by **Carole Horn**

Capture the vibrant colors of the rainforest in
this spectacular bracelet. Select beads in several
shades of green in both matte and shiny finishes
to create a rich surface. Embellish the cuff with a
few simple vines and leaves. Then, attach the
focal point: a spiky flower worked in a brilliant
contrasting hue of red, orange, or purple.

Rainforest
Bracelet

step*by*step

The finished bracelet should measure about 1 in. (2.5cm) larger than your wrist. My bracelet is 7 in. (18cm).

Flowers

[1] Using a comfortable length of Fireline, pick up five color E beads and tie the tail and working thread together using a surgeon's knot (Basics, p. 10 and **figure 1**).
[2] Go through the bead next to the knot. Pick up one bead between each of the five beads in the circle (**figure 2, a–b**).
[3] Working in circular peyote (Basics), stitch a total of six rows, stepping up at the end of each row. Keep the tension tight as you stitch, so the beads form a small tube.
[4] Pick up nine Es and one C. Skip the C, and sew back through the last E (**figure 3, a–b**). Pick up seven Es and sew through the first of the nine Es and the up bead. Exit the next up bead (**b–c**). Snug up the beads to make them stand.
[5] Repeat until there are five petals.
[6] To create the spikes, hold the five petals up toward the center. Sew through the same up bead that started the first petal and pick up nine Es and one C (**figure 4, a–b**). Skip the C, sew back through the nine Es, and go through the next up bead (**b–c**). Continue making spikes around the row.
[7] Drop down one row and make a spike in each bead. Repeat. It takes about 40 spikes and five center petals to make a full flower.

Herringbone band

For maximum contrast, I start with the darkest green and work so the lightest green falls in the middle of the bracelet. The instructions for the specific color changes in the bracelet below are given here, but you can easily design your own version. Keep in mind that once the first half is finished, simply repeat the colors and number of rows in reverse to mirror it. To introduce each new color, alternate one pair of new color beads with one pair of the old color for three rows before completely changing over to the new color.
[1] Start with a ladder of 16 two-bead stacks (Basics) using color D. Sew through the first, last, and first stack to join the ladder into a ring.
[2] Work in tubular herringbone (Basics and **figure 5**) through the top bead of each of the two-bead stacks for ten rounds. Step up to start each new round.
[3] To increase, pick up two Ds and sew down through the top bead of the next stack (**figure 6, a–b**). Pick up one C and sew up through the top bead of the next stack (**b–c**). Repeat around the tube.
[4] Pick up two Ds and sew down through the top bead of the next stack, as before (**figure 7, a–b**). Pick up two Cs and sew up through the top bead of the next stack (**b–c**). Repeat around the tube. You have now increased the bracelet band from 16 to 32 beads.

MATERIALS
bracelet 7 in. (18cm)
- seed beads, size 11º
  20g lime matte (A)
  15g lime AB shiny (B)
  15g dark green mix shiny (C)
  15g forest green matte (D)
  15g bright color for flower and buds (E)
  5g earth color for vines (F)
- **7** pressed-glass leaves
- Fireline 6 lb. test
- beading needles, #12

[5] Work two rounds of herringbone stitch, alternating two Ds and two Cs (**figure 8**).
[6] To stitch the gradient pattern in the bracelet shown below, work as follows:
Rounds 15-20: color C.
Rounds 21-23: alternate two Cs and two Bs.
Rounds 24-32: color B.
Rounds 33-36: alternate two Bs and two As.
[7] Continue in herringbone in A until the tube is about 2¼ in. (6cm) shorter than the desired length. Then work the gradient pattern in reverse (rounds 36–15), followed by two rounds that alternate two Cs and two Ds.

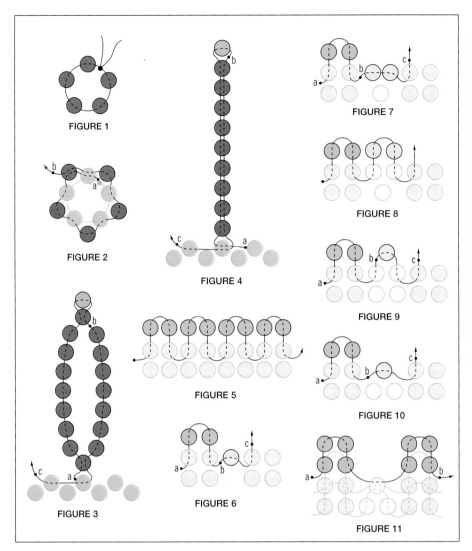

FIGURE 1

FIGURE 2

FIGURE 3

FIGURE 4

FIGURE 5

FIGURE 6

FIGURE 7

FIGURE 8

FIGURE 9

FIGURE 10

FIGURE 11

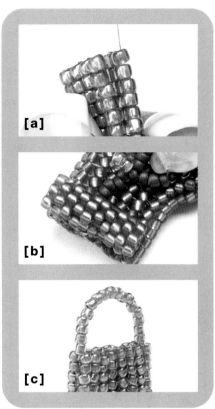

[a]

[b]

[c]

[8] The decreases at this end of the bracelet mirror the increases at the start. To begin, pick up two beads, sew down through the top bead of the next stack, and come up through the top bead of the following stack **(figure 9, a–b)**. For the second stitch, pick up one bead, sew down through the top bead of the next stack, and come up through the top bead of the following stack **(b–c)**. Repeat these two stitches around the tube. Step up to start the next round.
[9] Pick up two beads and sew down through the top bead of the next stack **(figure 10, a–b)**. Sew through the single bead at the top of the next stack and come up through the top bead of the following stack **(b–c)**. Repeat to the end of the round and step up.
[10] Work one more row as in step 9, passing through the single bead to prevent it from sticking out of the beadwork **(figure 11, a–b)**.

[11] Work in herringbone stitch over the 16 remaining beads for ten rows.
[12] Flatten the band and sew each end shut.

Peyote toggle
[1] Working in flat peyote (Basics), stitch a ten-bead band for ten rows, using Ds as at the start of the herringbone band.
[2] Roll the strip into a tube and zip up the ends **(photo a)**. Flatten the tube for your closure **(photo b)**.
[3] Anchor a new thread at one end of the bracelet. Exit at the middle near the edge row. Sew through two beads near the middle of the toggle and then sew back into the bracelet. Sew through a bead or two and repeat several times.
[4] To make the loop closure **(photo c)**, anchor a thread and exit at either folded edge. Pick up 18 Ds (enough to go over your toggle) and sew into several beads

at the opposite fold. Repeat to reinforce the loop.

Embellishment
[1] Anchor a thread near the toggle, exiting a few rows from the edge. Pick up four color F beads, sew through a bracelet bead and go back through the last vine bead. Repeat, branching off to the left side.
[2] Pick up a leaf and three Fs. Go through the last F on either stalk.
[3] To make a bud, pick up three Es and go through the last F on the other stalk.
[4] Add beads and leaves as desired. Repeat on the other end of the bracelet, leaving room to add the large flower.
[5] Anchor a thread at the loop end. Sew into several beads at the base of the flower and back into the bracelet, positioning the flower close to the bracelet's edge. Repeat until the flower is securely attached. ❍

Carole is a renowned instructor from New York. Reach her at (212) 682-7474.

Collier du Soleil

Stitch a radiant neckpiece with
hex beads and cubic zirconia teardrops

by **Anna Nehs**

Many ancient peoples worshiped the sun. Now, another divine example of solar power takes center stage. This neckpiece features faceted teardrops of cubic zirconia set in a herringbone collar. Wearing this knockout, you'll believe that the sun never sets on a good time.

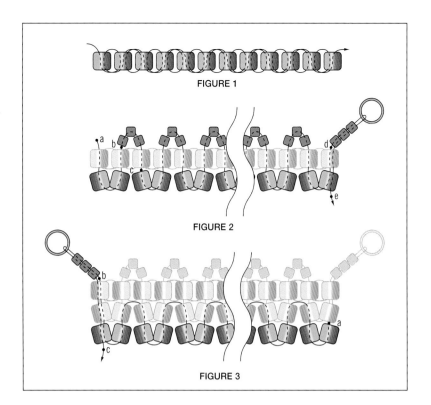

FIGURE 1

FIGURE 2

FIGURE 3

step*by*step

Choker

[1] Determine the finished length of your necklace (mine is 15 in./38cm), then subtract the clasp length to find the desired beaded length.

[2] Using a 3-yd. (2.7m) length of Fireline, leave a 6-in. (15cm) tail and make a 142-bead ladder (Basics, p. 10 and **figure 1**) with hex beads. Secure the tail with half-hitch knots between the beads (Basics) and trim the tail. Don't end the working thread.

[3] Start a new 3-yd. length of Fireline and sew through the first bead in the ladder, leaving a 10-in. (25cm) tail. Work in modified Ndebele herringbone stitch by picking up two hexes and sewing through the next bead (**figure 2, a–b**). Pick up three cylinder beads and sew through the next bead (**b–c**). Repeat across the ladder using hexes along the bottom edge and cylinders along the top.

[4] Pick up three cylinders and a soldered jump ring. Sew back through the three cylinders, the last bead in the ladder, and the last hex bead added (**d–e**).

[5] Work a second row of herringbone in hexes (**figure 3, a–b**).

[6] Finish the other end as in step 4 (**b–c**). Secure the threads and trim.

EDITOR'S NOTE: To make the dangles work out correctly, the ladder needs to be made with the correct number of beads. The gold/red collar requires a multiple of four, plus two. The silver/purple collar requires a multiple of eight, plus six.

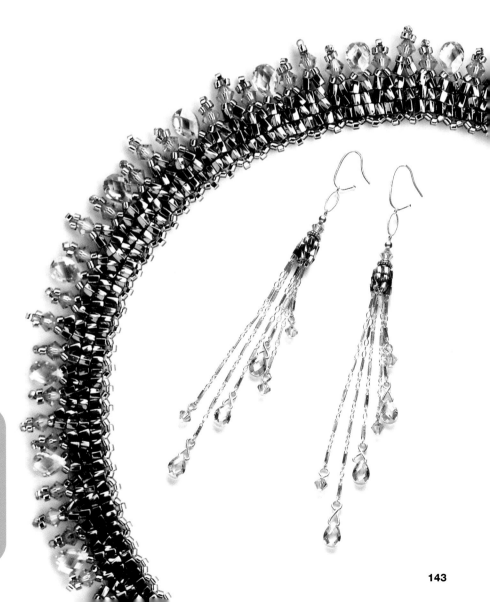

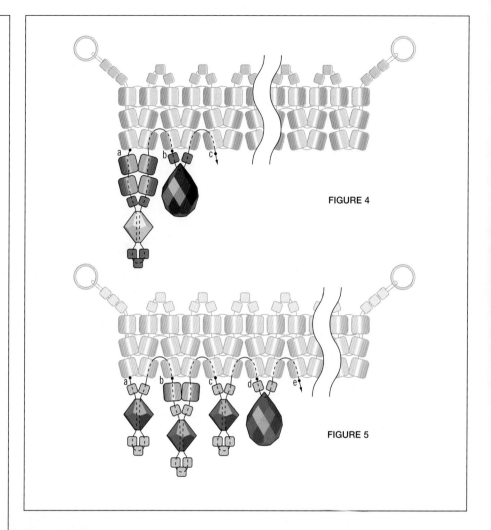

FIGURE 4

FIGURE 5

Embellishments
gold/red collar
[1] Leaving a 10-in. (25.4cm) tail, secure a new 3-yd. length of Fireline at either end of the collar. Pick up two hexes, a cylinder, a 4mm crystal, and three cylinders. Sew back through the crystal. Pick up a cylinder and two hexes. Sew through the next two beads in the previous row (**figure 4, a–b**).
[2] Pick up a cylinder, a teardrop, and a cylinder. Sew through the next two beads on the previous row (**b–c**). Alternate between crystals and teardrops to complete the row.
[3] To finish, reinforce the soldered ring when you reach the end of the row. Secure the working thread with half-hitch knots and trim. Repeat with the 10-in. tail on the other end.
[4] Attach the clasp to the soldered rings.

silver/purple collar
[1] Start a new 3-yd. length of Fireline.
[2] Pick up a cylinder, a 4mm crystal, and three cylinders. Sew through the crystal and pick up a cylinder. Sew through the next two hexes on the previous row (**figure 5, a–b**).
[3] Pick up a hex, a cylinder, a crystal, and three cylinders. Sew through the crystal and pick up a cylinder and a hex. Sew through the next two hexes on the previous row (**b–c**).
[4] Repeat step 2 (**c–d**).
[5] Pick up a cylinder, a teardrop, and a cylinder. Sew through the next two hexes on the previous row (**d–e**). Repeat steps 2–5 to complete the row.
[6] Repeat steps 3 and 4 of the gold/red collar to finish the ends.

Earrings
[1] Prepare the chain by cutting it into six graduated lengths, starting with ½ in. (1.3cm) and ending with 2½ in. (6.4cm) (**photo a**).
[2] String a crystal on a head pin and make a plain loop (Basics) above the crystal. Make three crystal dangles.

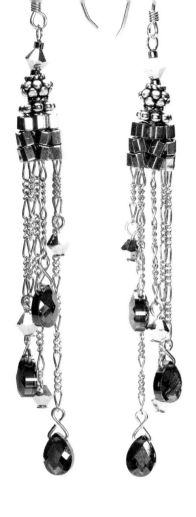

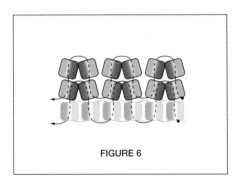

FIGURE 6

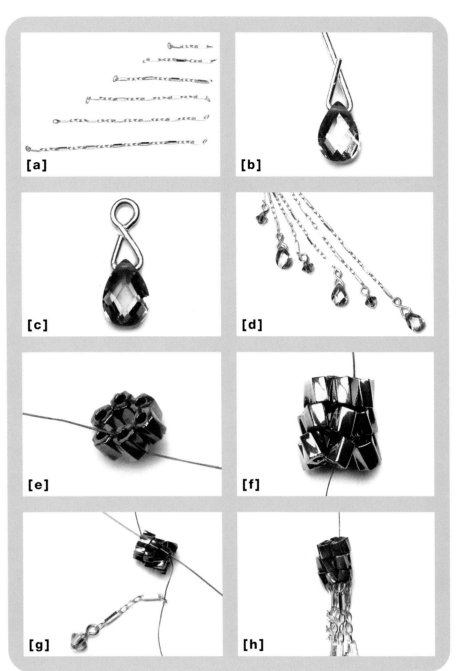

[a]

[b]

[c]

[d]

[e]

[f]

[g]

[h]

[3] Make a 45-degree bend ¼ in. (6mm) from the end of the wire and slide a teardrop to the bend. Bend the straight wire at a 45-degree angle to form a triangle over the bead **(photo b)**. Cut the wire about ⅛ in. (3mm) above the triangle and make a plain loop (Basics and **photo c**). Make a total of three teardrop dangles.

[4] Open the plain loops on the dangles and connect one to the end link of each chain cut in step 1 **(photo d)**. Close the loops and set aside.

[5] Start a 1-yd (.9m) length of Fireline and stitch a six-bead ladder, leaving a 6-in. tail. Connect the first bead to the sixth **(photo e)**.

[6] Work two rows of tubular Ndebele herringbone **(figure 6)**, exiting one of the hexes in the last row **(photo f)**.

[7] Sew through the top link on the shortest dangle and back up the stack of hexes that the thread is exiting **(photo g)**.

[8] Sew down through the next stack, pick up the second shortest dangle, and sew back up the same stack.

[9] Repeat step 8, attaching each remaining chain from shortest to longest. End with the needle exiting one of the hexes on the ladder **(photo h)**.

[10] Pick up a spacer, an accent bead, a cylinder, a crystal, a cylinder, and a soldered jump ring. Go back through all the beads and sew through the ladder opposite where the thread is exiting. Reinforce with a second thread path, secure the tails, and trim. Make a second earring to match the first. ◑

For more designs, visit Anna Nehs' website at beadivine.biz.

145

Ocean Cascade

An easy herringbone rope supports
a fringe of sea treasures

by **Lisa Olson Tune**

I'm always charmed by the luminous quality of pearls, and the endless combinations of their colors and shapes can suit virtually any project. While gazing at my pearl collection, I paired my light pink pearls with the organic, freeform, mother-of-pearl shapes called frangia and came up with this fabulous fringe cascade.

step*by*step

Herringbone rope

[1] On a 2-yd. (1.5m) length of Fireline, stitch a four-bead ladder (Basics, p. 10 and **photo a,** p. 10) using 8ºs, leaving a 12-in. (31cm) tail.

[2] Bring the fourth bead around to the first and come up through the first bead **(photo b).** Go through all the beads again to reinforce the ladder.

[3] Work in tubular herringbone (Basics) for 11 in. (28cm). Don't cut the thread.

[4] To insert the pearl accents, use your existing thread and string a spacer, a large pearl, a spacer, and two size 11º seed beads **(photo c).** Go back through the spacer, pearl, and spacer into the bead adjacent to where you started in the herringbone tube.

[5] Weave through a few beads, then go through the next bead in the tube and come up through the spacer, pearl, and spacer. Pick up two 11ºs, and secure them the same way by going back through the spacer, pearl, and spacer. Weave through a few beads and come back up through the spacer, pearl, and spacer. Exit an 11º.

[6] Stitch 2½ in. (6.3cm) of herringbone using 11ºs. Don't cut the thread.

MATERIALS

necklace 17 in. (43cm)

- **34** large freshwater pearls drilled top to bottom
- **67** small freshwater pearls drilled top to bottom
- strand graduated natural mother-of-pearl frangia (Fire Mountain Gems, 800-355-2137, firemountaingems.com)
- **136** 4mm vermeil daisy-shaped spacers
- seed beads
  30g size 8º, copper-lined
  15g size 11º, copper-lined
- Fireline, 6 lb. test
- beading needles, #12
- vermeil clasp

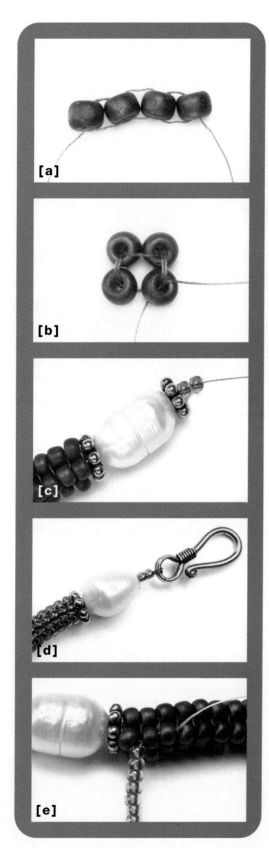

[a]

[b]

[c]

[d]

[e]

Clasp

[1] String a spacer, a small pearl, and two 11⁰s. Come through the ring on one end of the clasp and sew back through the beads. Repeat several times until the end of the clasp is secure (photo d). Weave down into the work and tie off the thread using several half-hitch knots (Basics). Trim the tail.

[2] Return to the start of the 8⁰ rope, thread the needle with the tail and add thread as needed. Finish the other half of the necklace to mirror the first.

Fringe

[1] Using a 60-in.(1.5m) length of Fireline, secure the end in the 8⁰ beads with several half-hitch knots and exit between the first and second bead in the end row.

[2] Pick up ten 11⁰s, a spacer, a small pearl, ten 11⁰s, a frangia, and ten 11⁰s.

[3] Go back up through the pearl, the spacer, the first ten beads in the fringe, and the adjacent two 8⁰s to the right in the rope (photo e). To add more heft, you can pick up an additional ten beads after coming out of the spacer and go through the two 8⁰s directly.

[4] Pick up 35 11⁰s, a spacer, a large pearl, and an 11⁰. Skip the last bead, go back through the pearl, the spacer, and five beads (figure, a–b).

[5] Pick up five beads, skip the last bead, and go back through the first four beads of the branch and the next five beads on the main stalk (b–c). Continue making five-bead branches every five beads for a total of six branches. Go back up through the beads in the stalk and through the adjacent two 8⁰s to the right in the rope.

[6] Repeat steps 4 and 5, starting with 30 11⁰s and a small pearl. Make a total of five five-bead branches on the main stalk.

[7] Repeat the fringe pattern along the same row of 8⁰ rope, ending with a frangia. If you're increasing the frangia size as you work towards the center,

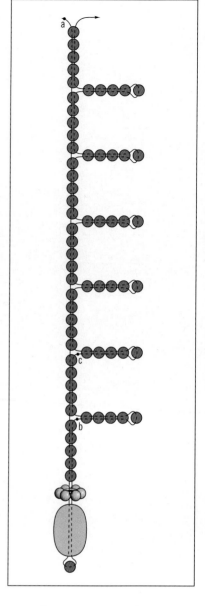

remember to start your decrease at the halfway point. ●

Lisa is a prolific beader from Portland, Oregon. Reach her via email at tunebdbdbd@aol.com.

EDITOR'S NOTE:
When working the fringe, start with smaller frangia and place the largest in the middle. You may want to use Nymo B instead of Fireline for a more flexible fringe.

Fringe adds movement to an undulating bracelet *by* **Hattie Newman**

Crave the wave

step*by*step

Base and closure

[1] Using 2 yd. (1.8m) of Power Pro, pick up five cube beads. Work odd-count, flat peyote (Basics, p. 10) until the peyote band wraps around your wrist. (My bracelet has 49 rows.)

[2] Position the needle so it exits a bead near the middle of row 6. Pick up four size 11º seed beads of any color, the button, and four seeds, then sew through the center base bead **(figure 1)**. Repeat the thread path twice. Tie a half-hitch knot between beads (Basics) and trim the tail.

[3] Secure 2 ft. (61cm) of Power Pro in the base beads opposite the button end. Come out the second bead along the edge. Pick up 34 11ºs, or enough to fit around the button. Go through the center base bead, retrace the thread path, and go through the next base bead **(figure 2)**. Tie off and trim the tail.

Fringe

[1] Start a 2-yd. piece of Power Pro, and exit the center bead on a long edge. Pick up one 8º, then two Bs, an A, two Es, a B, an E, a C, three As, and two Fs. Pick up a drop and repeat the pattern in reverse. Sew through the 8º and the base bead again **(figure 3)**.

[2] Repeat step 1, adding fringe to each cube, but delete one 11º from each side of each fringe as you go. Stop decreasing when you reach four 11ºs per side **(figure 4)**.

[3] Begin increasing by one 11º on

MATERIALS

Bracelet 7¾ in. (20cm)

- 25g 4mm cube beads, blue
- 25g 4mm drop beads, blue
- seed beads
  15g size 11º, silver-lined cobalt (A)
  10g size 11º, turquoise (B)
  10g size 11º, metallic blue (C)
  10g size 8º, blue (D)
  5g size 11º, silver (E)
  5g size 11º, amber (F)
- 5g triangle beads, size 100, transparent
- **35** 6mm flower beads, metal-coated
- ¾-in. (2cm) button with shaft
- Power Pro, 10 lb. test, moss green
- beading needles, #10 or #12

each side. When you reach the end, tie off, and start a new thread at the center. Continue to the other end.

[4] Work the other edge so the shortest fringes are opposite the longest ones.

Embellishment

[1] Start a 2-yd. piece of Power Pro, and exit near the loop at **point a (figure 5)**. Pick up a C, a D, a flower, a D, and a C **(a–b)**. Go through two base beads **(b–c)**, turn, and sew to **point b**. Repeat, ending before the button.

[2] Go through two base beads. Sew through the last flower, pick up two triangle beads, then go through the next flower **(figure 6, a–b)**.

[3] Pick up two Bs and go through the last flower again **(b–c)**. Pick up two Bs, and go through the next flower **(c–b)**.

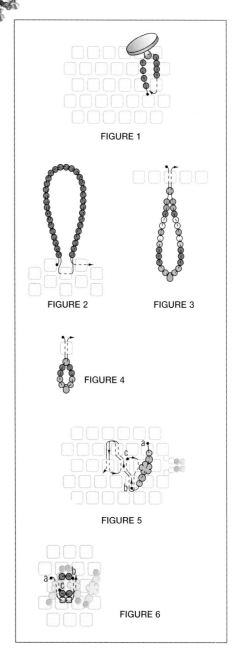

FIGURE 1

FIGURE 2   **FIGURE 3**

FIGURE 4

FIGURE 5

FIGURE 6

[4] Repeat until you finish the flower near the loop end. Secure the thread in the base and trim the excess. ●

Email Hattie at beadiac@hotmail.com.

Colorful

step*by*step

Blue peony bracelet

[1] Pick up four 6º beads on a comfortable length of Fireline. Work in even-count peyote (Basics, p. 10) until the band is the same measurement as your wrist. To end the thread, weave it into the beadwork and tie half-hitch knots (Basics) between beads. Trim the tail.

[2] To embellish the edges, anchor a new length of Fireline at one end of the band and exit the top corner bead. Pick up three drop beads. Go through the adjacent bead along the edge and exit the next bead (figure 1, a–b). Continue adding beads around the long edges of the band. Do not cut the thread or remove the needle.

[3] To make the loop closure, pick up enough 6ºs to fit loosely around your button, and exit the other 6º in the end row (figure 2, a–b). Add drop beads to the loop beads using peyote stitch (photo a).

[4] Anchor a 12-in. (30cm) length of Fireline in the middle of the band a few rows from the other end. Sew on the button, going through the shank several times to secure it. Weave in the thread and trim the tail.

Ladybug bracelet

[1] Pick up ten 8º seed beads and make a peyote band to fit your wrist as in step 1 of the peony bracelet.

[2] Trim the edges as in steps 2–3, using an 11º in a complementary color, a drop, and an 11º (photo b). When you get to the ends of the band, fill in the gaps between up beads with two 11ºs.

[3] Center the loop closure on one end using 30 11ºs in any color (photo c).

[4] Anchor the button on the other end as before (photo d).

[5] Embellish the ends with

[a]

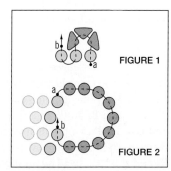

FIGURE 1

FIGURE 2

Closures

Dress up an easy peyote bracelet with a mix of festive buttons and beads. These bright florals and whimsical accents will be the center of attention at your next garden party.

by **Caren Schwartz**

[b]

[c]

[d]

[e]

colorful flowers and leaves **(photo e)**. Anchor 12 in. of Fireline where you want the first accent to sit. Pick up a flower, an 11º, and a 15º in any color. Skip the 15º and go back through the 11º and the flower. Go through several nearby beads and exit where you want the next accent to sit. When you are finished, secure the thread in the beadwork and trim the tail. ●

Caren hails from New York and is president of the Long Island Bead Society. Contact her via email at sendcarenemail@aol.com or visit her website at stringin-along.com.

MATERIALS

both projects
- Fireline 6 lb. test
- beading needles, #12

**blue peony bracelet
7 in. (18cm)**
- 20g size 6º seed beads, purple-lined teal
- 10g 4mm drops, clear
- peony-shaped plastic button with shank (joann.com)

ladybug bracelet 7 in.
- seed beads
  30g size 8º, lime AB
  10g size 11º, orange matte
  5g size 11º, purple-lined clear
  1g size 15º
- 10g 4mm drops, yellow AB
- lampwork ladybug button by Della Armstrong (916-922-0860; della@ dancingrabbitdesigns.com)
- assortment of resin flowers and pressed-glass leaves

Band together

Peyote squares frame crystals
in an elegant bracelet

by **Phyllis Fogel**

Subtle glamour makes this bracelet a standout. The delicate combination of
Japanese cylinder beads and small round crystals sits lightly on your wrist.
Choose beads with a quiet, monochromatic palette such as this one or select
a splashy contrast. You'll find that the peyote and brick stitch sections go
together quickly, even if you are new to off-loom weaving.

step*by*step

Beaded links

[1] Using 1 yd. (.9m) of thread, make a
nine-bead ladder (Basics, p. 10).
[2] Work in brick stitch for the
next nine rows as follows:
Rows 2–3: Pick up two seed beads for
the first stitch and one bead for each
stitch across the rest of the row **(figure
1, a–b)**. Each row contains nine beads.
Rows 4–10: Pick up two seeds for
the first stitch then one bead for the
next stitch **(b–c)**. Each row contains
three beads.
[3] Weave in the short tail, securing it
with half-hitch knots (Basics) and trim
the thread. Leave the working thread to
use later.
[4] Repeat steps 1–3, making a total of
14 L-shaped sections.
[5] Using the thread remaining

from step 3, connect two L-shaped
sections by sewing them closed with
peyote stitch **(figure 2, a–b and c–d)**.
[6] Sew through the beads from **points
d** to **e**. Go through a seed, pick up a
crystal, and go through a seed **(e–f)**. Sew
back through the crystal several times
for reinforcement, secure the thread
with half-hitch knots, and trim the tail.
[7] Repeat steps 5–6, connecting ten
more L-shaped sections.
[8] Connect two L-shaped sections
without adding a crystal. (This link
becomes the loop for the toggle clasp.)
[9] Start a new thread along the edge
of this link.
[10] Stitch seven rows in peyote stitch
(Basics), picking up three seed beads for
each row **(figure 3)**.
[11] Attach the seventh peyote row to
the edge of a crystal link, lining up the
beads as shown in **figure 3**.

MATERIALS
bracelet 7½ in. (19cm)
- 7g Japanese cylinder beads
- 6 5mm crystals
- SoNo, Silamide, or Nymo D
  conditioned with beeswax
- beading needles, #12

[12] Repeat steps 9–11 to connect the
remaining links.

Picot edging

[1] Weave through the beads to the
edge of the end link **(figure 4, point a)**.
Pick up three seed beads and go through
the next two edge beads **(a–b)**. Continue
to the end of the link **(b–c)**.
[2] Repeat step 1, adding picot edging
along the long sides of the links (see
photo, above). Don't cut the thread.

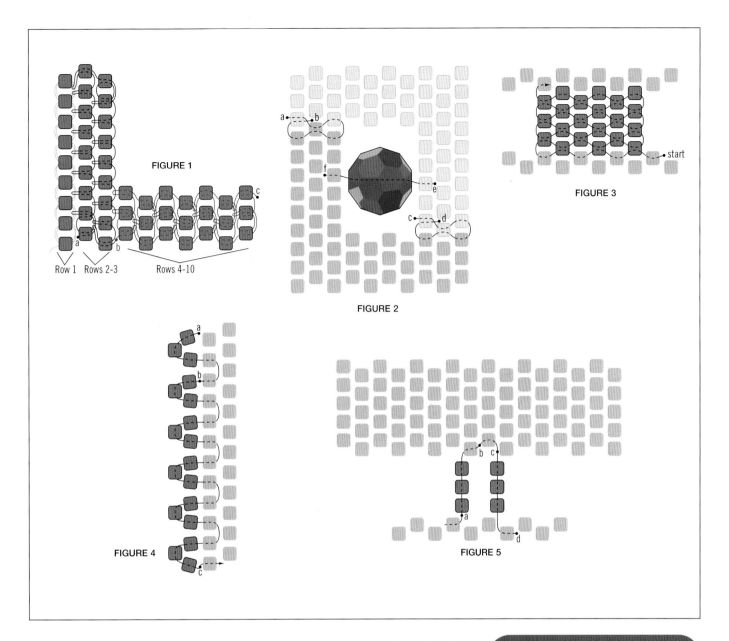

FIGURE 1

Row 1   Rows 2-3   Rows 4-10

FIGURE 2

FIGURE 3

start

FIGURE 4

FIGURE 5

Tubular clasp

[1] Start a new needle with 24 in. (61cm) of thread. Slide a stop bead to about 4 in. (10cm) from the end and go through it again in the same direction.

[2] String 16 seed beads and slide them to the stop bead. Stitch eight rows of flat, even-count peyote (Basics), picking up eight beads for each row.

[3] Zip up the long edges (Basics) to form a tube.

[4] Remove the stop bead, secure the tails with half-hitch knots, and trim the thread.

[5] Pick up the thread remaining from the picot edging, weave along the edge, and exit the fourth bead from the end **(figure 5, point a)**.

[6] Pick up three seed beads and go

through the eighth bead from the edge of the tube **(a–b)**. Go through the next seed **(b–c)**. Pick up three seeds and go through the corresponding bead on the bracelet **(c–d)**.

[7] Secure the clasp by retracing the thread path one or two more times, then weave in the tail. ❂

Contact Phyllis at cre8iveb@aol.com or (610) 820-9125.

EDITOR'S NOTE:
To increase the bracelet length by an inch (2.5cm), make one more crystal link. For a minor increase in length, simply adjust the bead count when attaching the toggle clasp.

Get CONNE

Peyote stitch rectangles
create a colorful necklace

by **Sonja Podjan**

This is a great design for experimenting with bead colors and finishes. Arrange your color choices before you begin. If you're not quite sure about the placement of each color, don't connect and close the links as you work. Instead, make the links first, arrange them until you like the way the colors flow, then sew them together to finish the necklace.

step*by*step

Refer to the pattern on p. 155 as you work.
[1] String a stop bead to 8 in. (20cm) from the end of a 1-yd (.9m) length of thread. Sew through the stop bead again.
[2] Pick up 20 beads and work flat, even-count peyote (Basics, p. 10) for six rows. This completes the first side of the link (rows 1–6).
[3] For side 2, stitch two beads per row for 11 rows (rows 7–17).
[4] For side 3, stitch two beads for two rows (rows 18–19). Then pick up 16

beads and push them against the last bead on row 18. Work a row of peyote with the beads just strung and the up beads from row 19 **(photo a)**. Continue working in peyote until this side is six rows wide (rows 18–23).
[5] Weave back through the beads and exit down through the third up bead from the bottom inside edge of side 3. See **point a** on the pattern.
[6] For side 4, work 11 two-bead rows as in step 3 to complete the last side of the link (rows 24–34).
[7] When you're ready to close a link, align the beads

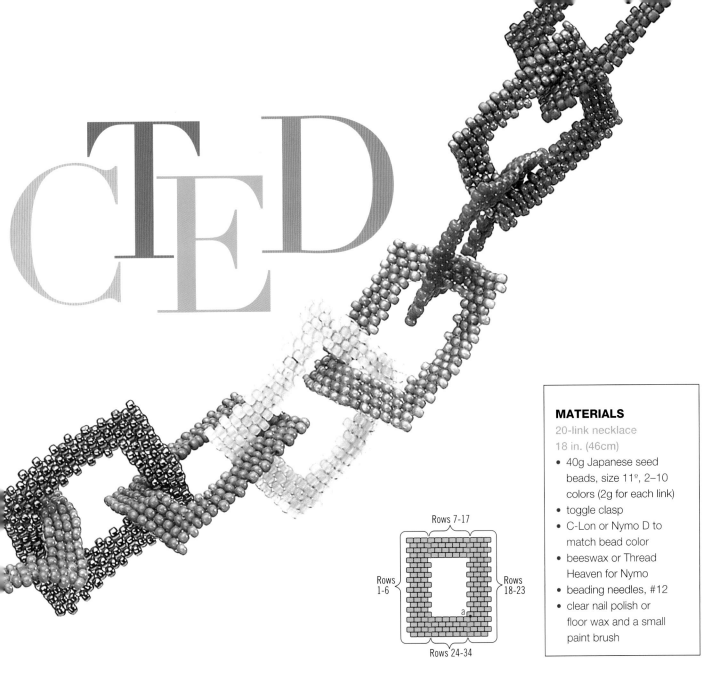

CTED

MATERIALS

**20-link necklace
18 in. (46cm)**

- 40g Japanese seed
  beads, size 11º, 2–10
  colors (2g for each link)
- toggle clasp
- C-Lon or Nymo D to
  match bead color
- beeswax or Thread
  Heaven for Nymo
- beading needles, #12
- clear nail polish or
  floor wax and a small
  paint brush

Rows 7-17

Rows
1-6

Rows
18-23

a

Rows 24-34

on row 34 with the beads on
row 6. Zip up the edge beads
(Basics) to stitch the sides
together. Secure the working
thread with half-hitch knots
(Basics) between a few beads
and trim the excess thread.

[8] To attach the clasp,
remove the stop bead and
thread a needle on the tail.
Pick up three beads, sew
through the loop on a clasp
half, and pick up three more
beads. Sew through the bead
the thread exits in the same
direction to form a ring
(photo b). Sew through the
beads again, secure the thread
in the beadwork, and trim.

[9] Repeat steps 1–6 and
make a second link.
[10] Connect the new link
to the previous link **(photo c)**.
Repeat step 7. Remove the
stop bead and secure the tail.
[11] Continue making and
connecting links until you
have a chain of 20. Attach
the remaining clasp half to
the end link as you did in
step 8.
[12] Lay the necklace as
flat as possible. Apply a
thin coat of floor wax with
a paint brush or use clear
nail polish on each link to
stiffen them. Let the links
dry, then rearrange them so

you can coat the parts of
each link that were covered
by other links. Let dry as
before, and add a second
coat if necessary. ●

*Sonja is the author of three
bead pattern books,* Split

Loom Magic, A Quilt
Around My Neck, *and*
Framed With a Little Help
From My Friends. *Contact
her at 8401 Hagar Shore
Road, Watervliet, Michigan
49098, (269) 463-5786, or
slpodjan@cpuinc.net.*

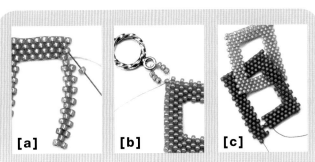

[a]   [b]   [c]

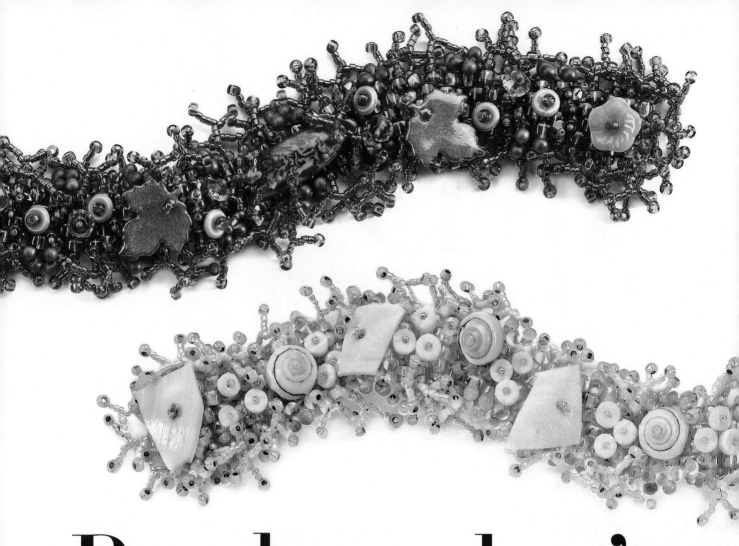

Beachcomber's Bracelet

Embellish a peyote band with a bounty of seaside treasures

by **Caren Schwartz**

You'll find me along the surf lines at the shore, collecting bits and pieces of interesting things. If there's a basket of various items at a bead store register, you'll see me sifting through it. This fringed, peyote stitch band takes that happy miscellany and turns it into something beautiful.

stepbystep

Base

[1] Center a needle on a 4-yd. (3.7m) length of conditioned thread and work with the thread doubled.

[2] Pick up four triangle beads and work in flat, even-count peyote stitch (Basics, p. 10) until the band fits around your wrist comfortably without the ends overlapping **(photo a)**.

[3] Weave the working thread back through the last few rows of the band, tie a few half-hitch knots (Basics) between beads, and trim the excess thread. Repeat with the thread tail.

Edge embellishment

[1] Secure 1 yd (.9m) of thread in the band by weaving through a few rows and exit a corner bead on the long edge **(figure 1, point a)**.

[2] Pick up an 8º seed bead, six cylinder beads, and an 8º **(a–b)**. Turn, skip the last 8º, and sew back through two cylinders **(b–c)**.

[3] Pick up three cylinders and one 8º. Skip the 8º and sew back through the three new cylinders and the next two cylinders **(c–d)**.

[4] Pick up three cylinders and one 8º. Sew back through the cylinders, the first 8º, and the base bead **(d–e)**. Sew through the next edge bead on the base **(e–f)**.

[5] Repeat steps 2–4 for a total of five branch fringes.

[6] Pick up three drop beads and sew back through the edge bead and the next base bead **(f–g)**. Repeat for a total of three drop picots.

[7] Repeat steps 2–6 along the edge of the band, adding two or three branch fringes between two or three drop picots.

[8] Add branch fringe between the beads on the short edge of the band.

[9] Work the other long edge of the band as you did the first. Don't add fringe to the other short edge of the band. Secure the thread in the beadwork and trim the tail.

Top embellishment

[1] Start a new length of thread and secure it in the base beads at the fringed short edge of the band. Exit a center triangle bead near the end of the band.

[2] Sew up through the clasp bead, pick up three 15ºs, and sew back through the clasp bead and a triangle on the band directly below **(photo b)**. Retrace the thread path a few more times to secure the bead in place.

[3] Weave through a few beads on the band and exit a triangle where you will add the next embellishment. Continue adding surface embellishment across the length of the band, using one or three 15ºs, an 11º, or a cylinder, depending

on the size and shape of the bead. Space the larger beads across the length of the band with smaller beads between them.

Clasp loop

[1] After adding the last surface embellishment, exit the corner bead on the short edge without fringe **(figure 2, point a)**. Pick up two 15ºs, an 8º, a heishi, and enough 15ºs to go around the clasp bead twice plus ½ in. (1.3cm) **(a–b** and **photo c)**.

[2] Pick up a heishi and a drop **(b–c)**. Skip the drop and go back through the heishi, the 15ºs, the first heishi, and the 8º **(c–d)**. Pick up two 15ºs and go through the next two triangle beads, exiting the corner bead **(d–e)**.

[3] Pick up seven 8ºs, and go through the same two triangle beads **(e–f)**. Before you tighten the loop, position it around the strand of beads from the previous step **(photo d)**.

[4] Tighten the loop and retrace the thread path a few times. Secure the tail and trim. ●

Caren hails from New York and is president of the Long Island Bead Society. Contact her via email at sendcarenemail@aol.com or visit her website at stringin-along.com.

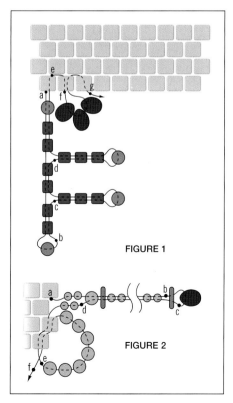

FIGURE 1

FIGURE 2

MATERIALS

bracelet 7½ in. (19cm)
- shell and heishi accent beads
  5 10–18mm
  20–25 4–6mm
- 10–18mm center-drilled bead or button for clasp
- 12g 3.4mm drop beads
- 18g triangle beads, size 5º (base)
- seed beads
  3g size 8º
  4g size 11º or Japanese cylinder beads
  1g size 15º
- Nymo D to match bead color, conditioned with beeswax
- beading needles, #12

[a]

[b]

[c]

[d]

Fleur du jour

Peyote flowers accent
bracelets and more

by **Sue Jackson and Wendy Hubick**

The technique used to make these beaded flowers is so versatile that once you make the strung floral bracelet, you will want to add flower embellishments to other beaded surfaces. The wonder bead pendant (to the right) and the beaded tassel and square-stitch bracelet (both on p. 160) are a few items we embellished with flowers. We hope these samples trigger your creativity and that you enjoy this technique as much as we do.

step*by*step

Base
[1] Start with a 2-yd. (1.8m) length of thread and string a stop bead to 24 in. (61cm) from the end of the thread. Go through the bead again in the same direction.
[2] Pick up six base-color beads and work in flat, even count peyote (Basics, p. 10) for 26 rows.

[3] Weave back through the beads to the approximate center of the peyote strip and exit the bead at **point a** on **figure 1**. Since you'll sew the peyote strip into a tube once the petals and leaves are attached, you can place the flower anywhere on the strip, but if you attach the flower toward the center of the strip, it is easier to hold as you work.

Flower
[1] Pick up seven petal-color beads. Position the beads against the peyote strip. Work a row of peyote for four beads (**figure 2, a–b**).
[2] Sew through the base bead and the first petal bead (**b–c**).
[3] Work the next row adding three beads (**figure 3, a–b**). Pick up a bead and sew through the next bead (**b–c**).

[4] Work down this side of the petal, adding three beads. Then sew through the base bead and the next two petal beads (**c–d**).
[5] Add two beads to each side of the petal (**figure 4, a–b**).
[6] Add a bead to each side of the petal and exit the base bead (**figure 5, a–b**).
[7] Repeat steps 1–6 and make a total of five petals.

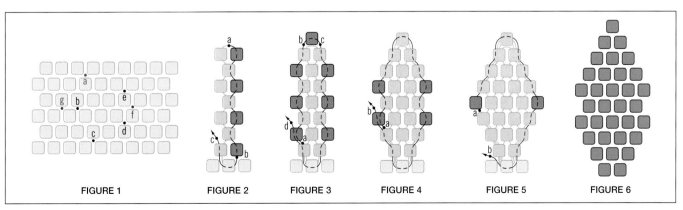

| FIGURE 1 | FIGURE 2 | FIGURE 3 | FIGURE 4 | FIGURE 5 | FIGURE 6 |

Position the remaining petals on the base at **points b–e** on **figure 1**.

[8] Exit a bead on the base at the center of the flower petals and attach the flower's center bead. Use short fringes, loops of seed beads, or a cluster of small stones or glass beads, if you want your flowers to have stamens.

Leaves

[1] Position the thread so it exits the bead at **point f** on **figure 1** and pick up nine leaf-color beads.

[2] Refer to **figure 6** and make the leaf the same way as the flower petals.

[3] Make a second leaf at **point g** on **figure 1**.

[4] Add two or three leaves the same shape as the flower petals and position them under the flower.

[5] Secure the thread in the beadwork with a few half-hitch knots (Basics) between beads and trim.

Finishing

[1] Thread a needle on the tail and sew the first and last rows of the base together to form a tube. Secure the thread in the beadwork and trim.

[2] Make two more flower beads.

[3] Cut a 10-in. (25cm) length of flexible beading wire. String an alternating pattern of flower beads (slide each tube over a 4mm bead to fill it) and stone beads to the center of the wire. Then string both ends of the bracelet with an alternating pattern of stone and silver beads until it is about 1 in. (2.5cm) shorter than the desired length.

[4] String a crimp bead, a 6–8mm bead, and a 4mm bead on one end of the wire. Bring the wire through a loop on the clasp and back through the beads just strung, the crimp, and one more bead. Crimp the crimp bead (Basics) and trim the wire tail.

[5] Repeat step 4 on the other end of the bracelet using the remaining half of the clasp. ●

Sue and Wendy teach bead classes around the country. Contact them via email at info@hummingbeads.com.

MATERIALS
bracelet 8¼ in. (21cm)

- Japanese cylinder beads
  1–2g petal color, each of several finishes
  1–2g leaf color, each of several finishes
  1–2g base color, same as leaf or petal
- **3–9** 2–4mm beads, center of flower
- **3** 4mm beads to fill peyote tube
- **14** 10mm stone beads
- **12** 10mm silver spacers
- **2** 6–8mm beads
- **2** 4mm silver beads
- clasp
- **2** crimp beads
- flexible beading wire, .012–.014
- Nymo D conditioned with beeswax or Fireline 6 lb. test
- beading needles, #12 or #13
- crimping pliers

Wire enhances a
sculptural peyote
brooch

Autumn leaves

by **Dottie Hoeschen**

Before becoming a beader five years ago, I had
been a painter for 25 years. Water, rocks, trees,
and leaves have been a recurring theme in my
work, and I never tire of exploring the constantly
shifting relationships among these elements.

My beadwork is more abstract than my painting
style, but my love of these earthy elements is
unchanged. You can see them in the shapes and
colors of my jewelry.

Once you master the leaves, experiment to see
what else you can create with them. My brooch
easily converts to a necklace by adding it to a
stitched neckband, or use individual leaves to
make a pair of playful earrings.

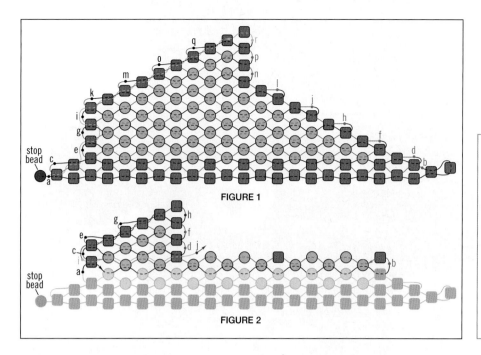

FIGURE 1

FIGURE 2

MATERIALS

- 50g size 11º seed beads, two or more fall colors
- 10g Japanese cylinder beads, one or more fall colors
- 10g size 5º hex cuts
- **12** or more assorted beads, 2–12mm
- Nymo B or D or Fireline 6 lb. test
- beading needles, #12
- 6 in. (15cm) 24-gauge wire
- pin back

step*by*step

Small amounts of thread show along the edges as you taper the leaves. To minimize its appearance, choose a thread color that closely matches your cylinder beads.

Basic leaf shape

[1] Thread your needle with a yard (.9m) of Nymo or Fireline and string a stop bead to the middle. Go through the bead again in the same direction to anchor it.

[2] String 24 cylinder beads. Turn, go through the second bead from the needle (figure 1, a–b), and work across the row in peyote stitch (Basics, p. 10) using cylinders until you reach the stop bead (b–c).

[3] Without picking up a new bead, go back through the last cylinder strung. Pick up a cylinder and work the next stitch. Work the next eight stitches using 11º seed beads in a mix of colors. Pick up a cylinder to make the last stitch (c–d).

[4] Without picking up a new bead, go back through the last cylinder. Pick up a cylinder and work one peyote stitch. Work the next eight stitches using 11ºs to complete the row (d–e).

[5] Pick up a cylinder and go back through the last 11º strung. Work the next seven stitches using 11ºs. Pick up a cylinder to make the last stitch (e–f).

[6] Without picking up a bead, go back through the last cylinder. Pick up a cylinder and go through the last 11º. Work the next seven stitches using 11ºs (f–g).

[7] Pick up a cylinder and go through the last 11º. Work the next six stitches using 11ºs. Pick up a cylinder to make the last stitch (g–h).

[8] Go back through the last cylinder again. Pick up a cylinder and go through the last 11º. Work the next six stitches using 11ºs (h–i).

[9] Pick up a cylinder and go through the last 11º. Work the next five stitches using 11ºs. Pick up a cylinder to make the last stitch (i–j).

[10] Without picking up a bead, go through the last cylinder. Pick up a cylinder and go through the last 11º. Work the next four stitches using 11ºs. Pick up a cylinder to make the last stitch (j–k). The edge of the leaf will begin to change shape.

[11] Without picking up a bead, go through the last cylinder. Pick up a cylinder and go through the last 11º. Work the next three stitches using 11ºs. Pick up a cylinder to make the last stitch (k–l).

[12] Without stringing a bead, go through the last cylinder. Pick up a cylinder and go through the last 11º. Work two stitches using 11ºs. Pick up a cylinder to make the last stitch (l–m).

[13] Without picking up a bead, go

through the last cylinder. Pick up a cylinder and go through the last 11º. Work the next two stitches using 11ºs (m–n).

[14] Pick up a cylinder and go through the last 11º. Work the next stitch using an 11º. Pick up a cylinder to make the last stitch (n–o). The edge of the leaf will change again.

[15] Without picking up a bead, go through the last cylinder. Work a cylinder and an 11º (o–p).

[16] Pick up a cylinder and go through the last 11º. End the row with a cylinder (p–q).

[17] Without picking up a bead, go through the last cylinder. Pick up a cylinder to make the only stitch (q–r).

[18] Pick up a cylinder and go through the last cylinder. Continue through the diagonal row of cylinders along the edge of the leaf and weave in and out of the last few cylinders, exiting the first one (r–a). Don't cut the tail.

[19] Remove the stop bead and thread the needle on this tail. Starting with step 3, stitch the leaf's second half as the mirror image of the first.

Leaf variation

Complete steps 1–4 of the basic leaf, then follow the steps below.

[1] Pick up a cylinder and go through the last 11º strung. Work the next eight stitches using 11ºs to complete the row (figure 2, a–b).

[a]

[b]

[c]

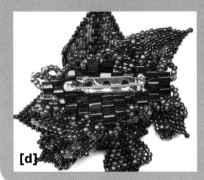

[d]

FIGURE 3

[2] Pick up a cylinder and go through the last 11º. Work the next two stitches using 11ºs, then a cylinder. Repeat, then finish the row with two 11ºs (b–c).

[3] Pick up a cylinder and go through the last 11º strung. Work two stitches using 11ºs (c–d). Your thread will be exiting a cylinder.

[4] Pick up a cylinder, turn, and go back through the last 11º strung. This begins to define one notch on the leaf's edge. Work the last two stitches using an 11º and a cylinder (d–e).

[5] Without picking up a bead, go through the last cylinder strung. Pick up a cylinder and an 11º to complete the row (e–f).

[6] Pick up a cylinder and go through the last 11º strung. Pick up a cylinder to make the end stitch (f–g).

[7] Without picking up a bead, go through the last cylinder strung. Complete the row with a cylinder (g–h).

[8] Pick up a cylinder and go through the last cylinder strung. Continue through the diagonal row of cylinders along the edge of the leaf (h–i). Go through the next cylinder along the edge and work across to the cylinder at **j**.

[9] Repeat steps 3-8 twice on this edge of the leaf. When the three sections are complete, work back to the cylinder next to the stop bead. Remove the stop bead and thread the needle on the long tail. You'll use the short tail to sew the leaf to the base.

[10] To stitch the other half of the leaf, repeat steps 3–4 of the basic leaf, then repeat steps 1–9 of this variation.

Leaf base

[1] Make a seven-bead ladder using 5º hex cuts (Basics and **figure 3, a–b**). Work in brick stitch (Basics) for five rows, decreasing to two beads (b–c).

[2] Repeat the rows of brick stitch on the other edge of the ladder.

[3] With your thread exiting one of the two end beads, pick up nine 11ºs. Go under the thread bridge above the edge bead in the previous row (c–d). Go back through the last 11º.

[4] Pick up eight 11ºs and continue as in step 3 (d–e). Repeat around the base until you reach the starting point. Weave in the tails and trim the ends.

Assembly

My brooch uses four basic leaves and two with variations.

[1] Sew the stem end of each leaf onto the center of the base with the remaining thread tails. Place the leaves so they overlap slightly and sew through the leaf and a base bead (**photo a**). Trim the tail. You'll hide any exposed threads in step 3.

[2] With the ends of the wire exiting toward the front of the leaf, center a 6-in. (15cm) length of wire through a base bead or two. String a mix of beads on the wire and bend the ends into decorative shapes (**photo b**).

[3] Sew an assortment of beads in the center of the leaves to embellish them and hide the joins (**photo c**).

[4] Stitch a pin back to the back of the leaf base (**photo d**). ●

Contact Dottie at stonebrash@juno.com.

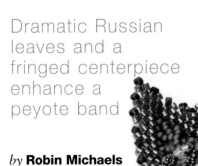

Dramatic Russian leaves and a fringed centerpiece enhance a peyote band

by **Robin Michaels**

Lacy Leaves

Rich hues in multiple colors add depth and dimension to this elegant bracelet. The Russian leaves work up quickly using a variation on peyote stitch and require a small amount of beads per leaf, making this a great technique for embellishing.

step*by*step

Peyote band

[1] Working with a comfortable length of thread, stitch a peyote band 18 beads wide (Basics p. 10 and **figure 1, a–b**), leaving a 10-in. tail. The band should fit comfortably around your wrist with the ends overlapping by about ½ in. 1.3cm).

MATERIALS
- Japanese cylinder beads
  15g for the base
  3g each of five colors for leaves
  3g each of two colors for fringe
- Japanese seed beads, size 15º
  2g each of five colors for veins
  3g for fringe
- 1-in. (2.5cm) mesh dome finding (ornamentea.com)
- 2 6–8mm plastic snaps
- conditioned Nymo D or Fireline 6 lb. test
- beading needles, #12

[2] Sew the two male halves of the snaps to one end of the band.

[3] Sew the two female halves of the snaps to the underside of the opposite end of the band to correspond with the male halves.

Leaves

Make five leaves in various colors, using two colors per leaf.

Sides

[1] Slide a stop bead to the middle of a 4-ft. (1.2m) length of thread. Sew back through it in the same direction.

[2] Pick up an accent color (AC) cylinder, five main color (MC) cylinders, an AC, and an MC. Sew back through the fourth MC (**figure 2, a–b**).

[3] Work two rows in peyote stitch, adding four MCs (**b–c**).

[4] Pick up an AC and an MC. Sew through the last MC added on the previous row (**c–d**).

[5] Work in peyote for one MC. Pick up an MC, an AC, and an MC. Sew back through the first MC so the other two beads sit side-by-side, with the AC closer to the tail (**d–e**). Work in peyote for one MC (**e–f**).

[6] Repeat steps 4 and 5 until you have nine ACs along the outer edge of the leaf (**f–g**). Don't trim the working

thread. You will use it to attach the leaf to the band.

[7] Remove the stop bead and thread a needle on the tail. Work the second half of the leaf to mirror the first (**h–i**).

Bottom

[1] Pick up three MCs and sew through two MCs on the other half of the leaf (**figure 3, a–b**).

[2] Pick up an AC and sew back through the same two MCs. Work in peyote for one MC (**b–c**).

[3] Pick up an MC and sew through the next two MCs. Pick up an AC, sew back through the same two MCs, and the last MC added (**c–d**).

[4] Work in peyote for one MC (**d–e**) and set the thread aside.

Veins

[1] Weave through the beads so the working thread exits at **point f**. Pick up 19 15ºs. Sew through the AC at **point a** in **figure 2**, two MCs, back through the AC, and continue through five 15ºs (**figure 3, f–g**).

[2] Pick up three 15ºs. Sew through the first inside AC on either side of the leaf and three MCs. Sew back through the AC, the three 15ºs, and the next 15º of the original 19 (**g–h**).

FIGURE 1

FIGURE 2

FIGURE 3

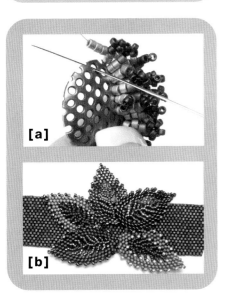

[a]

[b]

[3] Continue to add veins as in step 2, varying the number of 15ºs for each vein (h–i). Secure the thread and trim.

Centerpiece

Start a new thread and tie one end to the inside of the mesh dome finding. Exit one of the holes and pick up two MCs, an AC, and four 15ºs. Sew back through the first 15º. Pick up an AC and two MCs and sew through the next hole (photo a). Sew up through another hole and repeat until the finding is covered in fringe. Don't cut the working thread.

Assemble the bracelet

Refer to **photo b** as you position the leaves on the band. Stitch the leaves in place using the tail ends. Center the fringed dome over the leaves and stitch it in place. ◉

Robin owns Keep Me in Stitches. Contact her there at 77 Smithtown Boulevard, Smithtown, New York 11787, (631) 724-8111, or keepmeinstitches1@yahoo.com. You can also visit her website at keepmeinstitches1.com.

Bubble Bead Bracelet

Create several styles
of textured beads,
starting with a basic
peyote tube. Combine
the beads with simple
ladder stitch spacers
and string them on
a leather cord.

by **Jan Zicarelli**

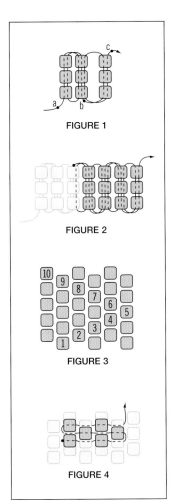

FIGURE 1

FIGURE 2

FIGURE 3

FIGURE 4

MATERIALS

bracelet 8 in. (20cm)

- 3g Japanese seed beads, size 8º, several colors
- 5g Japanese cylinder beads
- 16 3–4mm large-hole spacers
- 10 in. (25cm) 2mm leather cord
- 2 leather crimp tubes, 2.5mm hole (Rio Grande, 800-545-6566)
- toggle clasp
- 2 jump rings
- Nymo D in matching colors
- E-6000 glue or G-S Hypo Cement
- beading needles, #12
- chainnose pliers

step*by*step

Spacer beads

(make eight)

[1] Working with 18 in. (46cm) of thread, string six cylinder beads to 8 in. (20cm) from the tail end.

[2] Sew back up through the first three beads and down through the second three beads, creating a ladder of two columns with three beads each (Basics, p. 10 and **figure 1, a–b**).

[3] Pick up three beads. Sew down through the second column of beads and up through the new beads (**b–c**). Keep the thread tension tight and make sure the columns line up side-by-side. Continue until you have seven three-bead columns (**figure 2**).

[4] Sew the first and last columns of the ladder together to form a tube (**photo a**).

[5] To make a firmer bead, sew up and down the columns two to three more times.

[6] To end the thread, sew into a column of beads and come out between the second and third beads. Don't tighten the thread completely; leave about a ½-in. (1.3cm) loop near the beadwork. Brush a small amount of glue on the loop, then pull it through. Trim the excess thread. Repeat with the tail left in step 1 (**photo b**).

Tube beads

(make three)

[1] On a 1-yd. (.9m) length of thread, string six 8º seed beads. Work in even-count, flat peyote for 10 rows (Basics and **figure 3**).

[2] Roll the beadwork into a tube and zip up the edge beads (Basics and **photo c**). Zigzag back through the row again.

[3] Secure the thread ends with a few half-hitch knots (Basics) between beads and trim the tails.

Bubble bead

(make four)

[1] Make a tube bead as described above, but increase the count from ten to twelve rows. Don't end the working thread.

[2] Mark the starting point for the embellishment by sliding a needle through one row of beads (**photo d**).

[3] Skip the edge beads and add two beads per row to the tube's surface (**figure 4**).

Assembly

[1] Apply a dot of glue to one end of the leather cord and slide it into the crimp tube. Squeeze the center of the crimp tube with chainnose pliers (**photo e**). Wipe off any excess glue.

[2] Slide the beads onto the cord as shown in the photo on p. 166 or as desired. Check the fit and adjust the number of beads as needed.

[3] Trim the other cord end to about ¼ in. (6mm) short of the bracelet's desired length. Apply glue to the end, slide the cord inside the crimp tube, and squeeze the crimp. Wipe off the excess glue and let dry.

[4] Use a jump ring (Basics) to attach a clasp section to the crimp tube. Repeat on the other end. ●

Contact Jan at jan.zicarelli@mchsi.com.

EDITOR'S NOTE:
Japanese size 8º seed beads tend to make a rounder, better-looking bubble bead than Japanese size 8º cylinders or Czech size 8º seed beads.

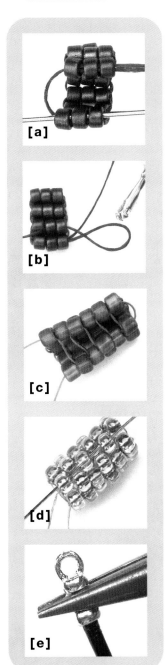

[a]

[b]

[c]

[d]

[e]

Ruffles and Ridges

Stitch a peyote tube bracelet with jaunty twists

Rows of peyote increases produce graceful, rippled edges along tube-shaped beaded beads. Make five, then string them with interesting accent beads to create a lively bracelet. There are no limits to the color combinations you can try for these beads, and feel free to substitute beads in other styles and sizes for the 11⁰s.

by **Beth Stone**

step*by*step

For an 8-in. (20cm) bracelet, make five ruffled tubes.

Tube

[1] Condition a 2-yd. (1.8m) length of Nymo (Basics, p. 10). I like to roll up half the length on cardboard to keep the Nymo manageable.
[2] String eight main color (MC) seed beads. Move them to the middle of the thread and work in flat, even-count peyote (Basics) for ten rows.
[3] Roll the beadwork into a tube and zip it closed (Basics), attaching row 1 to row 10.
[4] Sew through the beads so your needle exits the opposite end from the tail.

MATERIALS

bracelet 8 in. (20cm)

- Japanese seed beads, size 11°
  10g main color
  10g accent color
- **5** 8–12mm accent beads,
  various shapes, colors, and sizes
- **30** spacer beads, various sizes
- 10mm bead for button clasp
- Nymo D, conditioned with
  beeswax
- beading needles, #12
- head pin
- 12 in. (30cm) flexible
  beading wire, .014
- **2** crimp beads
- crimping pliers
- roundnose and chainnose pliers

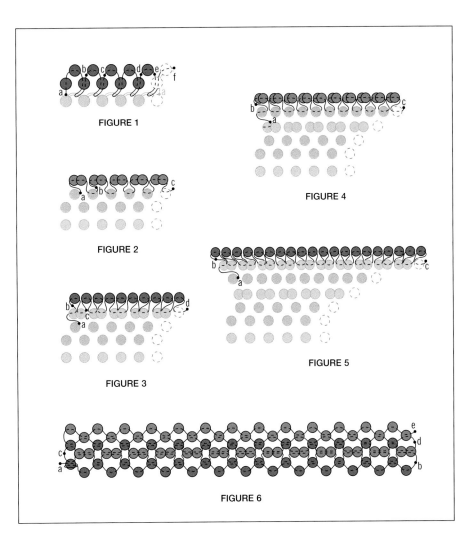

FIGURE 1

FIGURE 2

FIGURE 3

FIGURE 4

FIGURE 5

FIGURE 6

Ruffle

[**1**] Pick up three accent color (AC) seed beads. Go under the first thread bridge along the tube's edge and sew through the last bead to form a picot (figure 1, a–b).

[**2**] Pick up two ACs, go under the next thread bridge, and sew through the last bead added (b–c).

[**3**] Repeat step 2 twice (c–d).

[**4**] Pick up one AC (d–e), for a total of ten beads added.

[**5**] Sew down through the first AC in the row, and sew through the first two ACs (e–f).

[**6**] Pick up two MCs (peyote increase) and sew through the next AC on the picot row (figure 2, a–b).

[**7**] Repeat step 6 four more times, picking up a total of ten MCs (b–c).

[**8**] Step up through the first MC on the increase row (figure 3, a–b). Pick up one AC and sew through the next MC (b–c). Repeat nine times, picking up a total of ten ACs (c–d).

[**9**] Step up through the first AC on the AC row (figure 4, a–b). Pick up two MCs in every stitch across the row for a total of 20 MCs (b–c).

[**10**] Repeat step 8 (figure 5, a–b), picking up a total of 20 ACs (b–c).

[**11**] To secure your thread, sew through several beads, tie a half-hitch knot (Basics), repeat, and trim the excess thread.

[**12**] Repeat steps 1-11 on the other edge of the tube bead.

Toggle

[**1**] Pick up 26 ACs (figure 6, a–b). Pick up two MCs in every stitch across the row for a total of 26 beads (b–c).

[**2**] Stitch one row of peyote, picking up 13 ACs (c–d).

[**3**] Repeat step 2 twice, using MCs (d–e).

[**4**] Connect the short ends by sewing through several beads to form a twisted oval (see photo below). Secure the thread and trim the tails.

Stringing

[**1**] String a crimp bead and two MCs on the beading wire. Go through two outside MCs on the toggle, string two MCs, and go back through the crimp bead. Crimp the crimp bead and trim the excess wire.

[**2**] String 6½ in. (16cm) of spacers, ruffled tubes, and accent beads.

[**3**] String a crimp bead.

[**4**] String a 10mm bead on a head pin and make a wrapped loop (Basics).

EDITOR'S NOTE:
The directions make five ruffled tubes with two colors of beads. To make the bracelet more lively, select six seed bead colors with three sets of main colors and accent colors as shown on p. 168.

[**5**] String the loop next to the crimp, and go back through the crimp and the next few beads. Tighten the beads then crimp the crimp bead and trim the wire. ●

Contact Beth at bnshdl@msn.com or (248) 855-9358.

A touch of
red

by **Lynn Firth**

Enhance a
neckpiece with beautiful
flowers and leaves

I became fascinated by
beading when I came across an
issue of *Bead&Button* that had been
left in the needlecraft shop where I
worked in England. When Carol Wilcox
Wells' *Creative Beadweaving* arrived in the
U.K., all sorts of beading possibilities opened up
for me. Ten years later, I now have my own bead,
craft, and embroidery shop in a picturesque town in the
beautiful Dorset countryside. I'm not exactly sure where
the idea for this blooming neckpiece came from, but I
carried a clear vision of it in my head for a long time.
It was a triumphant moment when I held it up and knew
my vision had been realized.

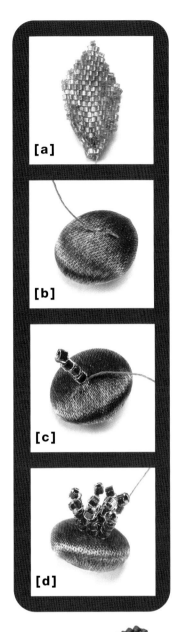

[a]

[b]

[c]

[d]

Small flower
Petal #1
[1] Start with a 4-yd. (3.7m) length of conditioned thread and string two cylinder beads to 6 in. (15cm) from the end. Sew back through the beads in the same direction, then position the beads side by side. Sew through the first bead again (figure 1, a–b, p. 172).

[2] Working in brick stitch (Basics, p. 10) pick up two beads and sew through the thread bridge from the previous row and up through the second bead (b–c).

[3] Pick up a bead and sew through the second bead from step 2 (c–d). Go down through the third bead under the thread bridge from the previous row and sew up through the third bead (d–e).

[4] Continue increasing one bead in each row for five more rows.

[5] After completing row 7, position the needle so it exits the second bead from the end (figure 2, a–b). Decrease row 8 to seven beads.

[6] Work rows 9–17 as follows:
Row 9: Eight beads
Row 10: Seven beads
Row 11: Eight beads
Rows 12–17: Decrease one bead on each row. Row 17 will have two beads.

[7] Sew through the edge beads (figure 3, a–b).

Petals #2–4
[1] The second petal is worked off the first. Pick up a bead, sew through the bead your thread is exiting, and continue through the new bead (b–c).

[2] Pick up two beads, sew under the thread bridge on the previous row, and through the second bead (c–d).

[3] Sew down through the edge bead on row 2 of the first petal, go under the thread bridge on the previous row, and sew back through the edge bead and the edge bead on the next row (d–e).

[4] Pick up one bead and sew under the thread bridge on the previous row and back through the new bead.

[5] Brick stitch two more beads on this row and end with the thread exiting the top of the last bead added.

[6] Work an increase on the next five rows as before, but anchor each row to the first petal as on rows 1–3.

[7] Repeat step 6 (rows 9–17) of the first petal.

[8] Repeat steps 1–7 to attach two more petals.

Petal #5
[1] Sew through the base bead on the first petal and back through the base bead on the last petal to make the first brick stitch row (figure 4, a–b). Sew through the base bead on the first petal again and go through the edge bead in the next row of the first petal (b–c).

[2] Pick up a bead, sew through the bridge from the previous row, and go back through the new bead (c–d).

[3] Sew through the edge bead in the second row of the last petal, go under the thread bridge from the previous row, and continue through the edge bead in this row and the next row (d–e).

[4] Continue in brick stitch for the next four rows, increasing one bead each row to connect the first petal to the fourth.

[5] Repeat the pattern in step 6 (rows 9–17) of the first petal.

MATERIALS
- Japanese cylinder beads
  3g for small flower
  7.5g for large flower
  3g for leaf
  3g for vine
  1g for stamen
- ⁷⁄₁₆ in. (11mm) diameter fabric-covered button
- conditioned Nymo D to match bead color
- beading needles, #12

Large flower
To make the large flower, increase the number of brick-stitch rows in step 4 of the first petal until the widest row is 15 beads across. Work six decrease rows alternating with six increase rows before you start the decrease rows for the other half of the petal.

Peyote leaf
[1] String a stop bead to the center of 1 yd (.9m) of thread. Go through the bead again in the same direction. Pick up 24 beads and sew back through the fourth bead from the needle (figure 5, a–b). Work a row of flat even-count peyote (Basics and b–c).

[2] Continue working in peyote until you reach point d.

[3] Pick up two beads and sew back through the last bead added on the previous row (d–e). Work peyote stitch to complete the row (e–f).

[4] Continue for two more rows (f–g).

[5] Decrease the bottom half of the leaf by working an odd-count peyote turn (Basics). Sew under the thread bridge next to the bead the thread is exiting. Then sew through the next two edge beads (g–h).

[6] Work the next four rows as shown (h–i).

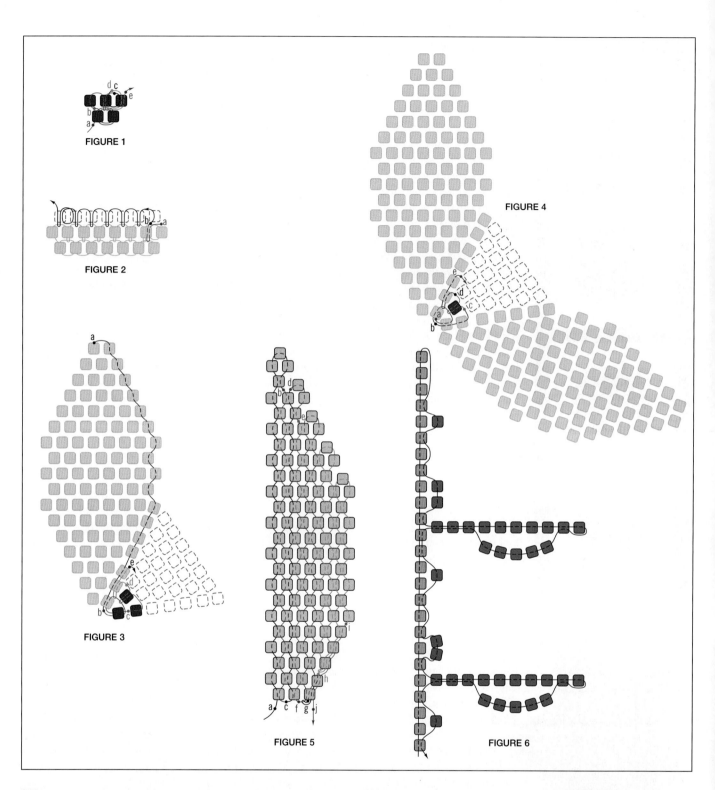

FIGURE 1

FIGURE 2

FIGURE 3

FIGURE 4

FIGURE 5

FIGURE 6

[7] Sew through the bottom edge of the leaf **(i–j)**, secure the thread with half-hitch knots (Basics), and trim.

[8] Remove the stop bead. Thread the needle on the tail and complete the other half of the leaf as a mirror image, starting with step 2.

[9] Sew the two bottom edge beads together to make a curve in the leaf **(photo a)**.

Stamens

[1] Secure 1 yd. of thread in the middle of the button **(photo b)**. Pick up four beads, skip the last bead, and sew back through three.

[2] Sew through the button fabric and exit next to the previous fringe **(photo c)**.

[3] Work in a spiral path from the middle out to the edges, adding as much fringe as desired **(photo d)**.

[4] Attach the stamen at the middle of the flower.

Vine

Secure 1 yd. of thread to a beaded rope or other surface to be embellished. Refer to figure 6 and the photo on p. 171 for suggested vine and leaf stitching. ●

Contact Lynn at Stitch n' Craft, Swans Yard Craft Centre, High Street, Shaftesbury, Dorset, SP7 8JQ, England, 44-1747852500, or lynnfirth@stitchncraft.co.uk.

Wonder Beads

2

Design and embellish hollow peyote beads

by **Sue Jackson and Wendy Hubick**

MATERIALS

one bead (37x24mm)
- 4g Japanese cylinder beads, each of two colors
- Nymo D
- beading needles, #12
- ¾-in. (1.9m) diameter mandrel or dowel

Hollow peyote Wonder Beads were originally featured in *Bead&Button* in April 2001. These exciting variations get their sturdiness from an additional layer of beads stitched onto the base. Once you master the basic design, the embellishment options are unlimited, as you can see in the bead samples below.

step*by*step

First, master the point-and-spike decrease by making a bead using the pattern shown on p. 175. This makes the beads shown on p. 173. Then use the blank template in figure 7 to create your own surface design. The three beads on this page have six-point ends. Change the pattern and number of rows to create beads of different sizes and shapes. To alter the bead's shape, change the number of points on each end. Three points make a triangular-shaped bead, and four points form a square.

Peyote tube

[1] Start with a comfortable length of thread and pick up 48 beads in a repeating pattern as follows: seven color A beads and one color B (**figure 1**, rows 1–2).
[2] Tie the beads into a ring around the mandrel with a square knot (Basics, p. 10), leaving an 8-in. (20cm) tail.
[3] Follow the pattern in **figure 1**, working in even-count, circular peyote (Basics). Once you have completed a few rounds, weave in the tail (no knots) and trim.
[4] Continuing in peyote stitch, make six points on each end of the tube as shown in **figure 2**. Stitch through the bead at the tip of each point twice to reinforce it.
[5] Remove the bead from the mandrel.

Embellishment

Add surface embellishment by working around the circumference of the peyote tube row by row.
[1] Embellish the tube by stitching the beads in the indicated ditches (spaces between beads) of the peyote tube (**figures 3** and **4**). You can sew in either direction, just make sure you work around the tube and that you pull each bead into place. You will hear a click when the bead is pulled snugly into a ditch.
[2] Weave the tails into the beadwork and trim.

Point-and-spike decrease

[1] Start a new thread and exit the bead at the tip of a point. Pick up three A beads and sew through the next point (**figure 5**). Repeat around the tube to make a ring of 24 beads, including the point beads.
[2] Retrace the thread path and pull the beads into a tight circle. Tie a half-hitch knot (Basics) to hold the beads in place. Sew through the next bead on the circle so

you are not working next to the knot.
[3] Work in circular peyote for a total of six rows, including the row created in step 2.
[4] For row 7, work a spike as shown in **figure 6** on every "up" bead for a total of 12 spikes. After you complete the last spike, sew through the first spike and exit the bead at the tip.
[5] Sew through the tip bead on each spike and pull them together to form a circle. Retrace the thread path and knot the beads in place.
[6] Embellish the ditches on the end rows as desired and secure the thread.
[7] Repeat steps 1–6 to finish the other end of the bead. ○

Sue and Wendy sell other Wonder Bead II designs. Visit hummingbeads.com to see more of their work or email them at info@ hummingbeads.com.

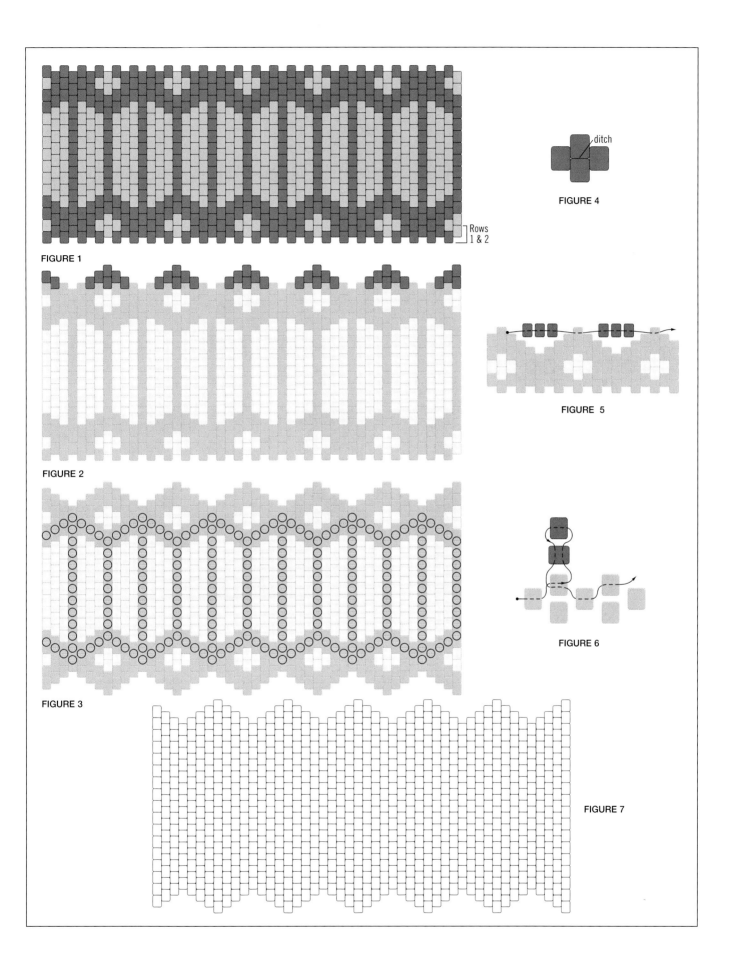

FIGURE 1

Rows 1 & 2

FIGURE 2

FIGURE 3

ditch

FIGURE 4

FIGURE 5

FIGURE 6

FIGURE 7

Window Dressing

MATERIALS

- seed beads, size 11º
  5g main color
  2g accent color
- **2** medium-weight focal beads
- variety of beads for embellishment (optional)
- Fireline, 6 lb. test
- beading needles, #12
- pair of earring findings (Rio Grande, riogrande.com)
- flatnose pliers

step*by*step

Peyote circle

[1] Thread a needle with 1 yd. (.9m) of Fireline. Pick up an even number of main color (MC) beads, enough to encircle your focal bead **(photo a)**. Tie them into a circle using a surgeon's knot (Basics, p. 10).

[2] Working in circular peyote (Basics), stitch around the ring. When you return to the first bead in the circle, step up to the next row (Basics and **photo b**). Stitch one more row.

[3] To work the fifth and final row, pick up two accent color (AC) beads as you make each stitch as in **photo c**.

Bail

[1] When you reach the last space in the outermost row, pick up six ACs to make the bail. Go through the first bead in the last row of the ring **(photo d)**. Do not cut the thread.

[2] Weave down through the beads and exit the first row directly underneath the bail **(photo e)**.

[a]

[b]

While I love long, fancy beaded earrings, I wanted to experiment with round or oval earrings with a focal bead in the middle. Inspired by Phyllis Dintenfass's lattice design in the October 2003 issue of *Bead&Button* magazine, I created these versatile seed bead earrings that allow you to add an element of surprise in the window. You won't be disappointed by all you can do with these little windows of opportunity.

by **Fran Morris Mandel**

[c]

[d]

[e]

[f]

Dangle
[1] Pick up two ACs, the focal bead, and one AC.
[2] Go back through the focal bead and pick up two ACs. Go through the adjacent bead in the first row and weave through several nearby beads **(photo f)**.
[3] Tie off your thread using half-hitch knots (Basics) and trim the tails.
[4] Open the loop on an earring finding, attach the bail, and close the loop.

[5] Make a second earring to match the first.

Variations
In the photo on p. 176, I used pearls as the focal beads and as the accent beads around the perimeter. Other options include small gemstones, nuggets, or stone chips for your focal bead.

In **photo g**, I used 5° hex beads around the perimeter. In **photo h**, the 6°s along the beaded edging add drama to the dangling green crystal. Focal beads that are drilled horizontally, like crystals and drops, are made to be the center of attention.

For a more fanciful look, try using bugle beads around the edge as in **photo i**. Pick up a bugle and 15°, then go through the bugle and the nearest bead in the row and continue around. If your bugles aren't large enough, add a 15° on either side to fill in the gaps. ●

Fran is from Lexington, Kentucky. Email her at franvmorris@yahoo.com.

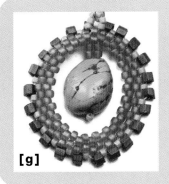
[g]

[h]

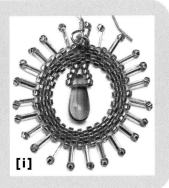
[i]

Ease into

Weave a sophisticated necklace
using peyote and pearls

by **Diane Dennis**

Elegance

During my down time between bead shows, when I have fun and play around with new ideas, I came up with the idea for this piece. The metallic beads work well with pearls and blend together in a feminine and elegant way. The Mabe pearl makes a sophisticated centerpiece, but this technique can easily be adjusted to other styles of cabochons, such as the face above.

step*by*step

Centerpiece

[1] Glue the pearl or cabochon to the center of the suede and let it dry completely. Trim the suede, leaving approximately ⅛ in. (3mm) around the outside.
[2] Start with a 2-yd (1.8m) length of thread and a #10 needle. Knot one end of the thread and sew through the suede next to the cabochon, working from front to back (photo a).
[3] Pick up two beads and sew back through the suede.
[4] Sew through the suede again, positioning the needle between the first two beads (photo b). Sew through the second bead.
[5] Repeat steps 3–4 and end with an even number of beads (photo c).
[6] Adjust the needle so the thread is doubled, securing the loose tail in the bead-work with half-hitch knots (Basics, p. 10). Trim the excess thread and sew through the next bead.
[7] Work in even-count circular peyote (Basics) for three rounds.
[8] On the fourth round, fold the beadwork up around the pearl (photo d).
[9] Work two to four more

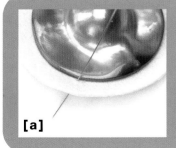

[a]

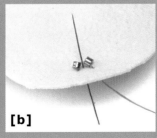

[b]

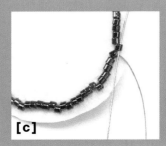

[c]

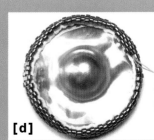

[d]

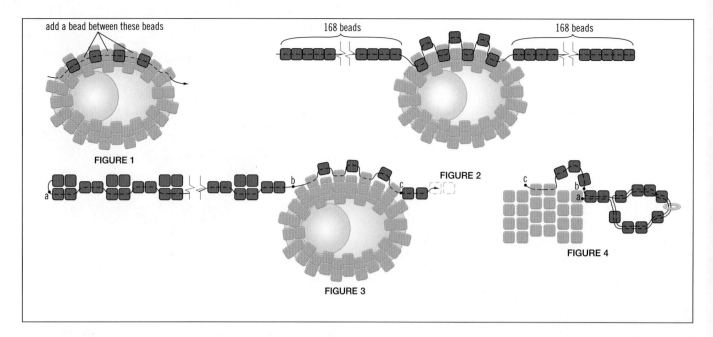

add a bead between these beads

FIGURE 1

168 beads   168 beads

FIGURE 2

a

b

FIGURE 3

c   b
a

FIGURE 4

rows, depending on the pearl's size, increasing the tension for each new row.

[10] Reinforce the last round with a second thread path.

[11] Sew through the beadwork and exit a bead on the second round at the approximate top center of the pearl. Peyote stitch four to six beads over the existing beads **(figure 1)**. These beads will connect the necklace to the pearl. Secure the thread and trim the tails.

Necklace

[1] Center the needle on a 6-yd (5.5m) length of conditioned thread and string a stop bead 6 in. (15cm) from the end.

[2] Pick up 168 beads. Sew through an end bead added in step 11 and work in peyote over the beads added in step 11 of the centerpiece (adding three new beads). Pick up 168 beads **(figure 2)**.

[3] Work back across the row in two-drop peyote (Basics) until you reach the pearl **(figure 3, a–b)**.

[4] Work across the up beads on the pearl in single-bead peyote **(b–c)**. Then work the second half of the necklace in two-drop peyote as before.

[5] Make an odd-count peyote turn (Basics) at the end of the row. Continue back in two-drop peyote, switching to single peyote across the top of the pearl. Work in two-drop peyote across the second half of the necklace. Repeat for four more rows.

[6] Decrease by working single peyote in every sixth stitch. Single peyote across the pearl and continue the decrease on the other half of the necklace.

[7] Repeat step 3.

[8] Repeat step 6.

[9] Secure the threads and trim the tails.

Closure

[1] Start with a 3-yd. (2.7m) length of thread and position the needle so it exits the end bead on the upper edge of the band. Pick up six beads, half the clasp, and four beads. Sew through the third through the tenth beads again to reinforce the clasp. Then sew through the first two beads strung **(figure 4, a–b)**.

[2] Pick up three beads and sew through the next two beads on the edge **(b–c)**. Continue adding beads around the edge of the necklace. When you reach the end, add the remaining clasp half and work the lower edge of the necklace as you did the upper edge.

[3] Secure the tails and trim.

Embellishment

[1] Start a 3-yd length of thread with a #13 needle. Secure the thread on the top edge of the necklace and exit any bead about a third of the distance from the pearl to the clasp.

[2] Pick up a bead, a pearl, and a bead. (Use more beads if you are using larger pearls.) Sew through a bead on the necklace close to where the needle is exiting. Embellish with pearls across the top of the necklace, starting sparsely but gradually clustering the pearls closer together as you approach the pearl. Continue embellishing around the curve of the pearl as desired.

[3] Secure the threads and trim the tails. ◉

Diane teaches at Star's Beads in Vienna, Virginia. Contact her at bdedennis@starpower.net.

EDITOR'S NOTE: If the necklace does not lay flat, gently press and stretch the decrease areas. Also, before adding the pearl embellishment, you can coat the back of the piece with clear acrylic to protect the finish on the metallic beads.

Pearls and crystals embellish a
two-tiered cabochon pendant

One on One

by **Diane Dennis**

Doubling up a gorgeous stone or pearl cabochon
with a striking agate slice provides beaders with the
perfect opportunity to show off. By keeping the palette
earthy and essentially monochromatic, this asymmetrical
design radiates a subdued, natural elegance, despite its
dramatic proportions.

step*by*step

Bezel the cabochons

[1] On a piece of Ultrasuede,
center the small cabochon
above the larger cabochon,
leaving about ¼ in. (6mm)
between the two.
[2] Apply a thin layer of glue to
the back of each piece and set
them in place. Let the glue dry.
[3] Thread a #10 needle on
a comfortable length of
conditioned thread, and knot
the end, leaving a 6-in. (15cm)
tail. Sew from the back to the
front of the Ultrasuede next
to the top cabochon.
[4] Pick up two cylinders and
sew through to the back of the
Ultrasuede. Sew back through
the Ultrasuede, positioning the
needle between the first two
beads **(figure, a–b)**. Sew through

the second cylinder **(b–c)**.
[5] Repeat step 4 around the
cabochon, ending with an even
number of beads. Sew through
the first bead in the round.
[6] Pick up a cylinder and work
even-count peyote stitch (Basics,
p. 10) for two or three rounds,
depending on the size of the cab.
[7] Change to a #13 needle and
work one to two rounds of
peyote using 15º seed beads.
[8] Repeat steps 4–7 with the
second cabochon.
[9] Connect the first rounds of
the bezels between the cabs by
working a row or two of peyote
stitch **(photo a, p. 182)**. Secure
the thread and trim.
[10] Lightly glue the back of
the pendant to a second piece
of Ultrasuede. Once the glue is
dry, carefully trim both pieces
of Ultrasuede as close to the

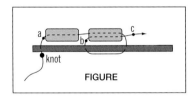

FIGURE

beaded bezel as possible. Don't
cut any threads.
[11] Start a comfortable length
of thread the same color as the
Ultrasuede, and whipstitch the
edges of the Ultrasuede close to
the bezel (Basics and **photo b**).
Secure the thread and trim.

Make the bail

[1] Secure a 1-yd. (.9m) length
of conditioned thread in the
bezel above the top cab. Exit
a bead on the second row, a
couple beads left of center.
[2] Using cylinders, work six to
ten beads (depending upon the

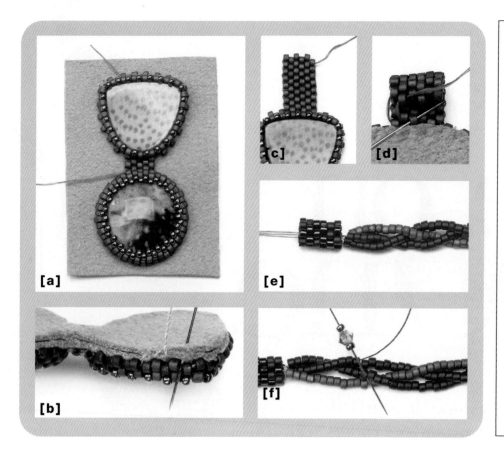

[a]

[c]

[d]

[e]

[f]

[b]

MATERIALS

necklace 19 in. (48cm)
pendant 3¼ x 2½ in. (8.3 x 6.4cm)

- 25 x 28mm cabochon
- 5–7cm agate slice or second cabochon
- 16 in. (41cm) strand 4–6mm pearls
- **15–20** 4mm bicone crystals or Czech glass beads (optional)
- 25g Japanese cylinder beads
- 8g seed beads, size 15º
- clasp or button with a shank
- **2** micro crimp beads
- **2** crimp beads
- flexible beading wire, .010
- Ultrasuede
- Nymo D, one color to match seed beads and one to match Ultrasuede, conditioned with beeswax
- beading needles, #10 and #13
- E-6000 adhesive
- micro and regular crimping pliers

size of your cabochon) in flat, even-count peyote for 16 rows **(photo c)**.
[3] Fold the strip of peyote so the last row is aligned with the first row of the bezel and stitch them together **(photo d)**. Secure the thread and trim.

Assemble the necklace

[1] Working with 1 yd. of conditioned thread, pick up six cylinders and work in flat, even-count peyote for six rows.
[2] Fold the peyote strip so the first and last row of beads are aligned. Zip up the two ends (Basics) to form a tube. Secure the threads.
[3] Make a second peyote bead and set them both aside.
[4] Cut three 24-in. (61cm) lengths of beading wire. String 12 in. (30cm) of cylinders on two of the wires and 12 in. of 15ºs or cylinders on the third wire. Center the beads.
[5] Tape the end of each strand next to the last bead stung. Bring the untaped end of all three wires together and string a micro crimp bead over the wires and against the beads. Crimp the crimp bead (Basics).

[6] Tape the crimped end to your work area; braid the three strands.
[7] Remove the tape from the unfinished ends, string a micro crimp over the three wires, and crimp it.
[8] Center the pendant on the braid. Then string a peyote bead over each crimp bead **(photo e)**.
[9] Working over all three wires, string cylinders on each end of the necklace until you reach the desired length minus the length of the clasp. My 19 in. (48cm) necklace has 4 in. (10cm) of cylinders on each side.
[10] Tape one of the wire ends. On the other end, string a crimp bead, a clasp half or button, and seven to ten cylinders. Bring the wires back through the crimp bead, tighten the wires, and crimp the crimp bead. Trim the wires close to the crimp.
[11] Repeat step 10 at the other end of the necklace, using the remaining clasp half. If you are using a button as your clasp, string enough cylinders after the crimp to fit around the button.

Add embellishments

[1] Working with a #13 needle, secure a comfortable length of conditioned thread in the peyote bead on the left side of the necklace. Then sew through a few cylinders on the braided portion of the necklace.
[2] Pick up one or two 15ºs, a crystal or pearl, and the same number of 15ºs. Sew through a bead on the next strand of the braid **(photo f)**.
[3] Sew through the next four to six beads and repeat step 2.
[4] Continue randomly adding pearls, crystals, and 15ºs along the top surface of the braid, around the top and right sides of the pearl, and down the left side of the agate.
[5] Once you reach the bottom of the agate, turn and work a second pass in the opposite direction. Repeat as desired. I make four passes, stitching into only about 1 in. (2.5cm) of braid above the pendant on the third and fourth pass. ●

Contact Diane Dennis via email at bdedennis@starpower.net.

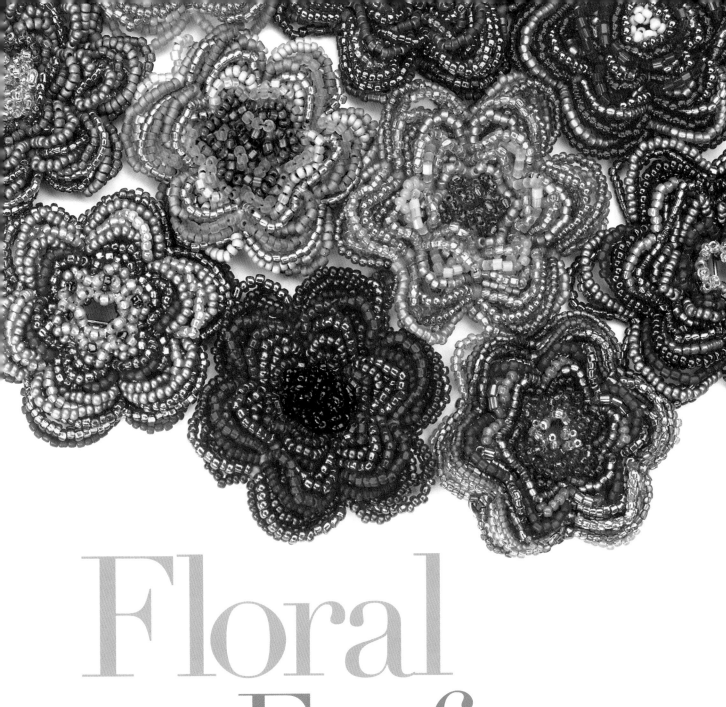

Floral
Fanfare

Weave colorful
netted posies

by **Allie Thompson**

Stylishly retro, fast, and fun, these flower brooches are a
breeze to make. Pin them on hats, scarves, jackets, shoes,
and shirts singly or in clusters. When choosing beads,
almost anything goes. Select a color, then find beads of
different shades, cuts, and finishes.

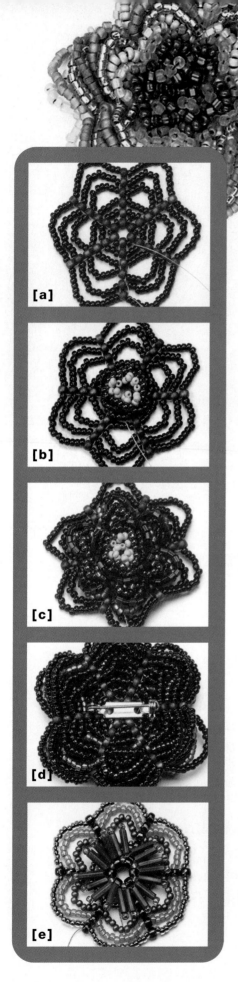

[a]

[b]

[c]

[d]

[e]

step*by*step

Flower base

[**1**] Thread your needle with a yard (.9m) of Silamide. If you are using Nymo, work with a yard of doubled thread. (To condition the Nymo, see Basics, p. 10).

[**2**] Stitch the flower's base as follows:

Round 1: String an 8º and an 11º six times, leaving a 6-in. (15cm) tail (**figure 1, a–b**). Sew through all the beads plus the first 8º again (**b–c**) to form a circle.

Round 2: Pick up one 8º (**c–d**), go through the previous 8º, then go through the new 8º again (**d–e**). Pick up three 11ºs and one 8º (**e–f**). Go through the next 8º on round 1 and back through the last 8º on round 2 (**f–g**). Repeat until you have picked up a total of 24 beads and are back at **point d**.

Rounds 3–6: Work as in round 2, but pick up five 11ºs between the 8ºs isn round 3, nine 11ºs in round 4, 12 11ºs in round 5, and 15 11ºs in round 6 (**figure 1** and **photo a**).

Petals

[**1**] Weave through the beads to reach round 1 on the base. Exit an 8º.

[**2**] Add three layers of beads on top of each base round. Use different shades of 11ºs for each petal layer.

Round 1: Pick up three 11ºs, then go through the next 8º on the base round (**figure 2, a–b**). Repeat around to **point a**. Make a second layer, passing through the same 8ºs but picking up four 11ºs. Repeat for a third layer, but pick up five 11ºs (**figure 2** and **photo b**).

Round 2: Go through an 8º on the next base round (**figure 3, a–b**). Pick up five 11ºs, then go through the 8º on the base round (**b–c**). Repeat around to **point b**. Make the second layer with six 11ºs between 8ºs. Make the third layer with seven 11ºs between 8ºs (**figure 3**).

Round 3: Go through an 8º on the next base round. Pick up eight 11ºs for the first layer, nine 11ºs for the second, and ten 11ºs for the third (**photo c**).

MATERIALS

flower brooch 2 x 2 in. (5 x 5cm)

- 1g seed beads, size 11º, 5–9 different shades
- 1g Japanese seed beads, size 8º to match 11ºs
- Silamide or Nymo D conditioned with beeswax or Thread Heaven
- beading needles, #12
- safety pin or pinback

Round 4: Work as in the previous rounds, but pick up 11 11ºs, 12 11ºs, then 13 11ºs for each layer.
Round 5: Repeat, but pick up 14 11ºs, 15 11ºs, then 16 11ºs.
Round 6: Repeat, but pick up 17 11ºs, 18 11ºs, then 19 11ºs.

Pin attachments

I like the durability of a safety pin, but feel free to opt for a pinback. Use the thread tails to sew the pin onto the back of the flower (photo d). Go through the 8ºs and thread bridges, but do not sew through the 11ºs. Weave in the tails, knot them with half-hitches (Basics), then trim the excess thread. ●

Contact Allie at (925) 672-3114,
creativecaravan@earthlink.net.

EDITOR'S NOTE:
For a center variation, use bugles for the first petal layer (photo e). Pick up a bugle and 11º seed bead. Skip the seed, sew through the bugle again, then go through a base bead. Repeat around. After all the petal layers are added, the bugles stand up, resembling stamens.

FIGURE 1

FIGURE 2

FIGURE 3

Snap it up

Finish a netted cuff with a grand flourish

Turn the tables on the commonplace task of hiding the closure. Showcase it! This vibrant cuff does just that with an embellished, interlocking clasp. The band can be netted using beads in a mix of sizes, shapes, and colors, and is framed with a picot edging. With drama to spare, it will make any day a special occasion.

by **Marilyn K. Lowe**

stepbystep

Mesh band

Use large-hole beads for the first and last two rows to accommodate the extra thread needed to attach the clasp.

[1] Thread a needle with 4 yd. (3.7m) of waxed Nymo and use the thread doubled. Pick up a stop bead, slide it 18 in. (46cm) from the tail, and go through it again in the same direction once or twice to keep it in place.

Row 1: Pick up one A bead, three Bs, 15 As, three Bs, and four As. Turn, go through the second A from the needle, and pull tight (figure 1, a–b).

Row 2: Pick up two As and one B. Skip three beads on the previous row and go through the fourth bead (b–c). Pick up three Bs, skip three beads on the

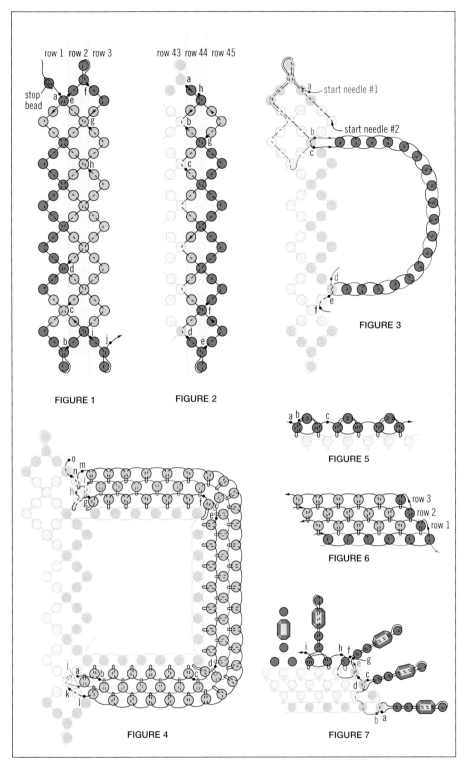

FIGURE 1

FIGURE 2

FIGURE 3

FIGURE 5

FIGURE 6

FIGURE 4

FIGURE 7

a B, an A, and a B and go through the center bead on the next net **(b–c)**. Repeat four times **(c–d)**. Pick up three As, turn, go through the second A from the needle, and pull tight **(d–e)**.

Row 45: Pick up three As and go through the center bead on the first net **(e–f)**. Repeat four times **(f–g)**. Pick up three Bs and go through the center bead of the end net **(g–h)**.

[2] Retrace the thread path through the last row, making several half-hitch knots (Basics, p. 10) between beads. Glue the knots. When dry, go through the next two beads. Trim the tails.

Clasp – loop end

[1] Remove the stop bead and thread both tails through one needle. Weave through several nets on the end rows **(figure 3, a–b)**, exiting at **point b**.

[2] Thread a second needle with 3 yd. (2.7m) of Nymo, wax it, and use it doubled. Secure the thread in the netting and exit at **point c**. The needles now exit from opposite ends of the same bead.

[3] Make a cross-needle-weave ladder to start the clasp. On one needle, pick up an A. Cross through the A with the other needle. Pull tight. Add 17 more As to the base. With both needles, cross through the center bead on the edge row's fifth net **(b–d, c–e)**. Push the base beads tightly against each other and curve the beads into an arc.

[4] Tie a half-hitch knot with the needle at **point d**. Do not cut the thread. With the other needle, go through the next bead on the row **(e–f)**. Pull tight.

[5] Using the same needle (with the longer thread), change to brick stitch (Basics). Pick up a B, go under the thread bridge between the end bead of the base and the connecting bead on the netting. Sew back through the B **(figure 4, a–b)**. Pull tight.

[6] Stitch five more beads up the base **(b–c)**, then increase by adding a second B to the same thread bridge **(c–d)**.

[7] Continue in brick stitch for seven more beads **(d–e)**, then increase as in step 6 **(e–f)**. Stitch six more beads to the base **(f–g)**.

[8] To connect to the netting, go through the third B on the edge row, under the thread bridge, and back through the B **(g–h)**.

previous row, and go through the fourth bead **(c–d)**. Repeat four times **(d–e)**. Pick up three As, turn, go through the second A from the needle, and pull tight **(e–f)**.

Row 3: Pick up two As and one B and go through the center bead of the first three-bead net **(f–g)**. Pick up three Bs and go through the center bead on the next net **(g–h)**. Repeat four times **(h–i)**.

Pick up three As, turn, go through the second bead from the needle, and pull tight **(i–j)**.

Rows 4–43: Repeat row 3. (Increase or decrease the number of rows to fit your wrist. Keep in mind that the clasp adds ¾ in./2cm to the length.)

Row 44: Pick up two As and one B and go through the center bead of the first net as before **(figure 2, a–b)**. Pick up

[9] To turn, go through the next B on
the netting, under the last thread bridge
on the previous row, and back through
the B (h–i). Continue in brick stitch
using Bs, increasing over the increases
in the previous row (i–j).

[10] Go through the center B on the
netting, under the thread bridge, and
back through the B (j–k).

[11] Go through the end B on the
netting (k–l). Work a third row of brick
stitch (l–m), with two increases over the
previous increases.

[12] Go through the first B on the
netting, under the thread bridge, and
back through the B (m–n). Go through
the adjacent A (n–o).

[13] Work the next brick-stitch row
with a picot edge using A beads. Work
one stitch (**figure 5, a–b**), then pick up
two beads. Go through all three beads
again, under the next thread bridge, and
back through the third bead (**b–c**).
Repeat around the clasp. If you run out
of thread, use the thread that you left
uncut in step 4. Secure the threads.

Clasp – connecting end

[1] Stitch the connecting end of the
clasp the same as the loop end with
these changes: Make the cross-needle
base 25 beads long, but don't attach the

end bead to the bracelet. Set one needle
aside. Work three rows of brick stitch
with B, as before, but simply turn at the
unattached end to form a tapered edge
as shown in **figure 6**. Use an A as the
edge bead at the unattached end of each
row. Secure the thread.

[2] Using the needle and thread set
aside in step 1, start the decorative
fringe. Pick up two As, a 4mm bead,
and an A. Turn, skip the last A, and go
through the 4mm bead and two As.
Pull tight. Go through the end base
bead, so the thread is exiting in the
same direction as before (**figure 7, a–b**).

[3] Go through the next base bead, the
second bead in the first brick stitch row,
and the end bead of the second brick
stitch row (**b–c**). Make a second four-
bead fringe, go through the base bead
(**c–d**), and continue through the first
bead on the third brick stitch row (**d–e**).

[4] Pick up an A and work one brick
stitch between the first and second
beads in the third row (**e–f**). This is the
first bead of the fourth row. Make
another four-bead fringe (**f–g**). Go down
through the first bead on the third row,
up through the second bead on that
row, and through the first bead of the
fourth row (**g–h**).

[5] Work two A beads in brick stitch.
Make another four-bead fringe, go
down through the first of these brick
stitch beads and up through the second
(**h–i**). Repeat, adding a total of nine
four-bead fringes.

[6] Continue in brick stitch as in step 5,
but make the next two fringes with one
A, a 4mm bead, and one A.

[7] Complete this row with the same
picots as in the loop end of the clasp
(**figure 5**).

[8] Sew a snap half onto the beads near
the unattached end (**figure 8**). Hide the
thread in the beads so nothing shows on
the other side. Secure the thread.

[9] Turn the bracelet over so the snap
faces down and overlaps the edge of the
netting (**figure 9**). Sew the other snap
half to the netting where it meets the
top snap.

[10] Put the bracelet on your wrist
with the snap on the bracelet facing
out and toward your hand. Connect
the clasp and snap it closed. Adjust
the bracelet so the clasp pieces fit.
Note where the clasp halves cross,

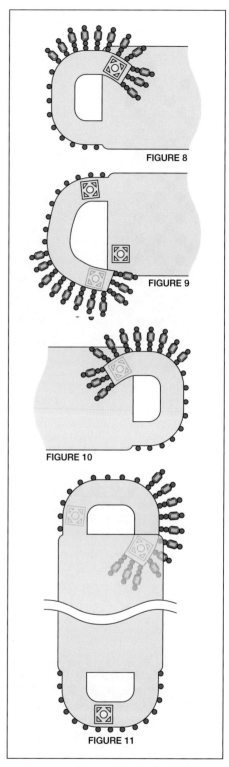

FIGURE 8

FIGURE 9

FIGURE 10

FIGURE 11

remove the bracelet, and sew both
halves of the second snap in place
(**figures 10 and 11**). ☉

*Marilyn K. Lowe can be reached at
emkaylo@optonline.net.*

Floral Finish

This lariat can be adapted for a variety of styles and is a great way to learn tubular netting and two- and three-drop peyote. You can have a lot of fun experimenting with a wide variety of fringe possibilities and bead combinations.

A netted lariat features tassels blooming with colorful accents

by **Leslee Frumin**

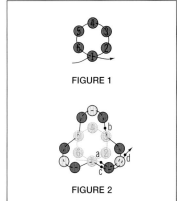

[a]

FIGURE 1

FIGURE 2

step*by*step

Netted rope

[1] Using 1 yd. (.9m) of Fireline, pick up six main color (MC) 11º seed beads. Leaving a 12-in. (30cm) tail, bring the beads into a circle and tie a surgeon's knot (Basics, p. 10). Go through the

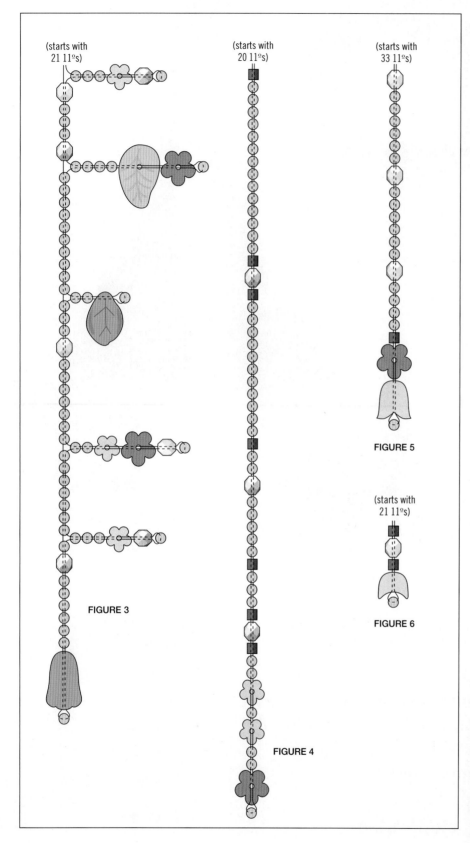

(starts with 21 11ºs)

(starts with 20 11ºs)

(starts with 33 11ºs)

FIGURE 3

FIGURE 4

FIGURE 5

(starts with 21 11ºs)

FIGURE 6

first bead in the circle **(figure 1)**.

[2] Pick up an MC, an accent color (AC), and an MC. Skip bead 2 and go through bead 3 **(figure 2, a–b)**. Repeat around the circle, skipping beads 4 and 6, and exit bead 1 **(b–c)**. Step up through the MC and AC in row 2 **(c–d)**.

[3] Pick up an MC, an AC, and an MC and go through the next AC on the previous row. Continue this pattern for 47 in. (1.2m). Keep the tension even. To end the thread, make several half-hitch knots (Basics) between beads. Don't cut the thread.

Peyote bell

[1] Using a comfortable length of Fireline, pick up 14 triangle beads. Pull the beads into a circle and check to see that it fits snugly over the tube. Adjust as necessary, making sure there are an even number of triangles in the circle. Go through the first bead in the circle. Don't cut or knot the thread, so you can adjust the circumference later when you put it on the rope.

[2] Working in circular peyote (Basics), stitch three rows using triangles.

[3] After stepping up to start the fourth row, use two MCs in place of each triangle. Continue in two-drop peyote for eight rows, treating each pair of 11ºs as one bead when stepping up. An armature, such as a small cork **(photo a)**, can help hold the bell shape.

[4] After the eighth row, switch to a combination of alternating two- and three-drop peyote (three 11ºs instead

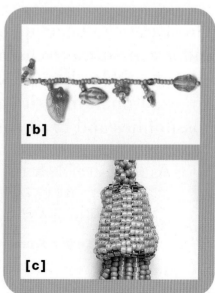

[b]

[c]

of two) to widen the bell. You want to create a flare without causing a bulge.

[5] When the bell is the desired length, switch to triangle beads for the final two rows. Make several half-hitch knots between beads. Don't cut the thread. Make the second bell identical to the first.

Fringe

Use a comfortable length of thread such as conditioned Nymo or Silamide. Stitch into several beads near one end of the netted tube and secure the thread. Exit one of the end beads in the tube and start the fringe. Below are two tassel variations. The 11ºs can be various colors or even a matte/shiny combination of the same color.

Branched fringe (p. 189)

[1] Pick up the following as shown in **photo b** and **figure 3**: 21 11ºs, a round faceted fire-polished bead, three 11ºs, a round, 13 11ºs, a round, 15 11ºs, a round, six 11ºs, a pressed-glass flower, and an 11º.

[2] Skip the last bead and go back through the flower, six 11ºs, the round, and one 11º.

[3] Pick up three 11ºs, a small flower, a round, and an 11º.

[4] Skip the last 11º and go back through to the main fringe.

[5] Continue up the fringe, adding beads as in **figure 3**. Use a variety of

pressed-glass accent beads.

[6] When you get back to the top, stitch into several beads in the tube, exit a bead at the end of the tube, and start another fringe. Continue adding fringe to the desired fullness. When finished, stitch into the tube, secure the thread, and trim the tail. Attach the peyote bells, as described in Connections, before fringing the other end of the tube.

Tiered fringe (at right)

[1] Start in the center with the longest fringes and pick up the following as in **figure 4**: 20 11ºs, a triangle, 14 11ºs, a triangle, a round, a triangle, 11 11ºs, a triangle, two 11ºs, a round, five 11ºs, a triangle, three 11ºs, a triangle, a round, a triangle, two 11ºs, a small flower, an 11º, a small flower, two 11ºs, a large flower and an 11º.

[2] Skip the last bead and go back up through all the fringe beads and into the netted tube. Stitch through several beads and exit next to the first fringe. Repeat for total of seven long fringes.

[3] For the medium fringe: 33 11ºs, a round, six 11ºs, a round, six 11ºs, a round, four 11ºs, a triangle, a small flower, a tulip, and 11º **(figure 5)**. Repeat step 2 and make a total of 11 medium fringes around the long fringe.

[4] For the short fringe: 21 11ºs, a triangle, a round, a triangle, a tulip, and an 11º **(figure 6)**. Repeat step 2 and

make a total of 11 short fringes around the medium fringe.

[5] When the fringe is complete, stitch into the tube and end the thread as before. Attach the peyote bells, as described below, before fringing the other end of the tube.

Connections

[1] Slide a peyote bell (flared end first) down the tube until it caps the fringe **(photo c)**.

[2] Thread a needle on the tail from the bell and weave through the beads until you exit the bell's top. Sew into several beads in the tube until the bell is secured. End the thread as before and trim the tail.

[3] Slide the other bell (small end first) to the middle of the netted tube.

[4] Create an identical tassel on the other end of the tube.

[5] Slide the second bell over the top of the fringe. Before securing, make sure the second bell covers the same amount of fringe as the first so the tassels are even. Repeat step 2 to secure the bell. ◉

Leslee is from San Juan Capistrano, California. Reach her via email at leslee@lesleefrumin.com, by phone at 949-456-0718, or on the Web, lesleefrumin.com.

MATERIALS

lariat 55 in. (1.4m) including fringe

netted rope and peyote bells
- seed beads, size 11º
  60g main color
  50g accent color
- 2g triangle beads, size 10º or 11º
- Fireline 6 lb. test
- beading needles, #12
- small cork (optional)
- 6 in. (15cm) 20-gauge wire for cork (optional)

both tassels
- Nymo B or Silamide
- beeswax if using Nymo
- beading needles, #12
- G-S Hypo Cement

branched fringe
- 2g triangle beads, size 10º or 11º
- **50** (approx.) 3mm or 4mm round, faceted, fire-polished beads
- **45** 5mm flowers (front-to-back hole)
- **20** 7mm flowers (front-to-back hole)
- **10** 10mm flowers (top-to-bottom hole)
- **10** 12mm leaves (side-to-side hole)
- **7** 15mm leaves (front-to-back hole)

tiered fringe
- **65** (approx.) 3mm or 4mm round, faceted, fire-polished beads
- **22** 5mm tulips (top-to-bottom hole)
- **25** 5mm flowers (front-to-back hole)
- **7** 10mm flowers (top-to-bottom hole)

Create a colorful spiral necklace
with netting and seed beads

Primary Twist

by **Beth Stone**

After I got my hands on the elusive Russian beading book, *Art of Bead Weaving* by Maya Anufrieva, I went on a beading bender, eagerly trying out new stitches. This happy outcome takes its fabulous twirl from a stitch called "Russian spiral weave," a netting variant. But the streamlined style and vibrant colors are sheer American exuberance brought to bear on this Old-World technique.

step*by*step

Netted tube

[1] Start a 3-yd (2.7m) length of thread and pick up two 11º seed beads and one 8º three times, for a total of nine beads.
[2] Leaving a 1-yd. (.9m) tail, sew through all the beads again in the same direction to form a ring. Exit the first 11º (**figure 1, a–b**).
[3] Pick up an 8º and two 11ºs. Sew through the 11º after the next 8º on the ring (**figure 2, a–b**). Repeat around the ring (**b–c**). Step up through the first 8º and 11º (**c–d**).
[4] Repeat step 3 until you reach the desired length. For the necklace at right, I changed bead colors every 1½ in. (3.8cm). For the necklace on p. 192, I alternated 1½ in. of black and white seed beads with ¼ in. (6mm) of various colors.
[5] To close up the tube, stitch the last round, picking up an 8º instead of an 8º and two 11ºs. Sew through the three 8ºs just added a few times and cinch the tube closed (**photo a**). Secure the working thread by tying half-hitch knots (Basics, p. 10) between a few beads. Don't trim the thread. Set aside.

Clasp

[1] Thread a needle on the long tail and pick up 24 11ºs. Sew into a bead on the opposite side of the netted tube to form a ring (**photo b** and **figure 3, a–b**).
[2] Sew around the tube, following the thread path of the netting, and exit the bead below **point a** (**b–c**). Work one round of peyote over the new beads (**c–d**). Sew through the tube as before (**d–e**). Increase to two-drop peyote in the fourth round.
[3] Continue alternating a row of single bead peyote with a row of two-drop until the ring is the desired size. I usually work six to eight rounds. Secure the thread in the beadwork and trim.
[4] To make the toggle end of the clasp, start a 1-yd. length of thread. Pick up 20 11ºs and work flat, even-count peyote (Basics) for 12 rows.
[5] Fold the peyote strip so the first and last row of beads are aligned. Zip up (Basics) the two ends to form a tube.
[6] Flatten the tube and stitch an 11º between the up beads along both sides of the tube (**photo c**). Secure the threads.
[7] Working with the thread at the cinched end of the tube, pick up eight 11ºs. I like to use two colors.
[8] Sew through a bead or two at the center of the toggle bar. Pick up an 11º, skip the last 11º strung in the previous step, and sew through the remaining 11ºs (**photo d**).
[9] Sew through two 8ºs on the end of the tube and retrace the thread path from the 11ºs to the toggle bar.
[10] Reinforce the thread path a few more times, sewing through different 8º pairs on the end of the tube each time. Secure the thread and trim. ◉

Contact Beth Stone at (248) 855-9358 or bnshdl@msn.com.

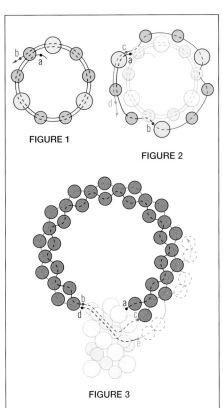

FIGURE 1

FIGURE 2

FIGURE 3

MATERIALS
necklace 18 in. (46cm)
- seed beads
  15g size 8º, two to six colors
  15g size 11º, two to six colors
- Nymo D conditioned with beeswax, or Fireline 8 lb. test
- beading needles, #12

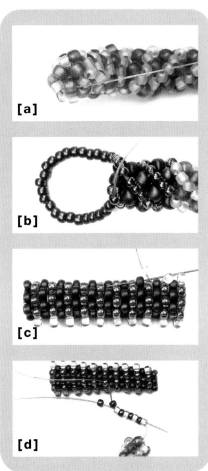

[a]

[b]

[c]

[d]

EDITOR'S NOTE: The open end of the netted tube will flatten as you weave through it to stitch the clasp's loop end.

Apple
Blossoms

Weave an embellished bracelet using
multiple techniques

by **Jacquelyn Scieszka**

One stitch blends seamlessly into the next in this
flower-embellished cuff. Start with peyote, then
work your way through Ndebele herringbone,
whipstitch, and a picot edging. And that's just the
base! Stitch oval pearls into flowers and attach
them to the base to complete this intricate piece.

step*by*step

Bracelet base

[1] Using a #12 needle on a
comfortable length of thread,
pick up 24 color A 11º seed
beads **(figure 1, a–b)** and
work in flat, two-drop
peyote (Basics, p. 10 and
b–c) for 153 rows. The last
five rows are the flap for
the snap closure, so the
bracelet ends will overlap
by five rows. If you add
length, you must end with
an odd number of rows.

FIGURE 1

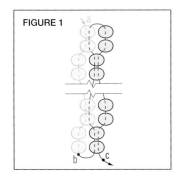

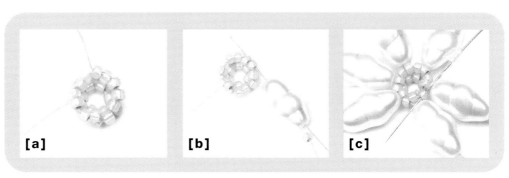

[a] [b] [c]

[2] Exit an end bead on either long edge of the band. Work along the edge in flat Ndebele herringbone stitch (Basics) in color B 11ºs for four rows **(figure 2, a–b)**, leaving the last five rows unedged, as shown on p. 196.

[3] Weave back through the last row of herringbone, looping back through beads as shown **(b–c)**, to create a thread bridge between each bead.

[4] Pick up a color C 11º, and sew under the thread bridge between the last two herringbone-stitched beads added in the last step **(c–d)**. Continue down the row, adding a bead to

each bridge **(d–e)**.

[5] Pick up a C 11º and sew back through the last two beads added **(e–f)**. Pickup another C 11º and go through the next two beads in the previous row. Repeat to the end of the row. **(f–g)**. Pick up a C 11º at the end of the row.

[6] Pick up two C 11ºs. Sew through the next bead **(g–h)**. Repeat this step to complete the row **(h–i)**.

[7] Add a picot along the edge of the bracelet by sewing back through the last bead added in the previous step **(point j)**. Pick up three color D 15ºs and sew through the last two beads added in the previous step **(j–k)**. Repeat

between every two beads on the previous row **(k–l)**.

[8] Repeat steps 1–7 along the other long edge, leaving the same five rows unedged.

Flowers

You can embellish the base with either of these flowers or both. Adjust the materials list as needed. The bracelets use five flowers each.

Seed bead and pearl flower (yellow, p. 196)

[1] Start a new thread and pick up six A 11ºs. Tie them into a circle with a surgeon's knot (Basics), leaving a 10-in. (25cm) tail.

[2] Sew through the bead next to the knot. Work in

circular peyote (Basics) for a total of four rounds **(photo a and figure 3, a–b)**. Tighten the beads to pull them into a cup shape, then exit a bead on the third round **(point c)**.

[3] Pick up a snail pearl and an A 11º. Sew back through the pearl and into the next bead on round 4 **(photo b and c–d)**. Repeat five more times for a total of six petals. Sew through to a bead on the fourth round between the petals.

[4] Add fringe between each bead in the third and fourth rounds by picking up three D 15ºs, an E 15º, D 15º, and an E 15º. Sew back through the first three D 15ºs and into the next bead in the third

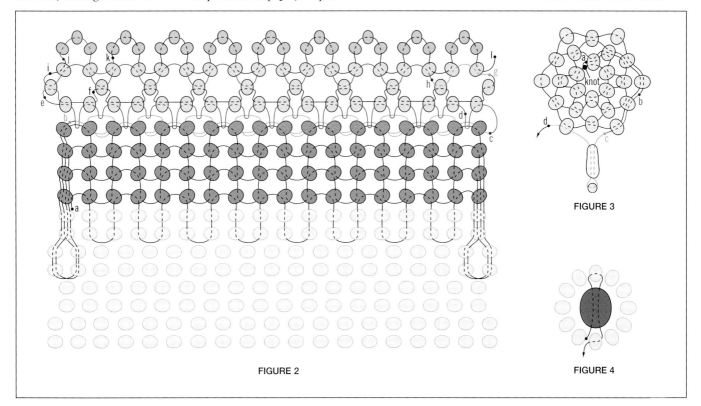

FIGURE 2

FIGURE 3

FIGURE 4

[d]

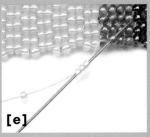

[e]

[f]

round (photo c). Repeat, making a total of 12 fringes between the beads in the third and fourth rounds.

[5] Exit one of the beads in the last round. Pick up a 4mm pearl, sew through the opposite bead in the last round, and sew back through the 4mm bead (figure 4). Secure the tail in the last peyote round.

Pearl and fire-polished bead flower (green and pink, p. 194)

[1] Repeat steps 1–3 of the seed bead flower.

[2] Complete two more rounds of circular peyote above the petals.

[3] Exit a bead in the fifth round of peyote and pick up a 3mm fire-polished bead and a matching 15°. Sew back through the 3mm and the next 11° in the fifth round. Repeat for a total of six 3mm beads.

[4] Exit a bead in the sixth round, pick up a 3mm bead, and sew through the next bead in the sixth round.

[5] Repeat step 4 of the first flower, but substitute the 4mm round for the pearl.

Assembly

[1] Lay the bracelet flat and determine the placement of the five flowers.

[2] Secure a new thread in a flower, exiting the first round of peyote. Position the flower on the base and sew through a few base beads, then back into the first round of peyote. Repeat a few stitches to secure the flower to the base, then sew through one of the petals and exit the 11°.

[3] Pick up an A 11° and sew through a base bead and back through the 11° and the pearl (photo d). Repeat to secure the remaining petals to the base.

[4] Repeat to attach the remaining flowers.

Fringe

Secure a new thread in the base and exit the first bead on the first row of herringbone. Pick up three A 15°s and a B 15°. Sew back through the three A 15°s and sew through the next bead in the vertical stack of herringbone (photo e). Repeat, adding fringe between each bead on all the herringbone rows.

Embellishment (optional)

Secure a new thread in the base and exit a bottom row edge C 11°. Pick up a seed pearl and sew through the next two C 11°s (photo f).

Continue adding seed pearls to this edge, then repeat on other edge.

Closure

Sew the male half of three snaps to the five unedged peyote rows, positioning them evenly across the top of the base. Sew the female half of the snaps to the underside of the base at the opposite end, so they line up with the male half of the snaps. ●

Contact Jacquelyn at 1042 Puritan, Birmingham, Michigan, 48009 or e-mail her at jmscieszka@aol.com.

MATERIALS

bracelet base 7 in. (18cm)
- Japanese seed beads
  30g color A, size 11°
  20g color B, size 11°
  15g color C, size 11°
  25g color D, size 15°
  10g color A, size 15°
  1g 4–8 accent colors, size 15°
  15g color C, size 15° (optional)
- 16-in. (41cm) strand seed pearls (optional)
- 3 8mm nylon snaps
- Silamide or Nymo D conditioned with beeswax
- beading needles, #12

first flower
- 36 13 x 7mm oval baroque snail pearls (landofodds.com)

- Japanese seed beads
  7.5g color D, size 15°
  3.5g color E, size 15°
  1g color A, size 11°
- 6 4mm pearls
- Fireline 6 lb. test
- beading needles, #12 or smaller

second flower (optional)
- 30 13 x 7mm oval baroque snail pearls
- 30 3mm fire-polished beads
- 30 Japanese seed beads, size 15° to match fire-polished beads
- 25 2–3mm rondelles
- 5 4mm round beads
- Fireline 6 lb. test
- beading needles, #15–13

EDITOR'S NOTE: Since you sew through the base rows so many times, use alternate paths when working the fringe and embellishment rows.

Beaded Lockets

Transform
your favorite
photos into
tiny treasures
using three easy
techniques

by **Carol Cypher**

My lockets start with
a basic embroidery
stitch. From there,
work your way into
brick stitch, then use
Ndebele herringbone
to make a great base
for embellishing.
You can stop here
and add a magnet
or pin finding to the
back, or try stitching
a cover in brick stitch
to make a locket
anyone will cherish.

step*by*step

Picture frame

[1] Place the adhesive side of the Page Pebble over the desired area of the photo. Trim the photo flush with the edge of the plastic dome. Trace the outline of the outer edge onto a piece of Stiff Stuff and trim it one bead's width away from the line. Trim the Ultrasuede the same size as the plastic dome **(photo a**, p. 199). Set aside the dome and Ultrasuede.

[2] Knot the end of a 2-yd. (1.8m) length of thread, leaving a 6-in. (15cm) tail. Sew from the back to the front of the Stiff Stuff between the line and the edge. Pick up two As and sew through to the back, two beads width away from the knot. Sew back through the first A **(figure 1, a–b**, p. 198, and **photo b)**. Sew through the second A and back up to the front, one bead's width away from the second A **(b–c** and **photo c)**.

[3] Pick up an A, sew through the previous A, and back up the new A **(c–d)**. Pick up an A, sew down to the back one bead's width away from the previous A, and then up to the front one bead's width away from the previous A **(d–e)**.

[4] Repeat step 3 around the line marking the circumference of the dome, ending with an even number of beads. Sew through the first bead in the round.

[5] Pick up two Ds and work a round of brick stitch (Basics, p. 10) as follows: Sew through the thread bridge between the next two beads on the previous round and back up the second D **(figure 2, a–b)**. Pick up a D and sew through the next thread bridge and up through the new D **(b–c)**. Repeat, adding one bead to each thread bridge. This round will fit snugly around the plastic dome.

[6] Turn the two rounds of beads inside out and glue the photo into the middle of the Stiff Stuff. Work one more row of brick stitch using Ds. To snug up the beads even more around the Page Pebble, you can substitute a round of one-bead edging in place of a row of brick stitch **(figure 3, a–b)**, which is shown on both round frames.

[7] Exit one of the A beads on the first round with the needle pointing towards the front side. Pick up two As and begin Ndebele herringbone (Basics) by sewing down through the next A in the base round **(figure 4, a–b** and **photo d)**. Pick up two As and sew up through the next A in the base row **(b–c** and **photo e)**. Continue to add a round of herringbone to both sides of the base row.

[8] Exit an A bead on the front round of herringbone with the needle pointing toward the front side. Work a round of circular herringbone in color B. Exit the first B on the new round.

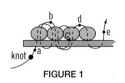

FIGURE 1

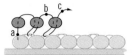

FIGURE 2

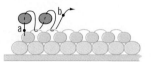

FIGURE 3

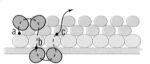

FIGURE 4

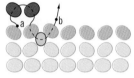

FIGURE 5

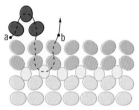

FIGURE 6

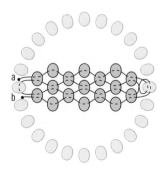

FIGURE 7

[9] Work a third round of herringbone in color C, with the following change: Pick up two Cs and sew down through the next bead. Pick up an E and sew up through the next bead (figure 5, a–b). Repeat to complete the round, exiting the first C added.

[10] Work the fourth round of herringbone in color C with the following change: Pick up three beads instead of two, sew down through the next two beads on the previous round, the E added in step 9, and up the next two beads on the previous round (figure 6, a–b). Repeat to complete the round. Secure the tails and trim.

[11] Glue the Ultrasuede to the back of the locket. Secure a new thread and exit a bead in the herringbone round on the back. Work a round of herringbone using color E beads.

FIGURE 8

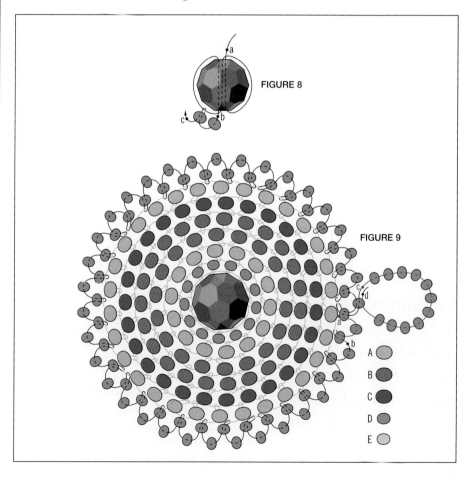

FIGURE 9

A
B
C
D
E

198

[12] Work another round of herringbone using only one E per stitch. Exit the first E added in this step.

[13] Pick up an E and sew through the next E. Repeat to complete the round. If too much thread shows between the beads, pick up a B between each E in the round.

[14] To add a pin back, you must construct a strip of flat, even count peyote (Basics) across the back of the locket (figure 7, a–b). Sew the pin back to the peyote strip.

Cover

[1] Start a 2-yd. length of thread. Sew through the 3 x 5mm bead three times to create two threads on the outside of the bead (figure 8, a–b).

[2] Work a round of brick stitch off the threads along the outer edge of the big bead (b–c) using color D.

[3] Work a round of brick stitch using color A. Work an increase for two rounds with color B and one increase round with color C. Work an increase round with color A. Add increase rows as needed until the cover completely covers the photo.

[4] Work a round of picot edging with color D (figure 9, a–b).

[5] Make a loop of 11 Ds on the picot round (c–d) to fit over a point along the outer edge of the frame.

[6] Sew around the picot edge and exit on the opposite side of the loop. Connect the locket to the frame in two places by picking up a D and sewing through one of the Es from step 9 of the picture frame (photo f). Make sure the cover is centered over the frame. Adjust the number of beads used to attach the cover if necessary. Center the loop over a point on the frame to be used as the closure. Secure the threads and trim. ◖

Carol teaches beadwork and feltmaking nationwide. Her schedule and kits are available at carolcypher.com.

EDITOR'S NOTE: Carol omitted the cover on the blue frame below so it can sit on a little stand instead of being used as a locket. To reinforce the points, work an extra D bead between the herringbone stitches after step 9 to keep the points in place.

MATERIALS

one locket or picture frame
- Page Pebble approx. ⅞ x ⅝ in. (2.2 x 1.6cm) oval or approx. 1 in. (2.5cm) round (scrapbooking or craft stores)
- Ultrasuede
- small photograph
- Japanese seed beads
  5g size 11º, each of three colors (A, B, C)
  5g size 15º, each of two colors (D and E)
- Lacy's Stiff Stuff
- E6000 glue
- pin finding (optional)
- beading needles, #12 or 13
- Nymo, size B or D

cover (optional)
- 3 x 5mm bead (or a round bead if using a round Page Pebble)
- Japanese seed beads
  1g size 11º, each of three colors (A, B, C)
  1g size 15º, color D

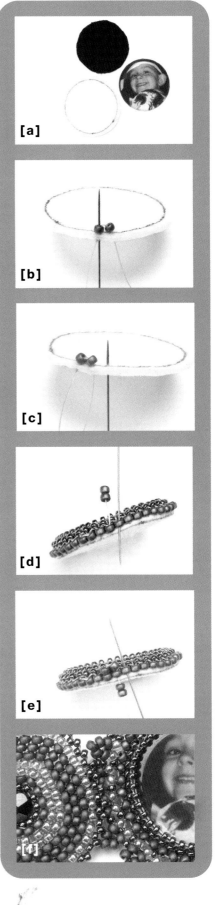

[a]

[b]

[c]

[d]

[e]

[f]

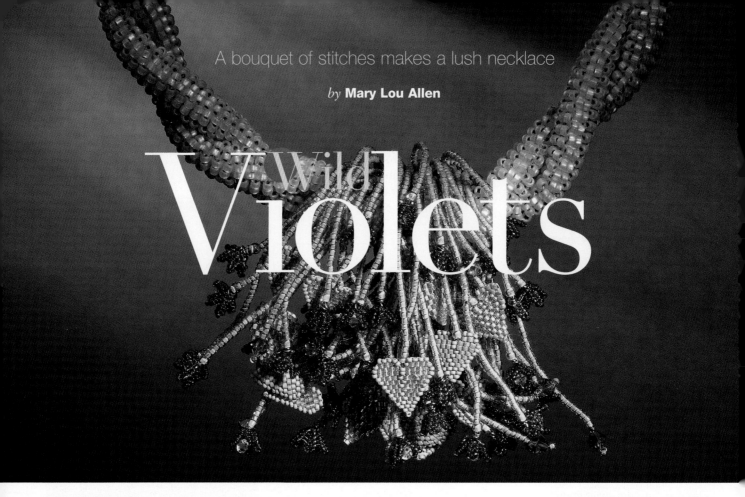

A bouquet of stitches makes a lush necklace

by **Mary Lou Allen**

Wild Violets

This perfect posy of a necklace contrasts the sleek undulations of a twisted, peyote stitch rope with a profusion of leafy blooms. The petite violets are made in Ndebele herringbone; the heart-shaped leaves in brick stitch. They work up so quickly, you'll feel like you're gathering them in a flower-strewn meadow.

step*by*step

Neckpiece

Peyote tubes

Work with comfortable lengths of doubled thread, securing the tails with half-hitch knots (Basics, p. 10) when ending and adding thread.

[1] Leaving a 12-in. (30cm) tail, pick up 12 8º seed beads and tie them into a circle with a surgeon's knot (Basics). Sew through the next two 8ºs **(figure 1, a–b)**.

[2] Pick up two 8ºs, skip two 8ºs on the ring, and sew through the next two 8ºs on the ring **(b–c)**. Repeat around the ring and step up through the first two 8ºs on the new round **(c–d)**.

[3] Continue working in two-drop peyote passes, stepping up after each round, until you reach the desired length. Mine is 26 in. (66cm) long. Do not knot or cut the thread Make a second tube the same length.

[4] Cut two pieces of electrical wire to the same lengths as your tubes and tape the ends **(photo a)**. Slide one wire into a tube. Pick up the thread where

[a]

[b]

[c]

FIGURE 1

FIGURE 2

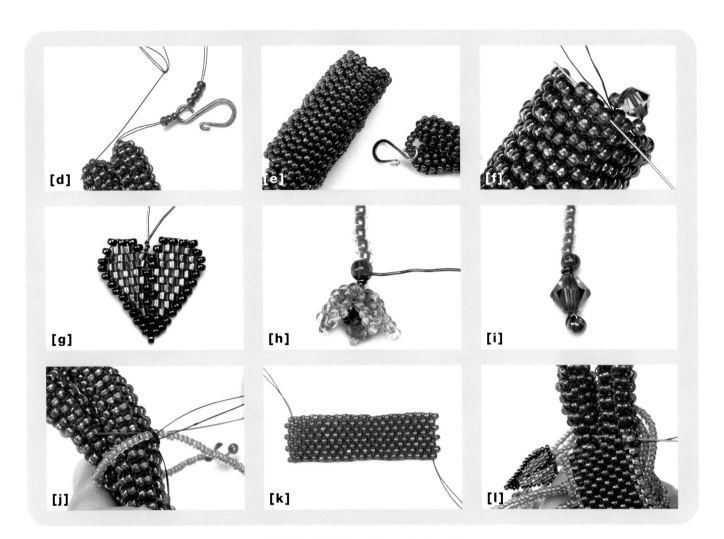

[d]

[e]

[f]

[g]

[h]

[i]

[j]

[k]

[l]

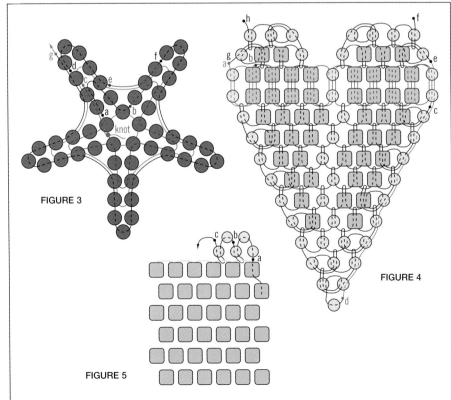

FIGURE 3

FIGURE 5

h

g

a

b

f

e

c

d

FIGURE 4

c b a

you left off and work a decrease in two more rounds by picking up one bead instead of two (figure 2, a–b and photo b). Reinforce the last round with several thread passes, but do not cut the thread. Repeat on the other end and with the other wire and tube.

[5] Twist the two tubes together, then stitch the pairs together at their ends (photo c). Sew back through to the last round.

[6] Pick up seven 8°s and half the clasp. Center the clasp over the 8°s and sew through the last round on the other tube (photo d). Reinforce the seven 8°s with several thread passes, then secure the tail. Repeat on the other end with the second half of the clasp.

clasp cover

[1] Work the clasp cover in the same manner as the neckpiece tube, but start with approximately 30 8°s in step 1 instead of 12. You may have to adjust the number of beads so the cover fits

MATERIALS

neckpiece and clasp cover 24 in. (61cm)
- Japanese seed beads
  180g, size 8º
  1g, size 15º
- **14** 6mm bicone crystals
- Nymo D conditioned with beeswax
- beading needles, #10
- 52 in. (1.3m) 10-gauge coated electrical wire
- plastic tape to match wire color
- clasp

flowers, leaves, and vines
- Japanese seed beads
  5g violet, size 15º
  5g green, size 15º
  35g green, size 11º
  40 green, size 8º
- 10g green Japanese cylinder beads
- **20** 4mm bicone crystals
- **6** 6mm bicone crystals
- Nymo B
- beading needles, #12
- 20 ft. (6m) 24-gauge green craft wire
- wire cutters

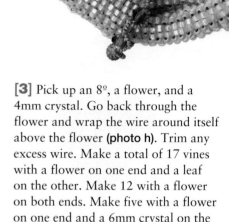

Center fringe

flowers

[1] On 24 in. (61cm) of thread, pick up five 15ºs. Leave a 6-in. (15cm) tail and tie the beads into a ring with a surgeon's knot. Sew through the next bead (**figure 3, point a**).

[2] Pick up four 15ºs and sew through the next bead on the ring (**a–b**). Repeat four more times to complete the round. Sew through two beads on the next stack (**b–c**).

[3] Pick up two 15ºs and work a round of tubular Ndebele herringbone (**c–d**).

[4] Work another round of herringbone with the following change: Pick up three beads per stitch instead of two and sew down through two beads (**d–e**). Sew up through two beads (**e–f**). Repeat to complete the round (**f–g**).

[5] Repeat the thread path through the last round, tying half-hitch knots between a few beads. Trim the working thread and secure the tail. Make a total of 45 flowers.

leaves

[1] On 1 yd. (.9m) of thread, pick up two 15ºs and two cylinders. Leave a 12 in. tail and sew back through the 15ºs and the cylinders to start a ladder (Basics and **figure 4, a–b**). Continue in ladder stitch the beads shown (**b–c**).

[2] Use cylinders and 15ºs to build the bottom half of the leaf in brick stitch (Basics and **c–d**).

[3] Weave through the edge beads and exit at **point e**. Work half of the leaf's top using 15ºs and cylinders as shown (**e–f**).

[4] Thread a needle on the tail and repeat on the other top-half of the leaf (**g–h**). Secure the tails and trim.

[5] Make a total of 17 leaves as in steps 1–4. Make eight of these leaves substituting cylinders for 15ºs and 11ºs for the cylinders.

vines

[1] Cut the wire into 34 pieces ranging from 8–12 in. (20–30cm) long. Take one wire through two rows of a leaf's ladder and secure the wire with a twist above the leaf (**photo g**).

[2] Pick up an 8º and enough 11ºs to cover the wire, leaving approximately 1 in. (2.5cm) exposed.

[3] Pick up an 8º, a flower, and a 4mm crystal. Go back through the flower and wrap the wire around itself above the flower (**photo h**). Trim any excess wire. Make a total of 17 vines with a flower on one end and a leaf on the other. Make 12 with a flower on both ends. Make five with a flower on one end and a 6mm crystal on the other (**photo i**).

[4] Drape a vine over the middle of the neckpiece. Start a new thread and secure the vine with a few stitches on the back of the tube (**photo j**). Repeat with the remaining vines, spacing them as desired. Alternate flowers and leaves so they fall at different lengths.

peyote patch

[1] Using 8ºs, make a flat, even-count peyote strip eight beads wide and 38 rows long (**photo k**) or long enough to cover the vines on the back of the neckpiece.

[2] Exit an edge bead on the last row. Make a picot trim along both edges by picking up three 11ºs and sewing through the thread bridge between the first two edge beads and back through the third 11º (**figure 5, a–b**).

[3] Pick up two 11ºs, sew under the next thread bridge and back through the second 11º (**b–c**). Repeat to complete the row. Repeat along the other edge.

[4] Position the strip over the stitches that attach the vines on the back of the neckpiece. Sew the strip in place (**photo l**). ●

Contact Mary Lou Allen at beachstones1@charter.net.

over both tubes. Work in two-drop peyote for 46 rounds, or as long as needed to cover the clasp plus a few rounds on each end of the neckpiece (**photo e**).

[2] With the thread exiting two 8ºs in the last round, embellish the tube by picking up an 8º, a 6mm crystal, and an 8º. Sew through the 8ºs the thread is exiting in the same dirction and the next four 8ºs on the edge (**photo f**). Repeat around the edge.

[3] Exit a crystal. String five 15ºs and sew through the next crystal. Repeat around the edge.

[4] Exit a crystal. Pick up ten 15ºs and sew through the same crystal again, the five 15ºs from the previous step, and the next crystal. Repeat around the edge. Secure the tails. Embellish the other edge to match.

[5] Open the clasp, slide the cover on one end of the necklace, close the clasp, and slide the cover over the clasp.

Beaded Garden

Weave a collection
of floral forms

by **Lisa Olson Tune**

Wanting to make a collage rather than a specific, defined structure, I started stitching a variety of interesting shapes in the hope that one day I would come up with an idea for putting them together. That day finally came, and my rather abstract bouquet is the result.

Shapes are a great way to fool around with stitches. One of the nicest things is that you can start and stop whenever you want without fear of losing your place. When you have enough pieces, sew the shapes together to create a centerpiece for a necklace or brooch. Consider adding a beaded cabochon to highlight your design.

Fan

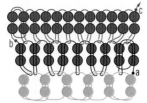

FIGURE 1

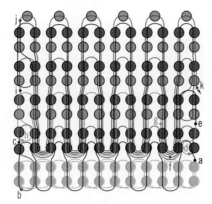

FIGURE 2

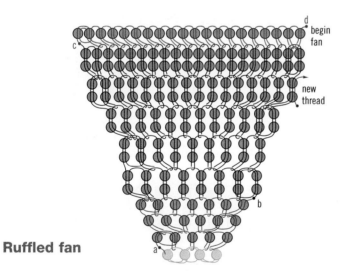

FIGURE 3

Ruffled fan

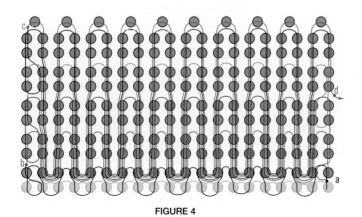

FIGURE 4

FIGURE 5

Large leaf

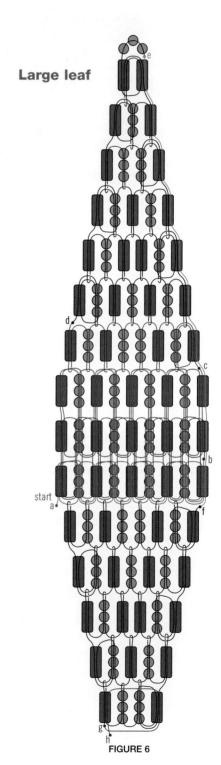

FIGURE 6

Small leaf

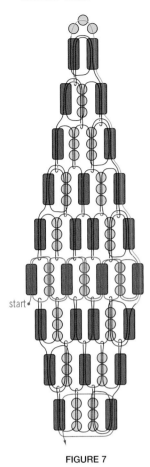

start •

FIGURE 7

Large flower

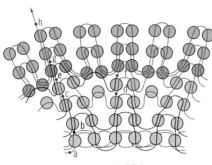

FIGURE 9

Small flower

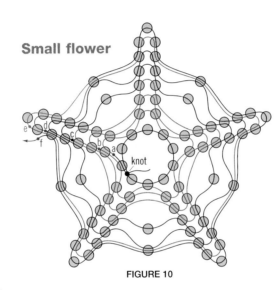

FIGURE 10

Twig

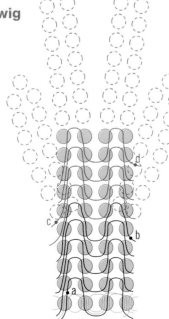

FIGURE 8

step*by*step

Work with about 60 in. (1.5m) of thread. Use Nymo O for the beaded shapes because of the many thread passes and size B for the strap.

Fan

Stitch the fans in two-bead brick stitch and modified herringbone. If you prefer to work in single-bead brick stitch, make twice as many rows.

[1] Make a ladder of six two-bead units (Basics, p. 10).

[2] On the second row, increase from six to nine stitches (**figure 1, a-b**).

[3] On the third row, increase to 12 stitches (**b-c**).

[4] Work one row of herringbone across the fan base, going up and down through both beads in each stitch (**figure 2, a-b**). To turn, come up the brick-stitch beads in the previous column, then jog over and come up the edge herringbone bead (**b-c**).

[5] Work a second herringbone row across the fan (**c-d**) and turn as shown (**d-e**).

[6] For the rest of the fan, pick up four beads for each herringbone stitch. To make the fan divide into "fingers," go down through the first herringbone row after picking up a group of four beads (**e-f**). Then come back up all the beads on the first side of the next stitch (**f-g**). Work across the row (**g-h**). Turn as shown (**h-i**).

[7] Work three rows as in step 6 (**i-j**).

[8] Finish the fan by adding one bead at the top of each finger (**j-k**).

Ruffled fan

The ruffled fan has a longer brick stitch section and a second herringbone layer.

[1] Start with a ladder of four beads.

[2] Work three brick-stitch rows, increasing to five beads in the first row, six in the second, and seven in the third (**figure 3, a-b**).

[3] Work five two-bead rows, increasing to eight stitches in the first, nine in the second, 12 in the third, 16 in the fourth, and 20 in the fifth (**b-c**).

[4] Finish the brick-stitch section with a row of 20 stitches (**c-d**).

Zigzag

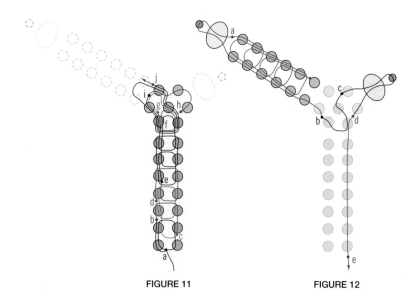

FIGURE 11

FIGURE 12

Spiral

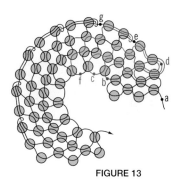

FIGURE 13

FIGURE 14

Pearl-studded rope

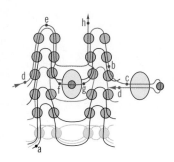

FIGURE 15

[5] Work one row of herringbone across the previous row (**figure 4, a-b**).
[6] Work the next four rows in four-bead-per-stitch herringbone as in step 6 of the fan (**b-c**).
[7] Finish the fan with a single bead at the top of each finger (**c-d**).
[8] To make the ruffle, refer back to **figure 3** and secure a new thread in the fan, exiting as shown. Then refer to **figure 5** and work a row of two-bead herringbone in front of the 16-stitch row as in step 4 of the fan (**a-b**).
[9] Work the next three rows in four-bead-per-stitch herringbone as in step 6 (**b-c**).
[10] End as in step 7 (**c-d**).

Large leaf

[1] Stitch a ladder alternating one bugle bead with a stack of three seed beads until you have five bugles and four stacks of seed beads (**figure 6, a-b**).
[2] Square stitch (Basics) two rows of beads onto the ladder (**b-c**).
[3] Decrease to eight stitches as follows: bugle, seeds, bugle, seeds, seeds, bugle, seeds, bugle (**c-d**).
[4] Work the next seven rows as shown (**d-e**).
[5] Go down through the bugles along the outer edge of the leaf and exit the edge ladder bugle (**e-f**).
[6] Work the bottom five rows in brick stitch as shown (**f-g**).
[7] Join the last bugle to the first on the end row to form a tube. End by coming back down the last bugle (**g-h**).

Small leaf

The small leaf is similar to the large leaf in its shape and construction. Stitch the small leaf in brick stitch as shown in **figure 7**, referring to the leaf instructions above, if necessary.

Twig

[1] Start with a four-bead ladder and join the ends to form a ring.
[2] Work four rows of tubular herringbone (Basics) for a total of five rows (**figure 8, a-b**). The fifth row is the base row.
[3] Use the same technique as in the fan instructions to make two

herringbone fingers (shown in red), going back down to the base row for each round. Make these fingers six to eight rows long and complete each with a single bead as before.

[4] At this point, you are exiting the bottom of the last bead in the base row again. Go up the first bead in the base row and work five rows of tubular herringbone (c-d). The fifth row in this group is the new base row.

[5] Work another pair of fingers off the new base row as in step 3 (shown in blue).

[6] Repeat steps 4-5, completing four sets of fingers.

Large flower

[1] Start with a six-bead ladder and join it into a ring (figure 9, a-b). Work two rows of tubular herringbone (b-c).

[2] Work the first part of an increase on the next row: Pick up two beads and go down the next bead to make the first herringbone stitch, pick up one bead, and come up the next bead (c-d). Repeat around, adding one bead between each stitch for a total increase of three beads (d-e).

[3] Work the second part of the increase on the next row by picking up two beads where you picked up one on the previous row (e-f). Complete the row with three increases (f-g). You now have enough beads to make six herringbone stitches. This is the base row.

[4] Make fingers five to six rows tall attached at the base as before (g-h shows two rounds). If you wish, you can work the last row or two by adding four beads per stitch as in the fan rather than two. Finish with a single bead at the top of each finger.

Small flower

Use size 14° seed beads.

[1] String ten beads and tie them into a circle with a surgeon's knot (Basics). Go through the first bead again.

[2] Pick up two beads, skip one, and go through the next. Repeat around the circle. End by going through the first bead on the circle and the first bead of the first row (figure 10, a-b).

[3] Work two rounds of herringbone on the pairs of beads added in the previous round (b-c).

[4] Increase one bead between each herringbone stitch on each of the next two rounds (c-d).

[5] Work the next round in herringbone, going through the increase bead on the previous row (d-e).

[6] Complete the short fingers with a single bead above each of the herringbone stitches. Work down through two beads and the increase bead as before (e-f).

Zigzag

[1] String four beads and tie them into a circle. Go through the first two beads again (figure 11, a-b).

[2] Pick up two beads and go through the third bead on the circle (b-c).

[3] Come back through the second bead and the first bead added (c-d).

[4] Pick up two beads, go down the second bead of step 2, and come back up the first bead of step 2 and the first new bead (d-e).

[5] Repeat step 4 until you've added six more rows (e-f).

[6] Pick up one bead and go down the second bead on the row below and up the first (f-g).

[7] To angle off, pick up two beads and go back through the single bead (g-h).

[8] Pick up two beads, skip the single bead, and come out the second bead added in step 7 (h-i). Go down the first bead added in step 7 and the first bead added before the single bead. Come up the adjacent bead, through the single bead and the second bead added in step 7 (i-j).

[9] Repeat steps 5-8 until you've made five to seven angled sections, ending with step 5.

[10] End the last section by stringing a pearl and a size 14° and go back through the pearl. Continue down the other side of the section (figure 12, a-b).

[11] To embellish the angles, sew down then up the last two beads of the previous section, and through the single bead (b-c). Go up the bead next to the new section on the two-bead corner, string a pearl and a 14°, and go

Fan

Ruffled fan

Large leaf

Small leaf

Twig

Large flower

Small flower

Zigzag

Spiral

Pearl-studded rope

down the other corner bead **(c-d)**. Continue down the side of the previous section **(d-e)**.

Spiral

The spiral uses flat even- and odd-count peyote stitch (Basics) and brick stitch. Pull the thread tight as you work so the outer edge curls under.

[1] String four beads and work two or three rows of even-count flat peyote stitch **(figure 13, a-b)**.

[2] Pick up two beads for the first stitch of the next row and make one more stitch. Peyote to the end of the row and back to the two beads added at the beginning of the row. Add a bead in peyote stitch between the two beads **(b-c)**.

[3] On this row, you change from even- to odd-count peyote. Pick up two beads and go through the last bead added on the row before. Add one bead each in the next two spaces **(c-d)**. Then work the modified turn as shown **(d-e)**.

[4] Work across the row, putting the third bead between the two beads at the start of the previous row **(e-f)**. Work the next row, adding two beads with the first stitch of the row and ending with a loop turn **(f-g)**.

[5] Repeat steps 3-4 until the spiral is about two complete revolutions or as long as you wish. You can work the modified turn shown in step 3 or the loop turn in step 4.

[6] Bring the thread out the first peyote stitch bead on the inside edge of the spiral **(figure 14, a)**. For a small spiral, work a row of brick stitch, using size 14ºs, along the thread loops on the inner edge **(a-b)**. For a large spiral, work one row of brick stitch with 11ºs and one with 14ºs.

[7] Finally, sew the top of the brick stitch row to the outer edge of the spiral to maintain its shape. If desired, trim the spiral with two- to three-bead spiked fringe.

MATERIALS
- seed beads, sizes 11º and 14º
- bugle beads, 4mm
- accent beads: shell heishi, 5-6mm and 3-4mm button-shaped freshwater pearls
- beading needles, #12 or 13
- Nymo beading thread, size O and B

Pearl-studded rope

[1] Start the rope with a four-bead ladder joined into a ring as in the twig.

[2] Work in herringbone to three or four rows past where you want the first pearls to be **(figure 15, a-b)**.

[3] Continue down the column to the first pearl's location **(b-c)**.

[4] String a pearl and a 14º. Go back through the pearl **(c-d)** and come up the next column to the top **(d-e)**.

[5] Go down the next column. Exit the same row as for the first pearl **(e-f)**.

[6] String the second pearl and seed bead and go back through the pearl **(f-g)**. Come up the next column to the top **(g-h)** and resume the herringbone tube.

[7] Place pearls at regular intervals, repeating from step 2. ●

Contact Lisa at oralee5olson@comcast.net.

Flaming Cuff

Attach a classic woven band to a bracelet form for a hot accessory

by **Ellen Friedenberg**

This bracelet design is adapted from a needlepoint pattern called bargello, or flame stitch. I was so pleased with the first bracelet, I made a series of them using various colors to represent gemstones. To enhance the flame effect of the design, I combine beads with different finishes and use silver-lined crystal or silver-lined gold beads for the main color of the pattern.

step*by*step

Metal cuffs are available in a variety of sizes. Adjust the number of warp threads and the pattern if you choose a cuff with a different width than we show here.

Weave the bracelet
[1] Thread the loom (p. 211) with 20 warp threads, keeping the tension even.
[2] Working with a comfortable length of thread, weave the repeating pattern at right for 77 rows or until it is ⅜ in. (1cm) longer than the metal cuff.
[3] Weave the working thread into the beadwork to secure it and trim.

End the warp threads
Choose one of the following options for ending the warp threads:
Option 1
[1] Before you cut the beadwork from the loom, center a 2-in. (6cm) piece of first-aid tape, adhesive side up, under the warp threads about ⅛ in. from the end of the beadwork.
[2] Fold the ends of the tape over the top of the warp threads, bringing them in slightly so the band of tape is narrower than the beadwork (photo a).
[3] Repeat steps 1–2 with the warp threads on the other end of the beadwork.
[4] Cut the beadwork from the loom, trim the warp threads just past the tape, and fold the bands of tape under the beadwork.

Option 2
[1] Cut the beadwork from the loom, leaving 2-in. (5cm) warp threads on each end.
[2] Cut a piece of two-sided tape and adhere it to the back of the beadwork near the edge.
[3] Take two or three adjacent warp threads, twist them together, and press them against the tape (photo b). Repeat with the remaining warp threads.
[4] Cut the warp threads about ½ in. (1.3cm) past the tape (photo c).
[5] Repeat steps 2–4 to finish the other end.

Assemble the cuff
[1] Cut a few small pieces of two-sided tape and adhere them to the underside of the metal cuff. Attach the piece of Ultrasuede so it extends ⅛ in. around the edges of the cuff (photo d). Trim the Ultrasuede if necessary.
[2] Place a few small pieces of two-sided tape on the top of the cuff. Center the beadwork on the cuff. It should extend past the edges of the cuff by one row of beads (photo e).
[3] Start a comfortable length of sewing thread, secure it in the beadwork, and exit an edge bead. Don't knot the thread.
[4] Stitch the Ultrasuede to the beadwork between beads (photo f). As you work around the cuff, you may need to sew around or through the corner beads to reposition your needle to start the next edge.
[5] Secure the thread in the beadwork as before and trim.
[6] Secure a comfortable length of Nymo in the beadwork and exit a corner bead.
[7] Pick up a triangle bead and stitch it to the side edge of the cuff. Continue adding a triangle bead between every other row of beads (photo g) on both sides of the cuff. ●

Ellen lives in New York City. Contact her via email at beaderella@nyc.rr.com.

MATERIALS
- Japanese seed beads, size 11º
  4g color A
  4g color B
  3g color C
  3g color D
- **80** triangle beads, size 8º or 10º
- 1 x 6 in. (2.5x15cm) metal cuff (www.moon dancedesigns.com)
- 1⅛ x 6⅛ in. (3x15.6cm) piece of Ultrasuede
- conditioned Nymo B or D to match beads
- sewing thread to match Ultrasuede
- beading needles, #10 or 12
- sewing needles
- loom
- 2-sided tape
- first-aid tape (optional)

A B C D

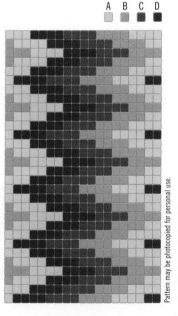

Pattern may be photocopied for personal use.

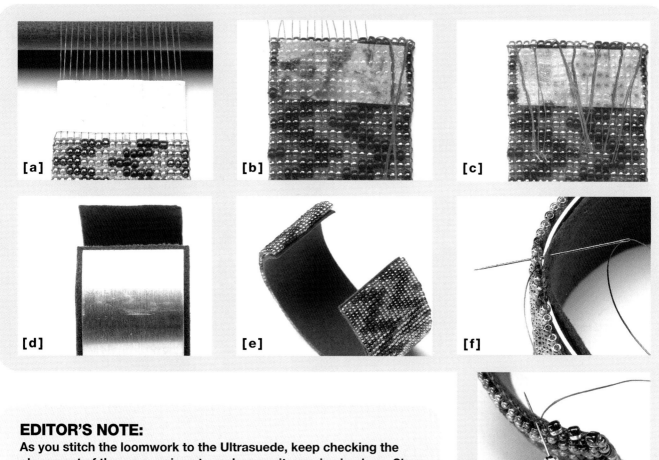

[a]

[b]

[c]

[d]

[e]

[f]

EDITOR'S NOTE:
As you stitch the loomwork to the Ultrasuede, keep checking the placement of the woven piece to make sure it remains in place. Since the tape doesn't adhere to the beads, the loomwork can easily slide down the metal form.

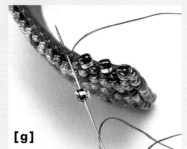

[g]

BASICS FOR LOOMWORK

FIGURE 1

FIGURE 2

knot

FIGURE 3

knot

FIGURE 4

knot

Set up the warp
[1] Tie the end of the spool of thread to a screw or hook at the end of the loom.
[2] Bring the thread over one spring and across to the spring at the other end of the loom. Wrap the thread around the back of the rod behind the bottom spring and back to the spring at the top of the loom.

[3] Continue wrapping the thread between springs, keeping the threads a bead's width apart, until you have one more warp thread than the number of beads in the width of the pattern. Keep the tension even, but not too tight. Secure the last warp thread to a hook or screw on the loom, then cut the thread from the spool **(figure 1)**.

Weave the pattern
[1] Tie the end of a 1-yd. (.9m) length of thread to the first warp thread just below the spring at the top of the loom. Bring the needle under the warp threads. String the first row of beads as shown on the pattern and slide them to the knot **(figure 2)**.
[2] Push the beads up between

the warp threads with your finger **(figure 3)**.
[3] Sew back through the beads, keeping the needle above the warp threads **(figure 4)**. Repeat, following the pattern row by row.
[4] Once you complete the last row, secure the working thread by weaving it into the beadwork.

Loomed
and
Layered

Multiple techniques enhance a woven band

by **Sharon Lester**

By incorporating a clever technique into your next loom project, you can eliminate the time-consuming step of weaving in the warp threads. The secret is to attach your clasp first. Once the loomwork is done, embellish the surface and add a decorative edging and fringe.

step*by*step

Set up the warp

Before you start, measure your wrist to determine how long to make your bracelet. Then, calculate the combined length of your clasp, bead tips, and accent beads plus 5 in. (13cm) for the loomed pattern and add ½ in. (1.3cm) for the rows that start and end the loomwork. Once you know this length, you'll know if you need to add or remove a few rows at each end of the pattern to make the bracelet fit.

[1] Cut nine 1-yd. (91cm) strands of Nymo. Divide the strands into sets of three and wax them (Basics, p. 10). Fold each set in half to determine the center point and tie three surgeon's knots (Basics) on top of each other to make a knot that will not slip through the hole on the bead tip. Thread all six tails into the bead tip so the knot sits inside **(photo a**, p. 214). Close the bead tips with your pliers. Repeat for the other two sets.

[2] Attach each bead tip to the clasp or three-to-one spacer. String a 3mm bead over all six strands in each set **(photo b)**.
[3] Tie an 8-in. (20cm) length of thread into a circle and attach it to the clasp with a lark's head knot (Basics). Wrap the other end of the circle around the tack on the loom's end roller or tape it to the roller. Loosen the wing nut on the side of the loom and turn it to take up slack until the clasp or spacer sits on top of the loom with the threads past the bar **(photo c)**. Tighten the wing nut.
[4] Set aside the first strand in the first set of six and seat the rest of the strands individually into the spring on the opposite side of the loom, wrapping the tails around the tack on this end. Secure the tails with tape. Repeat with the other two sets, leaving a space on the spring for the strands you set aside **(photo d)**.
[5] Thread a needle on the strand set aside from the first group and bring it under the first five strands. Pick up two seed beads and position the beads between the warp threads so there are

MATERIALS

one bracelet

- 10g Japanese seed beads, size 11º, each of four colors
- 10g Japanese fringe or teardrop beads (optional)
- **6–8** 3mm faceted accent beads for fringe (optional)
- **2** 4–5mm medium accent beads (optional)
- **7–8mm** flat or oval focal bead (optional)
- Nymo D to match bead color, conditioned with beeswax
- beading needles, #12
- **6** bead tips
- **6** 3mm large-hole round metal beads or crimps
- 3-strand clasp or 3-1 spacer bar (optional)
- clasp and jump ring if using spacer bar
- chainnose pliers
- G-S Hypo Cement or E6000
- bead loom

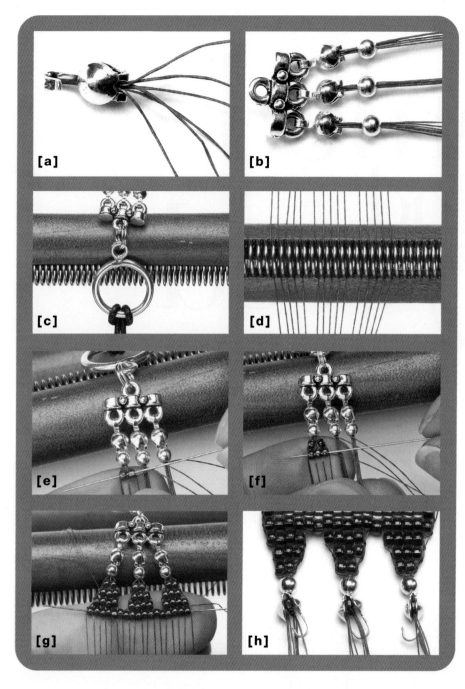

[a]

[b]

[c]

[d]

[e]

[f]

[g]

[h]

[1] Start with 2½ yd. (2.3m) of thread and weave through the last two rows of beads on the first set of warp threads. Add rows here, if necessary to increase the bracelet's length (Basics for loomwork, p. 211). Pick up 17 beads to start the pattern on p. 215 (photo g). Go back through the beads again. Follow the pattern for 66 rows. Once you've finished the pattern, add rows for length as at the start.

[2] Pick up four beads and position them between the warp threads with two warp threads next to the first bead and one warp thread on either side of the rest of the beads, as before. Go back through the beads.

[3] Pick up three beads and position them between the warp threads with two warps between the first two beads and one next to the third bead. Go back through the beads.

[4] Pick up two beads and position them between the warp threads with three warps next to the first bead, two next to the second, and one warp between them. Weave back through the last three rows and the first six beads in the last full row.

[5] Skip the first space of the next set of six warp threads and repeat steps 2–4 twice.

[6] Remove the piece from the loom. Working with three sets of six strands again, wax them if necessary. Then string the 3mm bead and bead tips.

[7] String a seed bead on three of each set of six strands and tie a surgeon's knot around it to secure the tails in the bead tips. Leave the tails if you want to add fringe (photo h). Otherwise, glue the knot and trim the tails. Close the bead tips.

Fringe (optional)

[1] Thread a needle on two strands. Pick up about 2 in. (5cm) of any color combination of seed beads, a 3mm bead, and a seed bead. Remove one of the threads from the needle and tie a surgeon's knot around the last seed bead. Rethread the needle and sew through the beads, tying half-hitch knots between beads. Trim the threads.

[2] Repeat, making as many strands of fringe as desired.

two warp threads on either side of the first bead and one warp thread after the second bead. Pass the needle back through the beads, making sure to push the beads up so the needle goes across the top of the warp threads (photo e).

[6] Pick up three seed beads and bring the needle under the same five warp threads and position the beads between the warp threads so there are two warp threads next to the first bead and one warp thread on either side of the other two beads. Go back through the beads as before (photo f).

[7] Pick up four seed beads and position them between the warp threads with one warp thread on either side of the beads. Go back through the beads as before. Remove the needle from the thread.

[8] Repeat these steps using the other two sets of six strands. Then incorporate the loose warp threads into the corresponding spaces on the spring.

Weave the pattern

Work with a comfortable length of thread and secure the tails with half-hitch knots (Basics) between beads when you add and end threads.

Edge embellishment (optional)

[1] Secure a new thread and exit the edge bead in the first row of the pattern. Pick up a seed bead and go through the next row (figure 1, a–b). Pick up a seed bead and sew through the next row (b–c). Continue adding beads in this manner until you reach the other end.

[2] For more elaborate edging, secure a new thread and exit one of the edge beads added above. Your needle should point toward the opposite end of the bracelet. Pick up a seed bead, adrop, and a seed bead, or three seed beads and sew through the next edge bead added in the previous step (d–e). Then add a seed bead and sew through the next edge bead (e–f).

Top embellishment (optional)

[1] Secure new thread in the beadwork and exit the center bead of the first flower design in the first row of flowers. Pick up a seed bead, sew through the center bead again, and sew through to the next center bead (figure 2, a–b). Continue adding beads to each flower. Move to the next flower row and repeat.

[2] Sew to the middle of the bracelet and come up through the end of the diamond shape. Pick up a focal bead and sew into the other end of the diamond. Then sew back through the focal bead, through the other end of the diamond, and back through the focal bead (figure 3, a–b).

[3] Pick up enough seed beads to surround the outside edge of one half of the focal bead. Go through the focal bead again (b–c). Repeat for the other half of the bead. To add a picot edge to these seed beads, go through the first seed bead, pick up three seeds, and sew through the third seed along the edge (c–d).

[4] Add two smaller beads on the other diamond shapes if desired, in the same manner as the focal bead.

[5] Weave to the other end of the bracelet and repeat step 1 to embellish the other flowers.

[6] Secure all the threads and trim. ●

Contact Sharon at 706 South Harrison Road, Houghton Lake, Michigan, 48629 or at mamalester@yahoo.com.

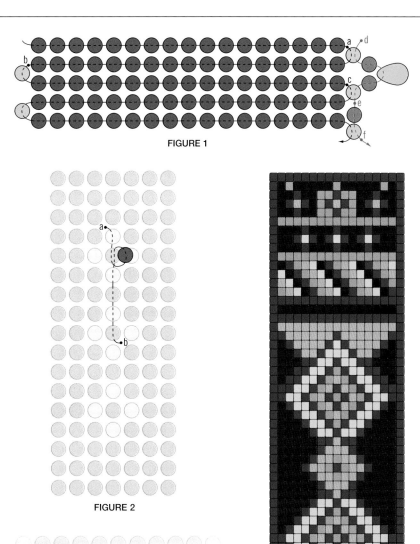

FIGURE 1

FIGURE 2

FIGURE 3

EDITOR'S NOTE: You may have to tighten your warp threads if they loosen up while you work. Unwind the loose ends from the loom and rewind them while pulling tightly. Tape the ends down. Also, I found that Japanese seed beads work better than Czech seed beads for loomwork. You can substitute Japanese cylinder beads, but they will change the length of the bracelet slightly.

Warp *Speed*

Accelerate loomwork projects with a clever new technique

by **Sandy Amazeen**

Finishing the long warp threads at the end of a loomwork project can be time-consuming and tedious. This inspired technique eliminates those threads, giving loomed beadwork a tantalizing new appeal. Sewing the ends into tubes to accommodate a custom-made slide clasp gives this piece a unique, contemporary look.

step*by*step

You must know the length of the project before you add the warp threads to the loom. There are about 12 rows of beads per inch (2.5cm) of length.

Set up the loom
[1] Tie a 2-yd. (1.8m) length of thread on the loom or a dowel with a surgeon's knot (Basics, p. 10).
[2] Pick up a size 11º seed bead and slide it up to the knot. Hold the bead in place and bring the thread around the back of the loom. Go through the loop of thread right next to the 11º and tighten the thread so it is snug against the loom (**figure 1** and **photo a**, p. 218).
[3] Repeat step 2 until you have lined up enough beads to equal the desired width of the bracelet and add two extra beads. My

design is 21 beads wide, so I used 23 bea to create the correct number of spaces (**photo b**).

Set up the warp
[1] Thread a needle onto a spool of Pow Pro or Fireline. Sew through the first 11º the top of the loom.
[2] Skip the first 11º on the bottom of th loom and sew through the second 11º. Sk the second 11º at the top of the loom and sew through the third 11º (**photo c**).
[3] Continue setting up the warp threads this way, pulling more thread off the spool as you need it. Exit the last bead on the to Leave 24-in. (61cm) tails on each end to for the clasp. Wrap the tails around the dowel to keep them out of the way, and t the ends.

Weave the pattern

[1] Start with a 4-yd. (3.7m) length of thread and tie it to the first warp thread, leaving a 6-in. (15cm) tail to weave in later. Bring the needle under the warp threads.

[2] Using one of the patterns shown, string the first row of beads and slide them up to the knot. Push the beads up through the warp threads and sew back through all the beads over the warp threads (photo d).

[3] Follow the pattern, keeping the tension even and the beads snug.

[4] When you finish the pattern, secure the tails with half-hitch knots (Basics) between a few beads. Snip the threads that hold the base row of beads in place. Every other bead will fall away, leaving a staggered pattern.

[5] If the bracelet is long enough, you can simply sew the end rows together to make a cuff. You can also finish off the ends with a sliding clasp. To start, weave a bead between each bead on the end row using the 24-in. tail (figure 2, a–b).

[6] Work five rows in square stitch (Basics), adding two beads with each stitch (b–c).

[7] Sew the last square stitch row to the last loom row to make a tube (photo e). Secure the threads in the beadwork, using half-hitch knots. Repeat on the other end of the bracelet.

Attach the clasp

[1] Make a decorative scroll at the end of an 8-in. (20cm) piece of wire (photo f).

[2] Position the wire in one of the square stitch tubes (photo g). Bend the scroll over so it is centered across the top of the bracelet (photo h).

[3] Bend the straight wire all the way back next to the beads (photo i).

[4] Slide the other tube over the wire, make a small loop, and trim the wire. ●

Contact Sandy at amamess@earthlink.net.

MATERIALS

- Japanese seed beads, size 11º, 5g each of 4 colors
- Power Pro 20 lb. test or Fireline 6 lb. test
- beading needles, #12
- loom (see editor's note)
- 2 ¼ in. (6mm) dowels, 6 in. (15cm) long (optional)
- 4 cords to attach dowels to loom (optional)
- 2 strong rubber bands (optional)
- chainnose pliers
- clasp
- 8 in. (20cm) 18-gauge wire, round or twisted

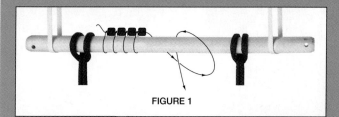

FIGURE 1

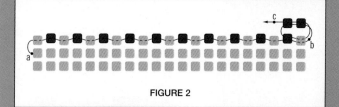

FIGURE 2

[a]

[b]

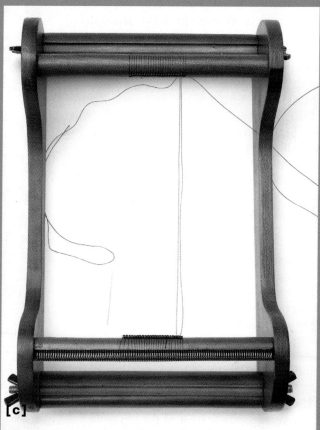

[c]

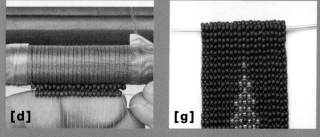

[d]

[g]

[e]

[h]

[f]

[i]

[j]

Tips & Techniques

Bead dish cover

I am a busy sports mom, and I like to take my bead projects with me. Since I use a porcelain bead dish, I normally scoop the beads into their original containers when it's time to go to the next event. I have tried using plastic lids from various containers and have yet to find one that fits snugly around the petal shape of the dish. A new kitchen wrap, Press 'n Seal by Glad (800-835-4523), has an adhesive on one side, and it sticks to smooth surfaces. Now, I simply cover my bead dish with a piece of Press 'n Seal and secure it by running my finger over the outer edge and divisions in the dish. Then I pull the excess wrap around the sides to the bottom. The beads stay in their individual compartments, and I can toss the tray in my bag and not worry about it. Occasionally, some beads stick to the wrap, but it leaves no residue on them.
– *Cindy Vaughn, Teague, Texas*

Project index

To keep track of projects and articles in *Bead&Button* and other publications, I make a copy of the table of contents (usually two pages), put it in a plastic sleeve, and keep it in a three-ring notebook. When I need inspiration or want to look up a specific project, I simply flip through my reference book to determine which issue I need to dig out.
– *Beth Tilley, Tacoma, Washington*

Modified Ndebele

Pick up four beads instead of two when working flat or tubular Ndebele, and you'll complete the piece in half the time. Attach each row to the bead below on the previous row as you normally would for Ndebele. – *B.J. Guderian, Colville, Washington*

Fixing mistakes

I use crimping pliers to break the occasional extra seed bead in my stitches when I miscount or pick up an extra bead. With chainnose pliers, I found that I was breaking beads and cutting threads. Now, when I use a crimping tool, I only break beads.
– *Diane Dennis, Nokesville, Virginia*

Tangle prevention

I use Fireline 4 lb. test and a #12 needle for almost all my beading. To prevent the tail end from wrapping and tangling around the working thread, I tie an overhand knot in it. The knot won't pull through the needle, but it goes through size 15° seed beads easily two or three times.
– *Jane A. Alley, Silver City, New Mexico* ●

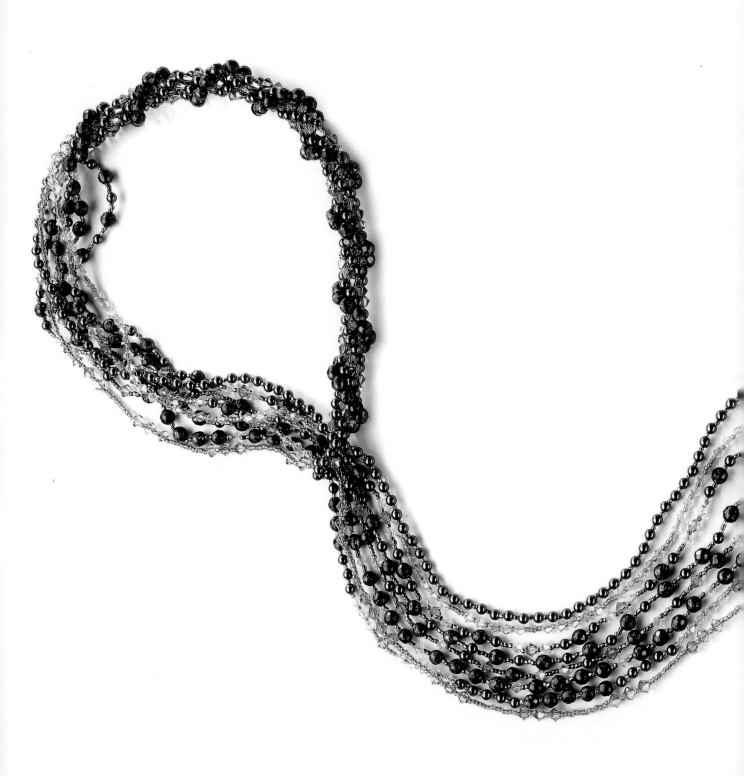

Crochet
Embroidery
Macrame

Crystal Crochet

by **Anna Nehs**

Crochet takes on a new twist with crystals and pearls

It's easy to become enamored with bead crochet. You can get wonderful results with different beads. This spiral gets its texture and sparkle from the pairing of pearls and crystals in various sizes.

step*by*step

Crocheted rope

[**1**] Thread a twisted wire needle with upholstery thread. To make the green necklace (p. 224), string a 6mm pearl, a 4mm pearl, a 5mm bicone, a 4mm pearl, and a 4mm bicone. Omit the second 4mm pearl if you are making the burgundy necklace. Repeat the bead sequence until you have used all the beads. Do not cut the thread off the spool until you are finished with the crochet.

[**2**] Leaving an 8-in (20cm) tail, work five chain stitches to start the green necklace and four to start the burgundy necklace. Connect the last chain to the first with a slipstitch (**figure 1**, p. 224).

[**3**] Work a round of bead slip-stitches (**figure 2**) into the round of chain stitches.

[**4**] For the next round, insert the hook to the left of the first bead and push the bead over to the right (**photo a**). Bring the thread over the bead in the first round (**photo b**). Slide down a bead and work a slipstitch (**photo c**).

[**5**] Repeat to complete the round. Continue to add rounds, working counter-clockwise, using all the beads strung. The beads will automatically form a spiral.

[**6**] Work a round of slip-stitches to complete the rope, then pull the thread through until you have an 18-in. (46cm) tail. Cut the thread.

[**7**] Thread a tapestry needle on the 8-in. tail. Weave the tail into the crocheted rope, tying half-hitch knots (Basics, p. 10) between a few beads. Trim the tail.

[**8**] Thread a tapestry needle with the 18-in. tail.

Green necklace: To make the loop, pick up 12 4mm pearls and sew into the last round of slipstitches (**photo d**). Reinforce the loop with a second pass of thread, then end the tail as you did before.

Burgundy necklace: Pick up the art bead and 15 4mm pearls. Sew back through the first 4mm pearl and the art

MATERIALS

both necklaces
- upholstery thread to match beads
- twisted wire needles
- crochet hook, size 7
- tapestry needle
- beading needles, #10 and 12
- Fireline 6 lb. test

green crochet rope
- **64** each of the following:
  6mm faceted pearls
  5mm bicone crystals
  4mm bicone crystals
- **130** 4mm crystal pearls

fringe
- **100** (approx.) each of the following:
  6mm faceted pearls
  5mm crystal bicones
  4mm crystal bicones
- **200** (approx.) 4mm crystal pearls

- hank or tube of any style of seed bead, size 10º–12º
- **3** small art glass beads
- **5** 6mm crystal rondelles
- **6** top-drilled crystal drops

burgundy crochet rope
- **109** each of the following:
  6mm faceted pearls
  5mm crystal bicones
  4mm crystal bicones
- **124** 4mm crystal pearls
- medium to large art glass bead

fringe
- **100** (approx.) each of the following:
  6mm faceted pearls
  5mm bicone crystals
  4mm bicone crystals
  4mm crystal pearls
  3mm crystal pearls
- hank or tube of any style of seed bead, size 10º–12º
- **14** 8mm round crystals

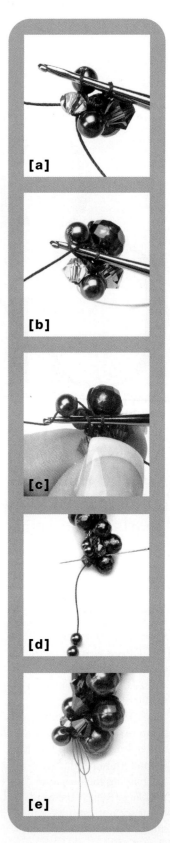

[a]

[b]

[c]

[d]

[e]

bead. Sew through the last row of slipstitches and reinforce the beads with a second thread path.

Fringe

[1] Determine the desired length for the fringe (my longest fringe is 24 in. (61cm). Multiply by four, then add 12 in. (30cm). Cut a piece of Fireline to that length. Fold the Fireline in half and thread a #10 needle over both ends. Sew through one of the stitches at the end of the crocheted rope. Pull the whole length through. Stop when you have about a 1-in. (2.5cm) loop **(photo e)**. Go through the loop with the needle and pull tight, making a lark's head knot (Basics) Remove the needle.

[2] Thread a #12 on one tail and string a pleasing assortment of crystals, pearls, and seed beads. At the end of the fringe, pick up a large crystal or bead and a seed bead. Skip the seed bead and sew through all the beads until you are back to the crocheted rope. Sew into the beads in the rope and tie a few half-hitch knots between beads. Trim the tail.

[3] Repeat step 2 to finish the remaining tail. Repeat steps 1–2, adding fringe as desired. ●

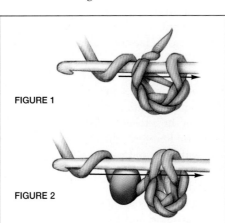

FIGURE 1

FIGURE 2

Anna is an associate editor at Bead&Button *magazine. Contact her at editor@beadandbutton.com.*

Silver

Crochet a two-toned rope with
oxidized sterling beads

by **Stephanie Riger**

Stitches

By keeping it simple and sterling, this necklace triumphs. The crocheted rope acquires a sophisticated appeal when made with sterling silver beads. Be sure to frame a bold centerpiece bead between the cones to retain the regal tone of this piece.

step*by*step

Oxidize the silver (optional)

I like the look of oxidized silver for the depth it gives the piece, but you can leave the beads shiny, if you prefer.

[1] String the beads temporarily onto string or fishing line. Tie the ends together with a knot, leaving a little slack in the line.

[2] Use liver of sulfur to achieve the desired patina, following the manufacturer's instructions.

[3] Rinse the beads in water, dry them, and polish them with steel wool. Rinse them again to remove any steel wool particles.

[4] Transfer the beads to Tuff Cord by tying the end of the line to the cord with a surgeon's knot (Basics, p. 10). Then slide the beads over the knot. You also can use a Big Eye or twisted wire needle to string the beads onto the cord.

Start the rope

The number of beads you'll use depends on how tightly you stitch. Working with average tension, you should be able to stitch one 6-in. (15cm) section with about 300 beads.

[1] To determine the length of each crocheted side, add the combined length of your clasp, cones, and focal bead. Subtract the total from 16 in. (41cm) or your desired finished length. Divide the resulting length in half. (My crocheted sections are 5½ in./14cm long.)

[2] Leaving an 8-in. (20cm) tail, make five chain stitches and join them into a ring with a slip stitch **(photo a and figure)**.

[3] Insert your hook into the first chain

stitch from inside to outside, slide a bead down to the stitches, and work a slip stitch **(photo b)**. Continue counterclockwise around the chain until you have stitched five beads into place.

[4] Continue around the tube, inserting the hook through the stitch on the left of the bead. Push that bead to the right

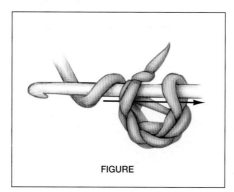

FIGURE

and bring the working thread over the top of it **(photo c)**. Slide a bead down to sit on top of that bead and work a slip stitch **(photo d)**.

[5] Continue adding rows as described above until you reach the length determined in step 1.

[6] To complete the rope, work a row

EDITOR'S NOTE: For comfort, wrap the handle of the crochet hook with a self-adhesive stretch bandage to pad it, or purchase a padded handle at your favorite craft store. Write the size of your hook on the new handle with a permanent marker.

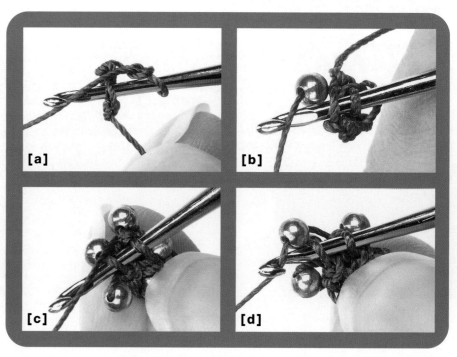

[a]

[b]

[c]

[d]

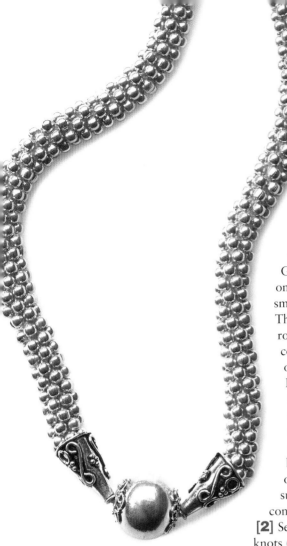

of slip stitches without adding beads (photo e). Cut the cord about 18 in. (46cm) from the end of the rope and pull it through the last stitch.

[7] Repeat steps 2–6 to make the second rope.

Connect the sides

[1] Thread a tapestry needle with the first rope's 18-in. tail. Go through the large opening on one cone, the focal bead, and the small opening on the second cone. Thread a needle on the second rope's tail and sew through the cones and focal bead in the opposite direction (photo f). Pull the tails to bring the ropes together. Then sew through one of the chain stitches on the end of the rope (photo g). Sew back and forth through the cones and beads using each of the stitches on each end of the ropes. Make sure the ends fit snugly in the cones and no cord shows.

[2] Secure these tails with half-hitch knots (Basics) and trim.

Attach the clasp

[1] Cut the wire into two 5-in. (13cm) pieces. Make a wrapped loop (Basics) at the end of one wire.

[2] Thread a tapestry needle with one of the 8-in. tails and go through the wire's wrapped loop. Sew back into the rope and through the wire loop (photo h), and pull to bring the loop next to the rope. Secure the tail with a half-hitch knot. Repeat two more times, then put a dot of glue on the knots.

[3] Slide the large opening of the cone over the wire and cover the end of the rope. Make the first half of a wrapped loop next to the cone, slide a soldered jump ring into the loop (photo i), and finish the wraps.

[4] Repeat steps 1-3 to finish the other end of the rope. ●

Contact Stephanie Riger through her website, picturetrail.com/greatjewelry.

MATERIALS

necklace 16 in. (41cm)

- 1 in. (2.5cm) silver focal bead
- **600** 3mm sterling silver beads
- **4** ¾ in. (2cm) silver cones
- Tuff Cord, size 3 (Shor International Corp., 914-667-1100, shorinternational.com)
- braided fishing line (optional)
- Big Eye or twisted wire needle
- crochet hook, size 7
- **2** tapestry needles
- 10 in. (25cm) 20–16-gauge silver wire
- S-clasp
- **2** soldered jump rings
- G-S Hypo Cement
- liver of sulfur (optional) (Rio Grande, 800-545-6566, riogrande.com)
- fine steel wool (optional)
- wire cutters
- roundnose pliers
- chainnose pliers

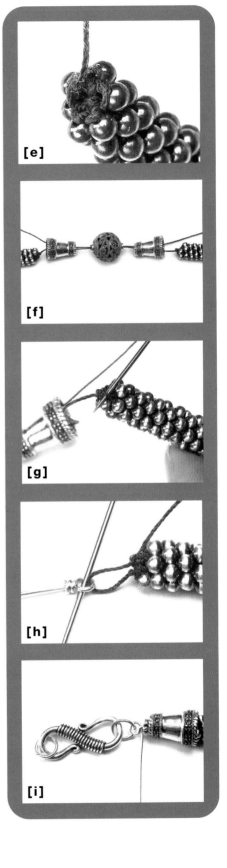

[e]

[f]

[g]

[h]

[i]

Falling for crochet

by **Linda Lehman**

Whether you're looking for a challenging bead crochet project or a relatively simple one, my lariat offers enough options to suit a range of interests. The version shown here consists of nine patterned sections of bead crochet connected with art glass beads, a peyote-stitch toggle, and bead caps worked in herringbone. To simplify the lariat, work with fewer colors, make fewer but longer sections, and buy the toggle and bead caps instead of making them.

step*by*step

Crocheted tubes

[1] Use a Big Eye needle to string 3-5 ft. (.9-1.5m) of beads onto the yarn. (To match the bead sequence in my lariat, refer to the sidebar on p. 230.)

[2] Leaving an 8-in. (20cm) tail, work eight bead chain stitches (**figure 1**, p. 231). Connect the chain into a circle with a slip stitch (**figure 2**, p. 231).

[3] Work in bead slipstitch (**figure 3**, p. 231) until the tube is 4 in. (10cm) long, if you plan to make a color change, or about 5½ in. (14cm), without a color change.

[4] Crochet a total of nine tubes.

[5] Block the tubes to prevent them from stretching: Pin one end to a terry cloth towel, pull slightly, and pin the other end. Dampen the tubes with water and let them dry overnight.

Bead connections

[1] Line up tubes in the correct color sequence. Thread one tapestry needle on the tail of the first tube and a second needle on the tail of another. Cross the needles through an 8mm bead (**photo a**, p. 230).

[2] Working with either needle, go through a bead on the end of the tube,

MATERIALS

54-in. (1.4m) necklace

- 30mm diameter donut (art glass donut by Kathy Perras/Itzart, kathyperras.com)
- **8** 8mm art glass beads (Kathy Perras)
- seed beads
  60g size 8º, 1 or more colors
  40g size 11º, 1 or more colors
  2g size 15º, 1 or 2 colors
- 2g Japanese cylinder beads
- **2** 5 or 6mm bicone crystals
- ball of #20 or 30 wt. crochet cotton or perle cotton, #8
- crochet hook, size 8-10 (to match yarn choice)
- Silamide or conditioned Nymo D (if not using 30 wt. cotton)
- eye pin
- **3** 6.5mm split rings
- Big Eye needle
- **2** thin tapestry needles
- beading needles, #10 or 12
- knitting needle, size 5, or other thin cylinder
- roundnose pliers
- chainnose pliers
- wire cutters

[a]

[b]

[c]

[d]

PATTERNS

Each tube in my lariat is worked in the following pattern: eight 11ºs in color A followed by an eight-bead alternating pattern of 11ºs in A and 8ºs in any color. To follow my design, change colors about 1½ in. (4cm) from the tube's end and finish using the new colors. Start the next tube using the color sequence from the end of the previous tube. Before sewing the tubes together, line them up in the correct color sequence.

CHANGING COLORS

To make a color change, slide the beads away from the stitches and cut the yarn, leaving a 6-in. (15cm) tail. Make one more chain stitch (no bead) and pull the tail through the loop on the hook to tie off the thread. Slide any beads that remain on the ball of yarn away from the cut end and string the next bead sequence.

To join the new yarn, insert the hook under the last bead added. Fold the new yarn about 3 in. (7.6cm) from the cut end. Grab the new yarn at the fold and pull the loop through to the inside of the crochet tube. Make a chain stitch (no bead), catching the yarn's working end and cut end. Pull the cut end until it comes loose. You will have two loose ends in the center of the tube. Work a few rows to make sure the new pattern is correct, then use a surgeon's knot (Basics) to tie the two ends tightly together inside the tube. Trim the ends about ¾ in. (2cm) from the knot. Continue in bead slip-stitch until the tube is the desired length.

then go through a bead a few stitches away. (They should be opposite each other). Go back through the 8mm bead **(photo b)**. Repeat with the other needle to connect the second tube. Tighten the yarn so the tubes press up against the 8mm bead **(photo c)**.

[3] Repeat twice, going through different beads each time.

[4] Repeat to connect the remaining tubes into a continuous rope.

Toggle

[1] Center a needle on 2 yd. (1.8m) of Silamide and work with doubled thread. Pick up 12 cylinder beads and go through them again to form a ring. Slip the ring onto a knitting needle or other cylinder.

[2] Work in tubular peyote (Basics, p. 10) until the toggle is about the same length as the donut's outer diameter. Keep the tension very tight. Secure both tails in the stitches and trim.

[3] Thread the needle with 1 yd. (.9m) of Silamide, pick up a 6º, and go through it again in the same direction. Sew through the peyote tube, lodging the 6º in the tube's center.

[4] String a bicone and a 15º. Turn, and go back through the bicone and the tube. Repeat on the other end of the tube **(photo d)**.

[5] Sew through the bicones and toggle several times to anchor the beads to the ends of the toggle. Secure the tails in the stitches and trim.

Bead caps

[1] Thread a needle with 2½ to 3 yds. (2.3-2.7m) of Silamide. Pull the ends so one side is 8 in. shorter than the other.

[2] Pick up eight 15ºs and slide them to

6 in. (15cm) from the end of the longer thread. Go through the beads again to form a ring. Tighten the thread and maintain a tight tension **(figure 4, a-b)**.

ROW 1 Begin working in Ndbele herringbone (Basics). Pick up two beads and go through the next two beads. Repeat, picking up four pairs of beads in this row **(b-c)**.

ROW 2 Adjust your needle and thread so the tail extends about 1 inch (2.5cm) below the last bead you've gone through. (You now will be working with doubled thread.) Go through the first bead added in the previous row, pick up two beads, and go through the second bead of the pair **(c-d)**. Pick up one bead and go through the first bead of the next pair. Repeat until you've picked up the last single bead **(d-e)**.

ROW 3 To step up and start the row, go through the first bead in rows 1 and 2 **(e-f)**. Work as in row 2, but add two beads between each pair instead of one **(f-g)**.

ROWS 4-6 Step up to start each row as before **(g-h)**. Pick up two beads and go through the next bead. Go through the first bead of the new pair added in the previous row, pick up two beads, and go through the next bead. Continue around the circle. The bead cap will begin to take on its cup shape in the sixth round (h-i).

ROW 7 Repeat Row 6, but pick up one bead between each pair of beads (i-j).

ROW 8 Pick up one bead instead of two and go back through the second bead of the pair. Pick up one bead and go through the next bead. Repeat around the circle (j-k). Reinforce the bead cap by sewing up and down each stack of beads. Weave in and trim the tails.

[3] Make a second bead cap.

Finishing

[1] Working on either end of the rope, weave the remaining tail into the tube. Thread a beading needle on 2 yd. (1.8m) of crochet cotton (if using #30) or Silamide and anchor it in the tube. String a bead cap, an 8º seed bead, and enough 11ºs to circle the edge of your donut. Go back through the 8º and the bead cap, tighten the thread, and secure it in the tube (photo e).

[2] Go back through the bead cap and 8º, string another loop of 11ºs around the donut, and go back through the 8º and bead cap. Secure the thread. Reinforce the loops by making at least one more pass through these beads.

[3] To finish the other end, thread a tapestry needle on the tube's tail. Sew through the eye of the eye pin to secure it in the tube. Trim the tail.

[4] Thread a bead cap and several 8ºs onto the wire. Make a wrapped loop (Basics) next to the end bead (photo f).

[5] Make a short chain using one or more split rings and attach them to the loop. Make sure the length of the toggle connection is at least half the length of the toggle bar.

[6] Stitch the end split ring securely to the center of the toggle (photo g). ●

Linda is the author of Bead Crochet Jewelry *(Schiffer Publishing, 2004). Contact her at (301) 439-2679 or lehman_linda@hotmail.com.*

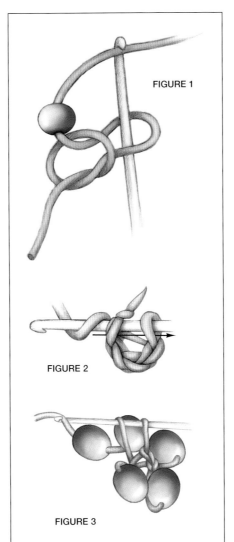

FIGURE 1

FIGURE 2

FIGURE 3

[e]

[f]

[g]

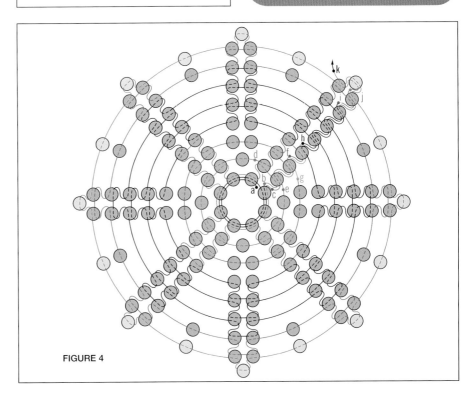

FIGURE 4

Brimming with possibilities

If you've tried colorful designs worked in traditional bead crochet, you know how much time and planning it takes to prestring hundreds of beads in their precise color sequence. My colorful beaded basket will introduce you to tapestry crochet, a technique that achieves the look of traditional patterned crochet with much less effort. In tapestry crochet, you string a single color of beads on each spool of yarn, then work with one color while carrying the others in the background. Since the motif does not have to be preplanned, the technique offers fantastic design potential.

Add tapestry crochet
to your stitch repertoire
by **Carol Ventura**

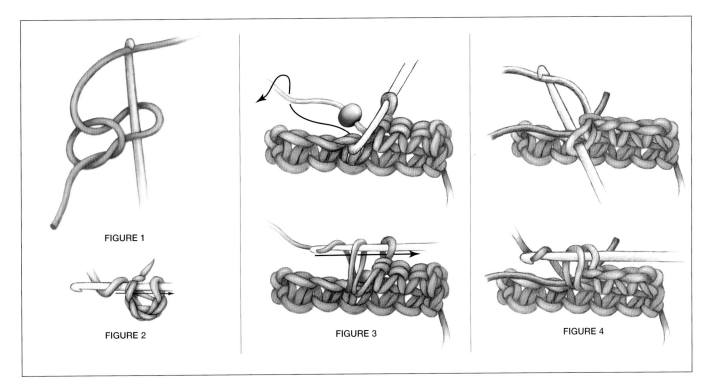

FIGURE 1

FIGURE 2

FIGURE 3

FIGURE 4

Gauge

8 stitches = 1 in. (2.5cm)
8 rows = 1 in.

step*by*step

This basket is worked as a spiral, so it can be difficult to tell where each round ends. To keep track, slip a safety pin or stitch counter into the top of the last stitch of each round or place a short piece of contrasting thread across the last stitch. Remove the marker as you come to it, and use it at the end of the next round.

[**1**] Using a twisted wire or Big Eye needle, string about half the amber beads onto the yellow thread. Slide the beads toward the cone, leaving 1 yd. (.9m) of thread without beads. Repeat with the full amount of amethyst beads on lilac thread, light blue beads on blue thread, and red beads on red thread.
[**2**] Using yellow thread, chain four stitches (**figure 1**). Join the ends into a ring by working a slip stitch (**figure 2**) into the first chain stitch.
[**3**] Work six stitches in bead single crochet (**figure 3**) into the ring and connect the last stitch to the first with a slip stitch. Crochet over the tail (**figure 4** shows how to hide or "carry" a second thread).

[**4**] Trim the yellow tail (not the working thread) and start to carry the lilac thread. Work the following rounds with amber beads and yellow thread. Remember to mark the end of each round.
Round 2: Increase in every stitch (12 stitches).
Round 3: Increase in every stitch (24 stitches).
Round 4: Increase in every second stitch (36 stitches).
Round 5: No increases in this round.
Round 6: Increase in every third stitch (48 stitches).
Round 7: Increase in every fourth stitch (60 stitches).
Round 8: Increase in every fifth stitch (72 stitches).
Round 9: Increase in every sixth stitch (84 stitches).
Round 10: No increases.
Round 11: Increase in every seventh stitch (96 stitches).
Round 12: Increase in every eighth stitch (108 stitches).
Round 13: No increases.
Round 14: No increases.
[**5**] Rounds 15–44 create the pattern motif on the side of the basket. Refer to the sidebar on p. 234 for instructions on tapestry crochet. The graph in **figure 5** (p. 234) shows the pattern motif. Untwist the threads occasionally by

suspending the basket by one thread while pulling on the other. Let the piece spin around.
Round 15: One amethyst bead, five amber beads. Repeat around.
Round 16: Two amethysts, four ambers. Repeat around.
Round 17: Three amethysts, three ambers. Repeat around.
Round 18: Four amethysts, two ambers. Repeat around.
Round 19: Five amethysts, one amber. Repeat around.
Round 20: Carry the yellow thread and

MATERIALS

8 x 3 in. (20 x 7.6cm) basket
- 4 180 yd. cones 3/2 pearl cotton: one each of yellow, lilac, blue, and red (Halcyon Yarn, 800-341-0282, halcyonyarn.com)
- seed beads, size 8º
  70g amber
  70g rainbow root beer (iridescent red)
  35g light amethyst
  35g light blue
- heavy twisted-wire beading needles or Big Eye needles
- steel crochet hook, size 1
- safety pin, stitch counter, or short piece of thread

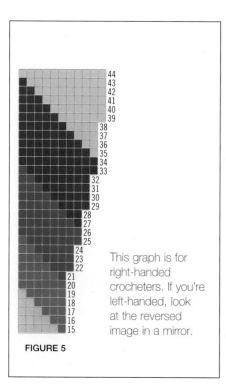

This graph is for right-handed crocheters. If you're left-handed, look at the reversed image in a mirror.

FIGURE 5

work 96 bead stitches with amethyst beads. Before crocheting the last 12 stitches, cut the yellow thread and begin carrying the blue thread. Finish the round's last 12 stitches.

Round 21: One light blue, five amethysts. Repeat around.

Round 22: Work two light blue beads in the first stitch (an increase), one light blue in the second stitch, then one amethyst in each of the next four stitches. Repeat around (126 stitches).

Round 23: Four light blues, three amethysts. Repeat around.

Round 24: Five light blues, two amethysts. Repeat around.

Round 25: Work two light blues in the first stitch, one light blue in each of the next five stitches, then one amethyst. Repeat around (144 stitches).

Round 26: Carry the lilac thread and work 132 stitches with light blue. Before crocheting the last 12 blue stitches, cut the lilac thread and begin carrying the red thread. Finish the round's last 12 stitches.

Round 27: One iridescent red, seven light blues. Repeat around.

Round 28: Two reds, six light blues. Repeat around.

Round 29: Work two reds in the first stitch, one red in each of the next two

stitches, then one light blue in each of the next five stitches. Repeat around (162 stitches).

Round 30: Five reds, four light blues. Repeat around.

Round 31: Six reds, three light blues. Repeat around.

Round 32: Seven reds, two light blues. Repeat around.

Round 33: Work two reds in the first stitch, one red in each of the next seven stitches, then one light blue in the next stitch. Repeat around (180 stitches).

Round 34: Before starting this round, load the remaining amber beads onto the yellow thread. Push the beads down, leaving a yard-long gap without beads. Carry the blue thread and work the next 168 stitches with red beads. Before crocheting the last 12 red beads, cut the blue thread and begin carrying the yellow thread. Finish the round's last 12 stitches.

Round 35: One amber, nine reds. Repeat around.

Round 36: Two ambers, eight reds. Repeat around.

Round 37: Three ambers, seven reds. Repeat around.

Round 38: Four ambers, six reds. Repeat around.

Round 39: Work two ambers in the first stitch, one amber in each of the next four stitches, then one red in each of the next five stitches. Repeat around (198 stitches).

Round 40: Seven ambers, four reds. Repeat around.

Round 41: Eight ambers, three reds. Repeat around.

Round 42: Nine ambers, two reds. Repeat around.

Round 43: Ten ambers, one red. Repeat around.

Round 44: Carry the red thread and work this round with amber beads.

[6] Cut the red thread flush against the basket. Make a slip stitch with the yellow thread and cut it, leaving a 6-in. (15cm) tail. Pull the tail through the loop. Weave 2 in. of the tail into the basket to secure it, then cut it flush against the basket.

[7] Turn the basket inside out so the beads are on the outside. Carefully

Tapestry crochet

Tapestry crochet is similar to single crochet, but it allows you to switch thread colors within the stitch.

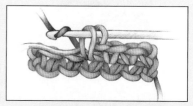

Go through the top two loops of the next stitch. Use the working thread to make the first single-crochet loop.

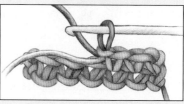

Yarn over with the carried thread and pull it through both loops.

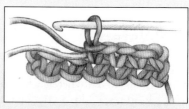

Continue working in the new color, carrying the previous color until it is needed.

steam the basket from the cloth side. Too much heat can break the beads, so work slowly.

[8] Now make your decision: Do you want the beads to be on the outside or the inside of the basket? ●

Carol learned tapestry crochet while serving in the Peace Corps in Guatemala, where she watched local residents making colorful shoulder bags. For more information about tapestry crochet or to purchase her book, More Tapestry Crochet, *visit her website,* tapestrycrochet.com.

Picture
perfect

Embroidered cuffs for
expressive cabs

by **Stella Broughton**

I was inspired to make a pictorial cuff bracelet when my husband gave me an agate cabochon from Quartzite, Arizona. Its pattern reminded me of a meadow with a big blue sky, and I beaded it accordingly. Since then, I've always been on the lookout for special cabs. Even those with abstract designs can be a great jumping off point for beading patterns and color combinations.

MATERIALS

- cabochon (Rio Grande, 800-545-6566, riogrande.com)
- approx. 3 x 10-in. (8 x 25cm) piece of Lacy's Stiff Stuff
- approx. 3 x 10-in. piece of leather or Ultrasuede (available at craft or fabric stores)
- assortment of seed beads, stones, and pearls to match cabochon
- beading needles, #12
- Nymo B beading thread to match beads
- set of snaps, size 4
- E6000 glue
- felt-tipped permanent markers
- soup can
- soft cloth
- wax paper
- rubber bands
- toothpick (optional)

step*by*step

Preparing the design

[1] To prepare the cuff, measure your wrist and add ½ in. (1.3cm). Cut a 2½-in. (6cm) piece of Lacy's to this length. On one end of the cuff, cut away the extra ½ in., leaving a ¾-in. (2cm) tab for the snap (photo a). Leave the other end straight. You will bead directly onto the Lacy's. To make the leather backing, place the Lacy's over a piece of leather or Ultrasuede, trace around it, and cut out an identical cuff from the leather. Put it aside.

[2] Glue the cabochon in the middle of the Lacy's with E6000 (photo b). Place the Lacy's on a piece of wax paper (cab side up) and cover it with a soft cloth. Weight it down with a heavy book and allow it to dry completely overnight. Allow the back to air dry if it's still wet, then remove any excess glue from around the cab with a toothpick.

[3] Consider the cab and draw your design in pencil to highlight significant markings. Fill in the lines with permanent markers to create color blocks that you will be able to bead over easily (photo c).

[4] Mark off a nonbeadable area on the straight end of the cuff. This area will contain the male portion of the snap and be covered by the beaded tab once the cuff is closed (photo d). Fill in the blank space with permanent marker to give it a little camouflage, but keep in mind it won't be visible when worn. With some skillful designing and a little planning, you can virtually hide the closure altogether (photo e) once the cuff has been snapped into place.

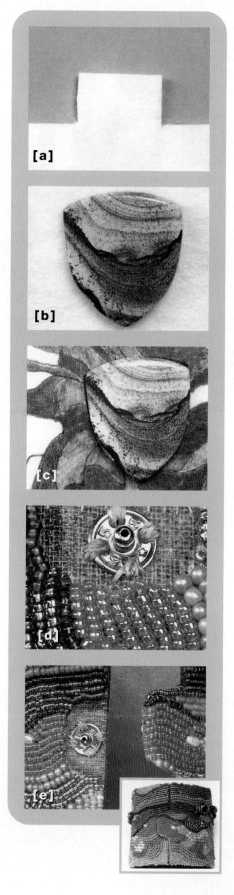

[a]

[b]

[c]

[d]

[e]

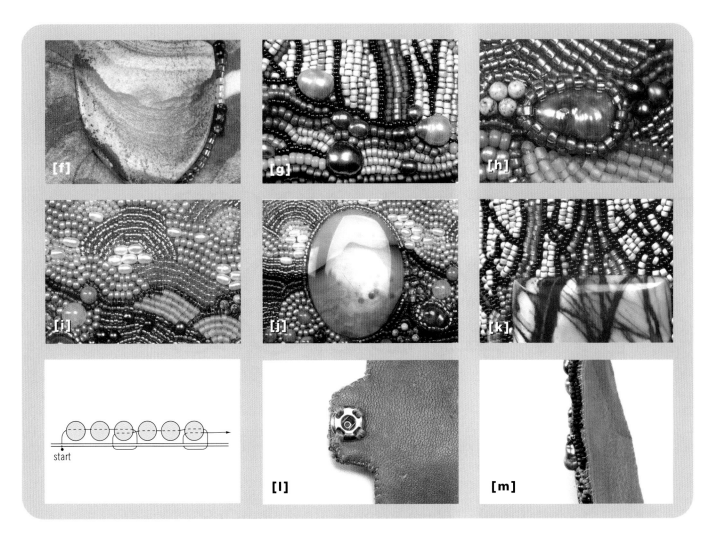

[f]

[g]

[h]

[i]

[j]

[k]

start

[l]

[m]

Stitching the beads

[1] Begin beading using beaded backstitch **(figure)**. Come up through the Lacy's along the edge of the cab. Pick up three beads and go through the Lacy's after the last bead. Come up through the Lacy's between the second and third beads. Go through the third bead, add the next three beads, and repeat.

[2] Even though your beads don't need to be all the same size, remember to use the right ones in each of the color blocks as you encircle the cab **(photo f)**.

[3] Bead your design using any combination of seed beads, pearls, small stones, or beads that will bring your picture to life. In the closeup **(photo g)**, small pearls in earth tones become boulders in the landscape.

[4] Add dimension using even-count circular peyote. (Basics, p. 10). I sewed the pearl on, then used 15º seed beads to build up around it **(photo h)**. Combining matte and metallic finishes also adds depth and texture.

[5] You can see how using rice pearls adds fullness to the clouds **(photo i)**. When beading around a curve, the smaller the beads, the more fluid your lines will be.

[6] When working horizontally, I bead the horizon line first, (such as in the outline of the mountain tops) so that it follows the natural line in the agate **(photo j)**. I then work each side of the cab separately.

[7] In the treescape **(photo k)**, I continued the vertical lines in the cab with closely matched seed beads. In this instance, I left out the embellishments to keep the lines seamless.

Finishing

[1] Once the beadwork is done, glue the Lacy's to the suede side of the leather cuff, leaving the edges and the areas for the snaps free of glue. Wrap the cuff around a soup can, then cover with a soft cloth and secure with rubber bands. Let it dry for 24 hours. The cuff should not be flattened out after this.

[2] After the two layers are joined, sew the snaps onto both ends. The female part is sewn to the back of the tab **(photo l)**. The male part is sewn to the front of the straight end **(photo d)**.

[3] Secure the edges of the two layers by whipstitching (Basics, p.10) them together **(photo m)**. Trim the Lacy's, if necessary, being careful not to cut the beadwork. Camouflage small exposed edges of the Lacy's with permanent marker. ○

Write to Stella at 1130 Deerfield Road, Prescott, Arizona, 86303, or e-mail her at seedbeader@juno.com.

Wraps Ribbon

Enhance a wire necklace with embroidered beads and fringe

by **Diane Hyde**

A plain metal neckwire comes alive when it is covered with a fiber braid and embellished with glass flowers and leaves. Wrapping the wire provides a base for stitching, so enjoy the freedom of adding colorful beads to any sturdy shape that you can wrap.

step*by*step

Necklace base

[1] Put a dab of glue at the midpoint (approximately) on one side of the wire base. Adhere the end of the braid to the wire, so the cut end points toward the V at the center **(photo a,** p. 240). Let the glue dry.

[2] Wrap the braid around the wire in a tight spiral, keeping the tension even and tight. Cover about half the previous wrap with each new wrap to create a firm, padded base for the embroidery **(photo b)**. Make the wraps closer together near the V to provide extra padding for the embellishment. Never allow the wire to show through the wraps. If you need to stop wrapping before you're finished, use an alligator-style clip to hold your work in place.

[3] Continue wrapping until the sides are symmetrical. Before you trim the end, secure the wraps in place by stitching the braid to itself on the back of the wire with thread that closely matches the fiber color. Cut off the excess braid and tack down the cut end as invisibly as you can, sewing on the back. Trim the thread close to the wraps when you're done.

Floral embellishment

[1] Anchor a new thread at the back of the V and work with it doubled. Use a series of tiny, nearly invisible (I call them "traveling") stitches to maneuver the thread to the front.

[2] Pick up a flower, a 4mm

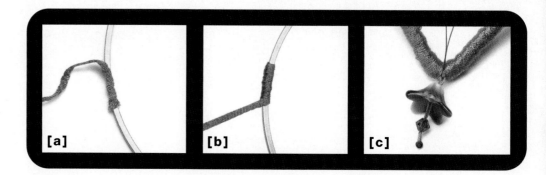

[a]   [b]   [c]

crystal, and a seed bead. Turn and go back through the crystal, flower, and braid **(photo c)**. Go through the beads and braid again at least one more time to secure the embellishment. Attach one flower on each side of the central flower **(photo d)**.

[3] Attach one large leaf bead on each side of the flowers **(photo e)**. Make your traveling stitches on the back of the neckpiece.

Fringe cluster

To make a cluster of fringe below the flowers, maneuver your needle to the V using tiny stitches as before. String each strand of fringe in a slightly different length, ranging from about 2½–3 in. (6.4–7.6cm). Keep the longer strands toward the center.

[1] For each fringe, blend the seed beads so they appear to change colors gradually from the neckpiece to the leaves and drops.

[2] As you reach the bottom of each strand, string a 4mm crystal, four seed beads, a leaf or crystal drop, and four seed beads. Go back through the 4mm crystal and the rest of the beads to the neckpiece **(photo f)**. Tighten the thread, but don't let the strand kink. Sew through the braid and start the next fringe.

[3] Make each fringe with a slightly different bead arrangement so the crystals complement each other when they hang together. When you make the last fringe (the amount is up to you), anchor the thread in the braid, but don't cut it if it is more than 2 ft. (61cm) long.

Cube picots

[1] If your working thread is less than 2 ft. long, start a new thread in the braid on the back of the neckpiece. Exit about 1 in. (2.5cm) up from the tip of the V.

[2] Pick up a cube, a 4mm crystal, and an 11º. Go back through the crystal, the cube, and the braid **(photo g)**. Straighten out the picot, if necessary, so it hangs pointing downward.

[3] Add picots at ⅛-in. (3mm) intervals or as desired. Secure the thread on the back of the neckwire.

[4] Start a new thread at the V and add picots on the unfinished section. Make sure the picots line up evenly on both sides. ◉

You can reach Diane at dianehdesigns@execpc.com.

MATERIALS

necklace 18 in. (46cm)

- **3** 14mm flower beads
- **2** 20mm leaf beads
- **3** or more 12mm leaf beads
- **5** 11 x 5.5mm crystal drops
- **22** 4mm crystal bicones
- **14** cube beads
- 5g seed beads, size 11º, each of two colors
- wire necklace base (Designers' Findings, dianehdesigns@ execpc.com)
- ¼ in. (6mm) rayon fiber braid (Designers' Findings)
- Nymo B or D to match braid color
- beading needles, #10 or 12
- E-6000 glue
- small alligator clip (optional)

EDITOR'S NOTE:
If your flowers droop or fall forward, brace them by stitching a short row of 11º beads behind or under them.

[d]   [e]

[f]

[g]

Heartfelt Embroidery

by **Karen Dismukes**

Showcase whimsical beaded pictures with a simple frame technique

Bold colors, clean design, and the fun of recycling frames offers an exciting outlet for your embroidery skills. But be warned, your walls won't stay bare for long.

step*by*step

Prepare the canvas

[1] Cut a 6½-in. (17cm) square piece of canvas. The opening in this frame is a 4½-in. (11cm) square. If you're using a different size, cut the canvas approximately 2 in. (5cm) beyond the frame opening to allow for wrapping the canvas around the backing. Fold masking tape over the edges to prevent fraying.

[2] To transfer the design **(figure 1**, p. 242) to the front of the canvas, draw the image on a piece of tracing

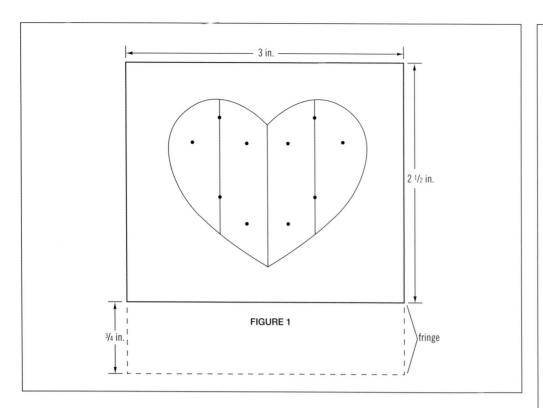

3 in.

2 ½ in.

¾ in.

fringe

FIGURE 1

MATERIALS
- 12mm accent bead
- **2** 6mm accent beads
- seed beads
  20g size 11º, blue
  10g size 11º, black
  5g size 11º, lime
  10g size 14º, light purple
  10g size 14º, dark purple
  3g size 14º, ivory
  4 size 8º, black
- Nymo D
- beading needles, #12
  sharps
- G-S Hypo Cement
- Col-Erase pencils
  (office and art supply
  stores)
- 7½ x 7½-in. (19 x 19cm)
  piece of canvas
- Poly-fil quilt batting
- 5¼ x 5¼-in. (13 x 13cm)
  frame
- tracing paper or vellum
- heavyweight cardboard
  to fit frame insert
- masking tape
- spoon

paper with a Col-Erase pencil. Lay the pattern with the pencil side down and burnish the drawing onto the canvas using the back of a spoon.

Bead the image

[1] Begin with the square border. Using a comfortable length of Nymo, come up in one corner of the square and pick up a black 8º, two black 11ºs, and a green 11º. Using beaded backstitch (Basics, p. 10), work the border clockwise in the 11º pattern until the square is completed. Remember to add an 8º in each corner. Working clockwise leaves less fabric to hold in your left hand if you're holding the needle in your right.

[2] Stitch the heart border. Come up through the bottom of the heart and pick up a larger bead or button and a green 11º. Go back through the larger bead and the canvas. Come up and backstitch counterclockwise with three green 11ºs and an

ivory 14º, repeating this pattern as you go around. Use your left thumbnail to help control the shape. Backstitching fewer beads at a time results in a more fluid curve. Place a large bead or button at the top of the heart, then complete the other side.

[3] For the striped pattern inside the heart, start with a vertical row in the center, and work your way out to each side. The inner stripes

have nine rows each, and the outer ones have eight. I used two shades of purple 14ºs and dotted the pattern with a few ivory 14º accents as illustrated in the pattern.

[4] To stitch the background, start with one bead in a corner and make arcs of beads fanning out from there **(photo a)**. **Figure 2** illustrates the progression of arcs that I used. Czech 11º beads for this technique work well because the size variations

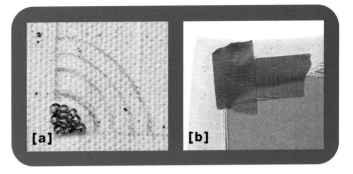

[a] [b]

FIGURE 2

make it possible to fill tight spaces with smaller beads. Add thread as needed, tying the ends off in the back and securing with a dab of G-S Hypo Cement.

[5] After the background is complete, work the fringe. Come up at the left end of the bottom border and stitch one fringe between each bead on the bottom row. Pick up ten black 11ºs, an ivory 14º, and a blue 11º. Go back through the ivory and black beads and the next bead in the bottom row of the border and repeat for another fringe. Pick up ten green 11ºs, an ivory 14º, and a blue 11º. Go back through the ivory and green beads and exit the next border bead. Continue the fringe pattern of two blacks and one green all the way across.

[6] To add the center embellishment, come up from the back in the center of the heart and pick up one larger bead or button and three 11ºs. Go back through the larger bead, tie off, and dab with G-S Hypo Cement.

Frame

[1] Remove the glass from your frame. Cut a piece of heavy-weight cardboard the size of the frame insert.

[2] Lay several pieces of Poly-fil quilt batting on top of the cardboard. The batting helps puff out the final image and adds to the piece's dimensionality.

[3] Tack down the beadwork onto the batting and cardboard. Tear about ten 1-in. (2.5cm) strips of masking tape to have at your disposal. Wrap the canvas around the board and batting, and tape it down in the back (**photo b**). The tape only has to hold long enough to get the picture into the frame before the back locks it in. ●

Karen is a talented beader and Design Studio Manager from Overland Park, Kansas. Send her an e-mail at kdismu1@hallmark.com.

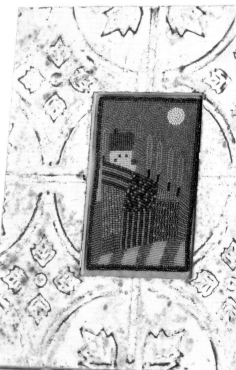

Donut Deluxe

Dress up
a donut with
an embellished
macramé
dangle.

by **Linnea
Lockwood-Gambino**

stepbystep

[1] Cut five 60-in. (1.5m)
lengths of cord. Fold each
cord in half and bring each
loop up through the donut
hole (**photo a**). Bring the ends
of the cord through the loop
and pull down, forming a
lark's head knot (**photo b**
and Basics, p. 10).
[2] Working from left to
right, number the cords
1–10. Separate cords 1–6 to
the left and 7–10 to the right.
Angle cord 6 over cords 5–1
(**photo c**). Working
from right to
left, make
double
half-
hitch
knots
(**figure 1**)
starting with
cord 5. Add a
5mm spacer
before making the knot
on cord 1.
[3] Angle cord 5 over cords
7–10. Working from left to
right (**figure 2**), make double
half-hitch knots starting with
cord 7. Add a 5mm spacer
before making the knot on
cord 10. Your first row
should look like **photo d**.
[4] Renumber the cords
1–10 from left to right.

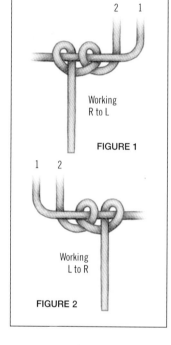

**Working
R to L**

FIGURE 1

**Working
L to R**

FIGURE 2

Repeat steps 3 and 4 without
adding spacers on cords 1
and 10. Keep the rows snug
against each other.
[5] To add center beads,
string five spacers (two 4mm
daisies, one 5mm spacer, two
4mm daisies) on cords 1 and
10, and string the rectangular
bead on cords 5 and 6 (**photo
e**). The remaining cords will
lie behind that bead.
[6] Angle cord 1 to the
center below the rectangular
bead over cords 2–5. Working
left to right, make double
half-hitches with cords 2–5.
[7] Renumber the cords.
Angle cord 10 to the center
over cords 9–5. Working
right to left, knot with
cords 9–5.
[8] Renumber the cords.
Place cord 1 over cords 2–6

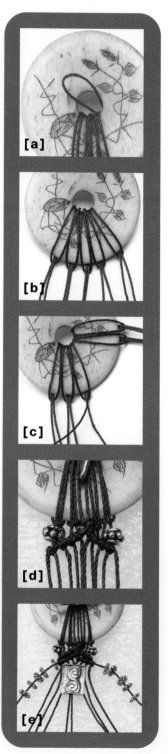

[a]

[b]

[c]

[d]

[e]

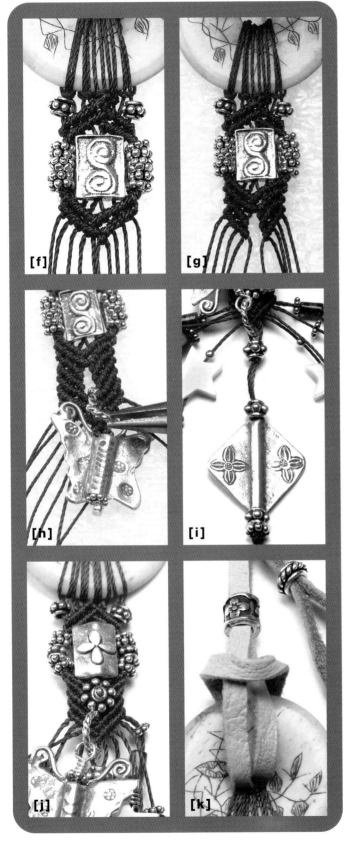

[f]

[g]

[h]

[i]

[j]

[k]

and knot with cords 2–6.

[9] Renumber the cords. Place cord 10 over cords 9–6 and knot with cords 9–6. Your piece should now look like **photo f**.

[10] Renumber the cords. Place cord 1 over cords 2–5 and knot with cords 2–5.

[11] Renumber the cords. Place cord 10 over cords 9–6 and knot with cords 9–6. The resulting buttonhole will hold the jump ring that attaches the silver butterfly **(photo g)**. Repeat steps 10 and 11.

[12] Renumber the cords. Place cord 1 over cords 2–5. Working left to right, knot with cords 2–5.

[13] Renumber the cords. Place cord 10 over cords 9–5. Working right to left, knot with cords 9–5.

[14] Repeat steps 6–9.

[15] Stack a 1mm bead, 4mm daisy, silver butterfly, and a 4mm daisy on a head pin and make a wrapped loop (Basics) at the top.

[16] Open the jump ring (Basics) and slide the loop with the butterfly on. Put the jump ring through the buttonhole, capturing the bottom two macramé rows **(photo h)**. Close the ring.

[17] Bring cords 5 and 6 together beneath the jump ring and string a silver diamond and other desired components on both cords **(photo i)**. This is the longest dangle. Make an overhand knot (Basics), trim the tail, and singe the end with a lighter. Create ascending dangles on each side as desired.

[18] The daisy-shaped spacer on the front **(photo j)** is added last. Using the same cording, sew up from the back where you want the spacer to sit. String a spacer and a stop bead larger than the hole in the spacer. Go back through the spacer, tie off, trim the tail, and singe carefully.

[19] Secure a length of deerskin cord to the top of the donut with a lark's head knot and slide a silver bead over both cords **(photo k)**. Add another silver stop bead near the ends and make an overhand knot at the end of each cord. ◗

Linnea lives in Clayton, North Carolina, and has kits available for purchase. E-mail linnea41@aol.com, call (919) 345-4157, or visit her website, linnayyah.com.

MATERIALS
dangle 4 in. (10cm)
- 40mm bone or stone donut
- 10mm Thai silver butterfly bead
- 20mm Thai silver diamond
- **4** 5mm silver spacers
- **30** (approx.) 4mm daisy-shaped spacers
- **10** (approx.) 1mm silver spacers
- assorted beads for dangles
- 3-in. (7.6cm) silver head pin
- 10mm twisted silver jump ring
- Conso beading cord, red
- 1-yd. (.9m) deerskin or suede cord
- chainose pliers
- roundnose pliers
- lighter

Tie _the_ Knot

Macramé a bracelet using three easy knots

_by_ **Dottie Hoeschen**

The bare arms of summer demand outstanding accents at the wrist, and this wonderful macramé cuff will undoubtedly attract much interest. Featuring a bold centerpiece button, it buzzes with a wonderful, casual vibe… as only macramé can. Created with just three basic knots, you can finish it in a jiffy – what a good reason to make more than one.

step_by_step

Bracelet

Work this bracelet upside down to make it easier to see the knots when you add the centerpiece button.

[1] To prepare the Styrofoam board, cut 12 slits along the bottom edge **(photo a)**. This helps keep the strands from tangling.

[2] Cut 12 1-yd. (.9m) strands of waxed linen. Tie them together in the middle with an overhand knot (Basics, p. 10 and **photo b**). Pin the knot to the board and arrange the strands as in **photo a**. To keep track of the strands, number their positions, left to right, 1–12.

[3] Tie a square knot (see illustration), using strands 4 and 9 over strands 5–8 **(photo c)**.

[4] Working left to right, use strand 1 and tie a row of double half-hitch knots (see illustration) over strands 2–12 **(photo d)**.

[5] Separate the strands into six sets

of two and string a cube over each set **(photo e)**.

[6] Repeat step 4 **(photo f)**.

[7] Separate the strands into two sets of six and put strands 7–12 aside. Working from the middle to the left, use strand 6 to tie a row of double half-hitch knots on a 45-degree angle over strands 5–1 **(photo g)**.

[8] Continue working from the middle to the left and use strand 6 to tie a row of double half-hitch knots over strands 5–2. Repeat for the next three rows, omitting the last strand each time **(photo h)**.

[9] Repeat steps 7–8 using strands 7–12, working from the middle to the right **(photo i)**.

[10] String seven 8° seed beads on strands 1 and 12 and a 6° over strands 6 and 7 **(photo j)**.

[11] Repeat steps 7–10, then repeat steps 7–9.

[12] Repeat steps 4–6 **(photo k)**.

[13] Untie the overhand knot and string

the centerpiece button over strands 5–8 **(photo l)**. Repeat steps 4–12 to complete the second half of the bracelet.

Button

[1] Using strands 4 and 9, make five square knots over 5–8 **(photo m)**.

[2] Using strands 1 and 12, make eight square knots over strands 2–11 **(photo n)**.

[3] Slide the button onto as many strands as possible, making sure to include strands 1 and 12. Tie an overhand knot to keep the button in place **(photo o)**. Trim the tails and dot the knot with glue. If some of the strands did not fit through the button, trim and glue them.

Loop

[1] Repeat steps 1–2 of the button instructions on the other end of the bracelet.

[2] Pick up the longest strand and wrap it around all the remaining strands until

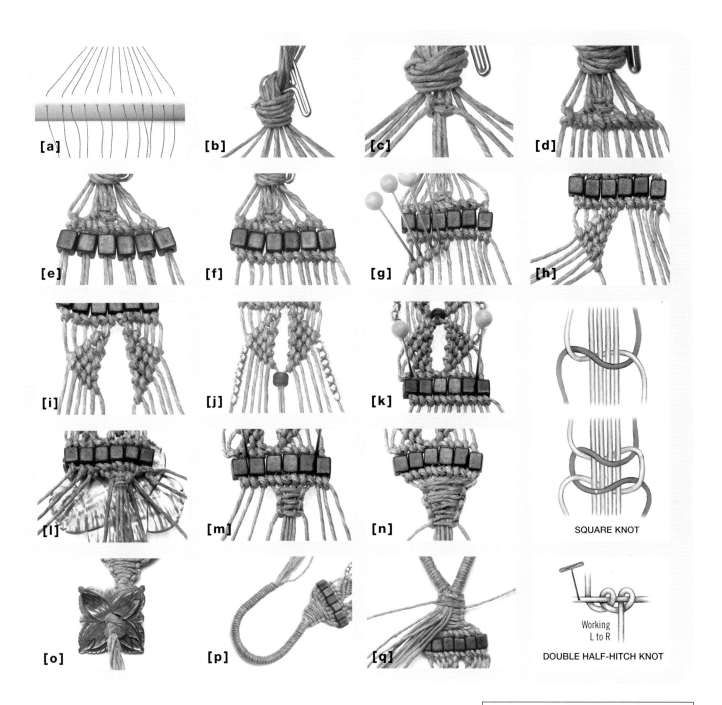

[a] [b] [c] [d]
[e] [f] [g] [h]
[i] [j] [k] SQUARE KNOT
[l] [m] [n]
[o] [p] [q] Working L to R
DOUBLE HALF-HITCH KNOT

the wrapped section is long enough to fit around the button (photo p).

[3] Pick up any two strands (except the one used for wrapping), curve the wrapped section into a loop, and make eight square knots over the square knots from step 1 (photo q). Trim the strands and glue the knots. ●

Contact Dottie via e-mail at stonebrash@juno.com.

EDITOR'S NOTE: If you cannot find a suitable shank button for the centerpiece, use a single-hole button instead. Put a head pin through the hole, then make a wrapped loop on the back to serve as a shank.

MATERIALS

bracelet 7 in. (18cm)

- 84 Japanese seed beads, sizes 8º and 6º
- 24 Japanese cube beads, 4 x 4mm
- 20mm button with shank
- 12mm bead or button for clasp
- waxed linen
- Styrofoam board
- T-pins or quilting pins
- G-S Hypo Cement

All tied
together

Knot cords with gemstones and silver
for a macramé necklace

by **Linnea Lockwood-Gambino**

Nothing makes me happier than creating new pieces of jewelry, and I believe
I've finally found my niche in knotting after designing wearable art for about ten
years. Although I primarily use traditional macramé techniques in my jewelry,
I also experiment with ways to create necklaces without knotting everything.

 As a result, this necklace features double half-hitch knots in its macramé
sides, a beaded section in back, and a focal bead surrounded by knots, with
amethyst, malachite, and Bali silver draped in the center.

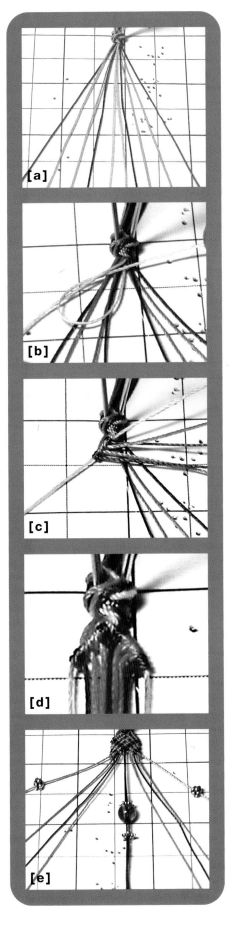

[a]

[b]

[c]

[d]

[e]

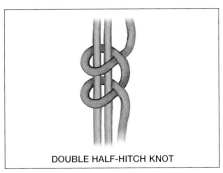

DOUBLE HALF-HITCH KNOT

step*by*step

Macramé sides

[1] Cut four 1-yd. (.9m) strands of celery green and two 1-yd. strands of hunter green, purple, and cream. Tie the cords together using an overhand knot (Basics, p. 10), leaving 2-in. (5cm) tails. Pin the knot securely onto a macramé board, then separate the cords in the order shown in **photo a**.
[2] Pin the four far-right cords to the board. Counting from the left, pick up the sixth cord, angle it to the left, then use the fifth cord to tie a double half-hitch knot around it **(photo b)**.
[3] Continue knotting to the left, using the fourth, third, second, then first cord around the sixth. When finished, the first knot will be the highest and the last knot, the lowest **(photo c)**.
[4] Unpin the right cords, then pin the five cords to the left. Counting from the left, pick up the sixth cord, angle it to the right, then use the seventh cord to tie a double half-hitch knot around it. Continue knotting to the right **(photo d)**.
[5] Repeat steps 2-4 until you have four rows completed on each side. To make the necklace longer than 16 in. (41cm), complete six rows on each side.
[6] Separate the cords and add one 3 x 4mm spacer to the far left and far right cords. On the two center cords, string a 7mm star spacer, a 6mm amethyst bead, and a 7mm star **(photo e)**. Slide the beads snugly against the knots.
[7] Place a T-pin below the left spacer to hold the bead in place. Pick up the far left cord, angle it to the right, then use the next cord to tie a double half-hitch knot around it **(photo f**, p. 250). Continue knotting to the right until you reach the fifth cord from the left.
[8] Remove the T-pin and place it below

the right spacer. Pick up the cord to the far right, angle it to the left, then use the adjacent cord to tie a double half-hitch knot around it. Continue knotting to the left until you reach the sixth cord from the left. Pick up that sixth cord, angle it to the left, then use the fifth cord to tie a double half-hitch knot around it **(photo g)**. Remove the T-pin.
[9] Repeat step 8 without pinning.
[10] Repeat step 7 without pinning. Continue past the center, making double half-hitch knots to the right until you reach the last two cords. On the next-to-last cord, string a 3 x 4mm spacer. On the last cord, string a daisy spacer, three seed beads, and a daisy spacer. Then knot these cords with the angled cord, pushing the beads up snugly to the previous rows **(photo h)**.
[11] Pin the five cords on the right. Counting from the left, pick up the fifth cord, angle it to the left, then use the fourth cord to tie a double half-hitch knot around it. Continue knotting to the left until you reach the last two cords. On the next cord, string a 3x4mm spacer. On the last cord, string a daisy spacer, three seed beads, and a daisy spacer. Then continue knotting the beaded cords with the far right cord, making the beads snug **(photo i)**.
[12] Unpin the sixth cord, angle it to the left, then use the fifth cord to tie a double half-hitch knot around it. Continue knotting to the left **(photo j)**.
[13] Using the cord now sixth from the left, angle it to the right, then use the seventh cord to tie a double half-hitch knot around it. Continue knotting to the right **(photo k)**. You have now completed one full section.
[14] Repeat steps 6-9, using a seed bead, 3 x 4mm spacer, and a seed bead on the left and right end cords and a scroll bead on the center cords **(photo l)**.
[15] Repeat steps 10-13, using the following bead combination: On the ninth cord from the left, string a daisy spacer, a malachite bead, and a daisy spacer. On the far right cord, string a seed bead, a pink crystal, a daisy spacer, a pink crystal, and a seed bead **(photo m)**. Mirror the other side by placing the same bead combination on the first and second cords from the left.

Center section

Adjust the bead count to accommodate your center bead.

[1] Add beads as shown in **photo n**.

CORD 1: Seed bead, daisy spacer, seed, daisy, hex bead, purple crystal, daisy, seed, small star spacer, seed, daisy, purple crystal, hex bead, daisy, seed, daisy, and seed.

CORD 2: Two seeds, hex bead, purple crystal, daisy, seed, small star, seed, daisy, purple crystal, hex bead, and two seeds.

CORDS 5 AND 6: Striped oval bead, large star spacer, focal bead, large star, and striped oval.

CORD 9: A 3 x 4mm spacer, daisy, two seeds, daisy, small amethyst bead, daisy, malachite bead, daisy, seed, 3 x 4mm spacer, three seeds, daisy, malachite bead, daisy, amethyst bead, daisy, two seeds, daisy, and 3 x 4 spacer.

CORD 10: Seed, hex bead, two seeds, daisy, purple crystal, daisy, small amethyst bead, daisy, malachite bead, daisy, small amethyst bead, 3 x 4mm spacer, dotted oval bead, 3 x 4mm spacer, small amethyst bead, daisy, malachite bead, daisy, small amethyst bead, daisy, purple crystal, daisy, two seeds, hex bead, and seed.

[2] Counting from the left, pick up the fourth cord, angle it to the left, then use the third cord to tie 14 double half-hitch knots around it. Pick up the seventh cord, angle it to the right, then use the eighth cord to tie 20 double half-hitch knots around it (**photo o**).

[3] String a 6 x 7mm spacer on the center of the knotted seventh and eighth cords.

[4] Place four T-pins closely together to secure the five cords to the right. Pick up the far right cord, angle it to the left, then use the adjacent cord to tie a

EDITOR'S NOTE: Use T-pins to secure your work in progress to get maximum control of the cord as well as the most consistent knots. When using T-pins, make sure to place them between rows; never pierce a knot with a pin. For additional strength, substitute alligator clips for T-pins.

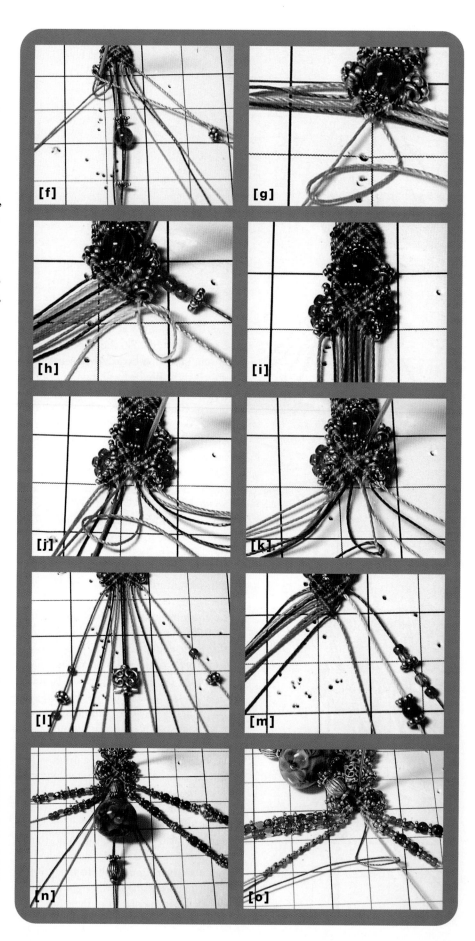

[f]

[g]

[h]

[i]

[j]

[k]

[l]

[m]

[n]

[o]

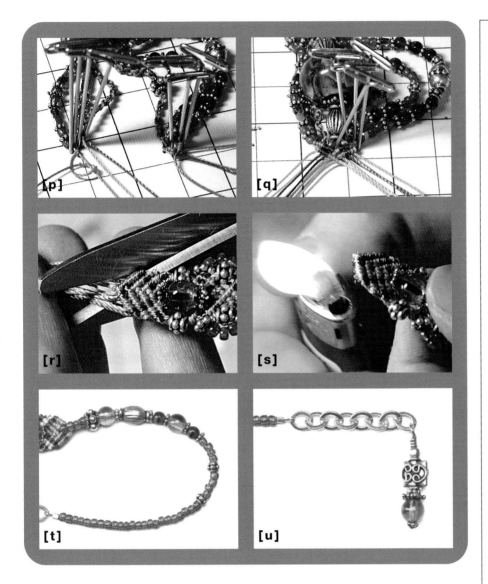

[p]

[q]

[r]

[s]

[t]

[u]

MATERIALS

16-in. (41cm) necklace

- 16mm focal bead (Da Beads, 708-606-6542,dabeads.com)
- Bali silver
  63 4-5mm daisy spacers
  30 3x4mm spacers
  8 5mm star spacers
  6 2mm hex beads
  4 3x5mm spacers, large-holed
  3 6x7mm spacers, large-holed
  3 7mm star spacers
  3 scroll beads, square
  2 10mm beads, oval with horizontal stripes
  9mm bead, oval with center dots
  4mm bead, round (optional)
- 2g Japanese seed beads, size 8º, purple
- 12 4mm malachite or dark green Czech glass beads
- 9 6mm amethyst beads, round
- 6 4mm amethyst beads, round
- 8 3mm fire-polished crystals, pink
- 6 3mm fire-polished crystals, purple
- Conso cord; bonded jewelry twine; or beading cord, size 8
  4 yd. (3.6m) celery green
  2 yd. (1.8m) cream
  2 yd. hunter green
  2 yd. purple
- 4 2mm crimp beads, silver
- 16 in. (41cm) flexible beading wire, .014
- head pin
- lobster claw clasp
- 1½-in. (3.8cm) cable chain
- macramé board
- 8 T-pins
- 2 alligator clips (optional)
- oblique cutter or scissors
- chainnose or crimping pliers
- roundnose pliers (optional)
- cigarette lighter

double half-hitch knot around it and continue knotting to the left. Then pin and knot the left side, working the knots from left to right (photo p).
[5] Remove the eight T-pins, then position and pin the two macramé sections together, forming a V. Knot a second row from right to left and stop in the middle, then knot from left to right (photo q).
[6] Work steps 2-15 of Macramé sides in reverse.

Beaded back
[1] On one end, cut the cords, leaving very short tails (photo r).
[2] Carefully seal the knots by melting the cords with the heat from a lighter (photo s).
[3] Pass an 8-in. (20cm) strip of beading wire through the center of the second and third rows from the end, leaving a 2-in. tail. String four purple seed beads on each end. String one crimp bead over both wires, tighten the beads, and crimp the crimp bead (Basics). Hide the crimp bead by stringing a 6 x 7mm spacer over it. Cut off the short tail, then string a mix of seed beads and spacers as shown in **photo t** or as desired.
[4] Loop the wire through the cable chain and go back through the last four seed beads. Tighten the beads, crimp the crimp bead, then trim the tail.
[5] Make an optional dangle by stringing beads on a head pin. Start a wrapped loop (Basics), then string the cable chain before finishing the wraps (photo u).
[6] Repeat steps 1-4 on the other end, substituting a lobster claw clasp for the cable chain. ●

Linnea lives in Clayton, North Carolina, with her husband and three cats. Contact her at linnea41@aol.com, (919) 345-4157, or linnayyah.com.

Fit to be Tied

Macramé knots define
a sophisticated neckpiece

by **Irina Serbina**

Keeping up with a crazy schedule can be stressful.
Looking for a change of pace, I was inspired by the
warmth of tiger-eye gemstones to return to my
childhood passion of creating beautiful macramé pieces.

stepbystep

Make the necklace

[1] Cut two 8-ft. (2.4m) lengths of cord.

[2] Pin the center of the two cords to a macramé board and make a 1½-in. (3.8cm) chain of alternating vertical half-hitch knots (figure 1 and photo a).

[3] Repeat steps 1–2.

[4] Bring one end of a chain through the donut hole so the first and last knots on the chain are on the outside edge of the donut. Pin the first and last knots on the chain to the macramé board. Repeat with the second chain (photo b).

[5] Pin the center of an 8-ft. cord (anchor cord) to the left of the knotted cords and bring the right half across the cords as shown in photo c.

[6] Hold the anchor cord in your right hand. Working from left to right, tie each vertical cord around the anchor cord with a clove hitch knot (CH) (figure 2). Keep the anchor cord straight as you work and pull up on it slightly as you tighten each CH so the knots are snug against the donut (photo d).

[7] Remove the pin from the anchor cord and pin it next to the last knot on the right of the row. Bring the anchor cord to the left across the vertical cords (photo e). Starting with the left half of the anchor cord, number the cords from left to right 1–10 (the anchor is cord 10).

Row 2: Make a row of CHs, working from right to left (figure 3).

Rows 3–5: Use cord 9 as the anchor and work CHs from right to left (photo f).

Rows 6–8: Use cord 1 as the anchor and work CHs from left to right with cords 2–9.

Row 9: Use the first left cord

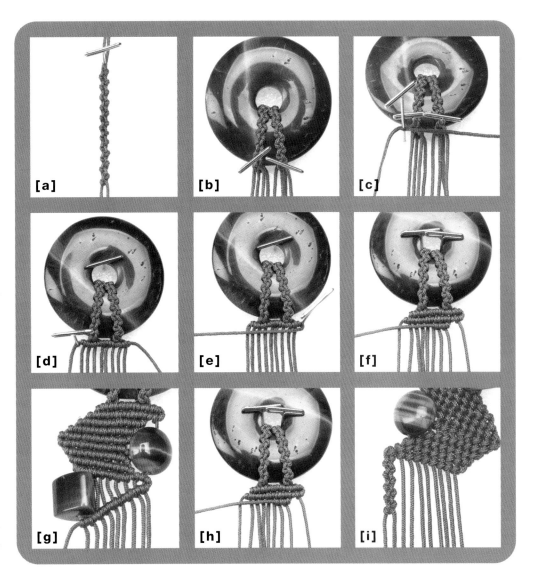

as the anchor and work CHs from left to right with cords 2–9. String an 8mm round bead on cord 10 and tie a CH (photo g).

Row 10: String a 10mm triangular shaped bead on cords 1 and 2 and pin it in place. If you are using a smaller bead or the hole isn't large enough to accommodate two cords, string it on the first cord.

Pin the anchor cord after the last knot on the previous row and bring it to the left diagonally across the vertical cords and below the triangle bead. Working from right to left, make a diagonal line of CHs (photo h).

Rows 11–12: Use cord 10 as the anchor cord and work CHs from right to left.

Rows 13–14: Use cord 9 as the anchor and work CHs from right to left.

Rows 15–16: Use the first left cord as the anchor and

work CHs from left to right with cords 2–9.

Row 17: Use the first left cord as the anchor and work CHs from left to right with cords 2–9. String an 8mm round bead on cord 10 and tie a CH.

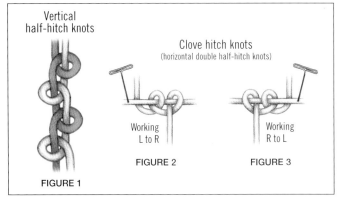

Vertical half-hitch knots

FIGURE 1

Clove hitch knots
(horizontal double half-hitch knots)

Working L to R

FIGURE 2

Working R to L

FIGURE 3

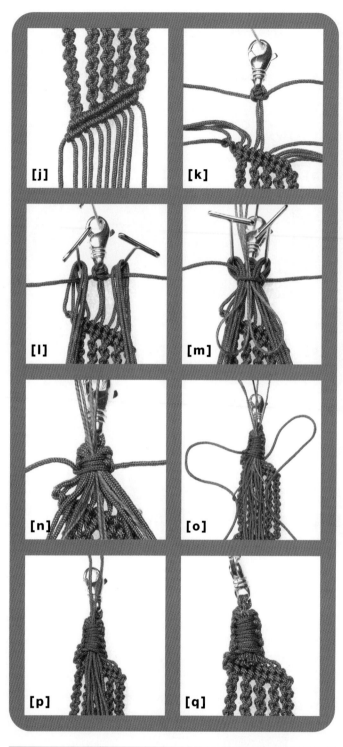

[j]

[k]

[l]

[m]

[n]

[o]

[p]

[q]

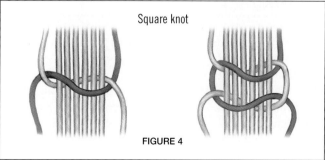

Square knot

FIGURE 4

Rows 18–19: Use the first left cord as the anchor and work CHs from left to right with all nine cords.

Rows 20–29: Repeat rows 10–19.

[8] Turn your work face down. Start with the left two cords and make a chain of vertical half-hitch knots (photo i) approximately 4¾-in. (12cm) long.

[9] Repeat step 8 with the remaining cords. Make each chain slightly longer than the first — the fifth chain is 5 in. (13cm) long. The chains graduate in length to continue the curve in the necklace.

[10] Turn your work face up, align the chains next to each other in order, and pin the end of each chain to the macramé board. Number the cords from left to right.

[11] Use cord 10 as the anchor and work a row of CHs from right to left. Repeat for a second row (photo j).

[12] Make the second half of the necklace the mirror image of the first.

Attach the clasp

[1] Turn the necklace face down and bring cords 5 and 6 through the loop on a clasp half in opposite directions. Position the clasp about ½ in. (1.3cm) from the last row of CHs. Tie a square knot (SK) (figure 4) just below the clasp to hold it in place (photo k).

[2] Fold the four cords on the left over cord 5 and pin the fold next to the clasp. Repeat with the right four cords and cord 6 (photo l).

[3] Cords 5 and 6 are the working cords, and the remaining cords are filler cords. Cut two 6-in. (15cm) cords, fold them in half, and add them, loops down, to the filler cords. Tie an SK around the filler cords (photo m).

MATERIALS

necklace 18 in. (46cm)

- tiger-eye donut with 40–50mm diameter
- 80 ft. (24m) nylon knotting cord (2mm diameter)
- 4 10mm triangular shaped tiger-eye beads*
- 6 8mm round tiger-eye beads*
- clasp
- macrame board
- T-pins or quilter's pins
- G-S Hypo cement
- *bead holes must be 2mm or larger*

[4] Tie 3–4 SKs. Remove the pins and pull the eight filler cords snug against the clasp (photo n).

[5] Continue making SKs until you reach the CHs.

[6] Thread the working cords through the loops in the 6-in. cords (photo o). Pull the ends of one 6 in. cord until the working cord has a 1-in. (2.5cm) loop. Repeat with the other cord.

[7] Apply glue to the loops and pull the cords all the way through the SKs (photo p). Allow the glue to dry and trim all the cords (photo q).

[8] Repeat steps 1–7 on the other end of the necklace. ●

Irina has kits for sale. Contact her at (415) 449-3508 or irina@macrameboutique.com. Visit her website, macrameboutique.com.

Tips & Techniques

Project organizers

I like to store my beading projects in canvas notebook pencil cases with a clear plastic front panel. These cases are inexpensive and sturdy enough to withstand needle piercings. They're large enough to hold all the materials needed for a project, and the clear panel makes it easy for me to find the project I want to work on.
– *Jill S. Banning, Newberry, Florida*

Eye exercises

Recently, my beading group had a guest who taught us many exercises to use while sitting and beading for long periods of time. The one we had the most fun with was an eye exercise — writing the letters of the alphabet with our eyes. It is easy enough and a lot of laughs if you happen to meet someone else's eye mid-letter.
– *Lynda Pedersen, Adelaide, Australia*

Untangling knots

To remove knots from nylon thread or cord, keep two sewing pins in your beading kit. Pierce the center of the knot with one pin and pick at it with the other. Jiggle the two pins apart and you should be able to untie the knot in seconds.
– *Maureen Harkins*

Patterns for lefties

If you are left-handed, stop struggling with patterns that are designed for righties. Instead of holding up a pattern to a mirror to reverse it, take it to a copy shop and have it copied onto a transparency for a mirror image of the original, one that is much easier for a left-handed beader to follow. The transparency can also be photocopied if you would like the pattern printed on paper.
– *Phyllis Muehlenthaler, Mesa, AZ*

Quick color clip

Color cards are a nice way to keep track of your beads, but they're inconvenient to carry. I also love the concept of beaded swatch samples, but that means having the time to bead them. So here is my solution.
String a single color of beads on a 1-in. (2.5cm) safety pin. (I used Dritz brand pins.) Make a small label for the color number and attach it to the other side of the pin. Slide the loop on the end of the safety pin onto a loose-leaf ring or split ring. Carry it in your purse or attach a chain or cord and wear it around your neck to keep your hands free as you shop. I also made one for my Austrian crystals.
– *Rafannette Dooley, Franklin, Texas*